BIOGRAPHIES
of
AMERICAN
WOMEN

BIOGRAPHIES
of
AMERICAN
WOMEN

AN ANNOTATED BIBLIOGRAPHY

Patricia E. Sweeney

ABC-CLIO

Santa Barbara, California
Oxford, England

Library of Congress Cataloging-in-Publication Data

Sweeney, Patricia E., 1950.
  Biographies of American women / an annotated bibliography /
Patricia E. Sweeney.
    p. cm.
    1. Women—United States—Biography—Bibliography. 2. United
States—Biography—Bibliography. I. Title.
  Z7963.B6S88 1990 [CT3260] 016.92072'0973—dc20 89-28277

ISBN 0-87436-070-6 (alk. paper)

97 96 95 94 93 92 91 90   10 9 8 7 6 5 4 3 2 1

ABC-CLIO, Inc.
130 Cremona Drive, P.O. Box 1911
Santa Barbara, California 93116-1911

Clio Press Ltd.
55 St. Thomas' Street
Oxford, OX1 1JG, England

This book is Smyth-sewn and printed on acid-free paper ∞.
Manufactured in the United States of America

This book is dedicated to
Elizabeth Kochanowsky Purcell (my mother)
and
Michael Paul Sweeney (my husband)

Contents

Preface

This annotated bibliography examines 1,391 biographies of American women that comprise at least fifty pages and are written in English. Books from the early 1800s through the present year are included. American women of all eras and all endeavors are covered by this bibliography; of the 700 women included, most are famous, many are noteworthy, and a few are notorious.

This reference book is intended for use primarily by a scholar or an educator studying the lives, roles, and histories of women in America. However, the younger student or general reader may find this book useful to identify interesting materials for reports or reading.

The women selected for inclusion in this bibliography were all born and raised in the United States, with the exception of our first English immigrants and a few later immigrants whose life experiences were chiefly American and whose adult careers are identified as being essential to U.S. history or culture; for example, English-born Elizabeth Blackwell is traditionally cited as the first woman physician in the United States. Conversely, a few women who were born and reared in the United States, but who spent their adult years abroad, are also included in this bibliography. Outstanding among these women are such figures as Jennie Jerome, later Lady Randolph Churchill, and Nancy Langhorne, later Lady Astor. Some contemporary U.S. women, especially those currently active in the performing arts, are not included in this work. Two reasons are behind this exclusion: in many cases the careers of these women have yet to be fully evaluated and established as deserving a permanent place in U.S. culture, and more importantly, the biographical books available on these women are almost universally ephemeral and badly produced.

Rather than limit my bibliographical entries very strictly to biographies, I have also included episodic accounts of women's lives: memoirs or portraits written by their family and friends, books that evaluate their careers or life works, and pertinent, unpublished doctoral dissertations. In this manner, many additional significant women, such as Mary Ritter Beard and Alice Dunbar-Nelson, have been included for study in this bibliography.

Not included as bibliographical entries are books either describing famous legal trials or re-creating notorious crimes. Also excluded are group or family biographies dealing with more than five individuals. Frequently the women discussed in such works are lost amidst the illustrious men in their families.

This bibliography is organized so that the user can find information easily. Each of the women is listed alphabetically, with her vital dates beside her name for clear identification. Under each woman's name appear, listed alphabetically by the authors' names, the various biographies on her. The text is cross-referenced to aid the user in dealing with either a woman known by both a maiden name and a marriage name, or one using a pseudonym. Similarly, any entry of a woman related to, a colleague of, or familiar with another woman is cross-referenced when a biography deals with both women simultaneously. An appendix to the text categorizes all the women included by profession or category. Those women with various jobs, or known in multiple roles, are listed under the most prominent or memorable profession.

Each of the 1,391 annotations informs the reader of that biography's worth to a researcher. In each case, I try to touch briefly on that book's scope, methodology, strengths, weaknesses, and any special features. One important piece of information about using this book could not be included anywhere else in its structure: many of the American women listed as entries are also the biographers of other women entered in this bibliography. Therefore, the user should consult this book's index to learn if a woman he or she is studying is also listed there as another woman's biographer. In this manner, the researcher may discover and employ for further study vital relationships between women.

Acknowledgments

I wish to thank Mr. Frank N. Magill, publisher of Salem Press, for granting me permission to reprint all the annotations for Julia Ward Howe and for Helen Keller. They originally appeared in Magill's *Great Lives from History: American Series*, published by Salem Press, copyright 1987.

I also wish to thank the entire staff of the Plumb Memorial Library in Shelton, Connecticut.

A

Abbott, Berenice   1898–

1 O'Neal, Hank. *Berenice Abbott: American Photographer*. New York: Mc-Graw-Hill, 1982. 255 pp.
O'Neal's book includes much useful information on Abbott's life and career; the biographical section is highly sympathetic to the photographer. Many of her photographs are reprinted here with commentary by Abbott herself.

Abbott, Emma   1850–1891

2 Martin, Sadie E. *The Life and Professional Career of Emma Abbott*. Minneapolis: L. Kimball Printing, 1891. 192 pp.
Martin, a close friend to Abbott, praises the singer's career too highly and in too sentimental a tone to be objective. However, she does present the facts of Abbott's life accurately.

Adams, Abigail   1744–1818

3 Akers, Charles W. *Abigail Adams: An American Woman*. Boston: Little, Brown, 1980. 207 pp.
Akers quotes at length from the first lady's 2,000 extant letters. He approaches her as a unique feminist and analyzes her life intelligently. One weakness of this book is its lack of formal documentation.

4 Levin, Phyllis L. *Abigail A. ams: A Biography*. New York: St. Martin's Press, 1987. 528 pp.
Levin paraphrases from her subject's letters to a great extent. Her focus is on the first lady's unusual role in America's early government. Unfortunately, Levin seldom discusses the influences on her subject.

5 Richards, Laura E. *Abigail Adams and Her Times*. New York: D. Appleton, 1917. 282 pp.
This is a rather sketchy biography in which Richards makes much use of the first lady's letters and her husband's diaries for information.

6   Whitney, Janet P. *Abigail Adams*. Boston: Little, Brown, 1947. 357 pp.

Whitney quotes frequently from Mrs. Adams's letters in drawing this sympathetic portrait of her. Whitney also uses a semifictional writing style, including such devices as imagined scenes and conversations, which renders her book less scholarly.

7   Withey, Lynne. *Dearest Friend: A Life of Abigail Adams*. New York: The Free Press, 1981. 369 pp.

All the stages of Mrs. Adams's life are covered by this book in sufficient detail. Withey focuses on Mrs. Adams's long marriage and her relationship to her husband. This book also makes use of the first lady's letters and journals to draw her portrait.

Adams, Louisa J.   1775–1852

8   Shepherd, Jack. *Cannibals of the Heart: A Personal Biography of Louisa Catherine and John Quincy Adams*. New York: McGraw-Hill, 1981. 440 pp.

Shepherd's biography is written mainly from Louisa Adams's viewpoint. He also takes a modern feminist approach in describing their marriage. The one weakness of this book is the author's reliance on surmised details.

Adams, Marion "Clover"   1843–1885

9   Friedrich, Otto. *Clover*. New York: Simon and Schuster, 1979. 381 pp.

Friedrich covers all of Clover's life, beginning with her classical education. He focuses on her marriage and highlights how the Civil War affected it. He believes that her husband drove her to suicide.

10   Kaledin, Eugenia. *The Education of Mrs. Henry Adams*. Philadelphia: Temple Univ. Press, 1982. 306 pp.

Kaledin omits some of the major facts of her subject's life while taking a thematic approach to that life. She theorizes that Clover had a major influence on her husband's writing.

Adams, Maude   1872–1953

11   Davies, Acton. *Maude Adams*. New York: Frederick A. Stokes, 1901. 110 pp.

Davies's book is based largely on interviews with people who knew or who worked with Adams. However, some of his interviewees are inaccurate about the facts of Adams's career.

12 Patterson, Ada. *Maude Adams: A Biography*. New York: Meyer Brothers, 1907. 109 pp.

Patterson, who acted in approximately the same era as Adams, is able to describe evocatively the atmosphere of the theatre of those days.

13 Robbins, Phyllis. *Maude Adams: An Intimate Portrait*. New York: G. P. Putnam's Sons, 1956. 308 pp.

The biographer was Adams's friend for approximately 50 years, yet her account is fairly objective. However, no new details of Adams's life are provided in this book. In order to depict Adams's career, Robbins relies on quotations from theatrical reviews.

14 ———. *Young Maude Adams*. Seattle: Jones, Stan Publishing, 1959. 163 pp.

Robbins, in this sequel to her biography of the actress, focuses on Adams's early career (1877–1891), when she played a large number of juvenile roles.

Addams, Jane   1860–1935

15 Davis, Allen F. *American Heroine: The Life and Legend of Jane Addams*. New York: Oxford Univ. Press, 1973. 339 pp.

Davis's purpose in writing this book is to free the true Addams from the myths about her. He is very successful in meeting his goal; his scholarship is excellent.

16 Levine, Daniel. *Jane Addams and the Liberal Tradition*. Madison: The State Historical Society of Wisconsin, 1971. 277 pp.

Although much of this book deals with Addams's thought, Levine opens with seven biographical chapters. He describes well her life at Hull House and the personal growth achieved through her work.

17 Linn, James W. *Jane Addams: A Biography*. New York: Appleton-Century, 1935. 457 pp.

Since this authorized biography written by Addams's nephew focuses on her professional rather than her private life, it does not attempt to evaluate her character. Linn researched Addams's private papers in order to prepare this detailed text.

18 Tims, Margaret. *Jane Addams of Hull House, 1860–1935: A Centenary Study*. New York: Macmillan Publishing, 1961. 166 pp.

Tims reassesses Addams's life and work from the vantage point of 1960. She describes Addams's complex personality fairly well, but she is overly admiring of Addams's work at Hull House instead of being objective.

Agassiz, Elizabeth Cary   1822–1907

19   Paton, Lucy A. *Elizabeth Cary Agassiz: A Biography*. Boston: Houghton Mifflin, 1919. 423 pp.

This book reprints many letters written by Agassiz as well as important documents relating to her life. Paton details her subject's work with and travels with her husband. She also describes Agassiz's personality well.

20   Tharp, Louise H. *Adventurous Alliance: The Story of the Agassiz Family of Boston*. Boston: Little, Brown, 1959. 354 pp.

Tharp describes in this book the marriage of Louis and Elizabeth Agassiz and their life of scholarship together. The reader is also shown their home life and Elizabeth's ancestry, each in some detail.

Akeley, Delia   1875–1970

21   Olds, Elizabeth F. *Women of the Four Winds: The Adventures of Four of America's First Women Explorers*. Boston: Houghton Mifflin, 1985. 263 pp.

In this well-researched book, Olds quotes from the journals these four women kept. She details clearly their achievements as well as their personal lives. The book has a useful scholarly apparatus.

Alcott, Abigail   1800–1877

22   Salyer, Sandford. *Marmee: The Mother of Little Women*. Norman: Univ. of Oklahoma Press, 1949. 209 pp.

Salyer's objective account of Alcott's life is based on sound scholarship. He describes her character especially well; the Fruitlands experiment and how it affected her are explained at length.

Alcott, Louisa May   1832–1888

23   Anthony, Katharine S. *Louisa May Alcott*. New York: Alfred A. Knopf, 1938. 315 pp.

This is an incomplete biography that contains some minor factual errors; the book is most thorough on Alcott's childhood. It also presents a controversial psychoanalysis of her that includes comments on her entire family.

24   Cheney, Ednah D. *Louisa May Alcott: Her Life, Letters, and Journals*. Boston: Roberts Brothers, 1889. 404 pp.

Cheney writes a basic biography of Alcott, then evaluates the autobiographical elements in Alcott's books. Cheney was a friend to Alcott and always depicts the author as a hard-working, morally superior woman. The book also reprints many selections from Alcott's diaries and letters.

25 Elbert, Sarah. *A Hunger for Home: Louisa May Alcott and "Little Women."* Philadelphia: Temple Univ. Press, 1984. 278 pp.

Elbert employs a feminist approach to Alcott's life and writing in this book, which is always sympathetic to her. Elbert is especially concerned with detailing how Alcott was personally and professionally influenced by the reform movements of her era.

26 MacDonald, Ruth K. *Louisa May Alcott*. Boston: Twayne Publishers, 1983. 111 pp.

This is one in a large series of books on noted American authors of all eras, which serve as an introduction to each writer and her works. Each volume contains at least one biographical chapter to open the study, followed by a few analytical chapters on the literature addressed to a beginning college student. Also included is a chronology of the author's life, extensive notes, and a set of annotated bibliographies (primary and secondary). Most of the books in this series are very well written.

27 Moses, Belle. *Louisa May Alcott, Dreamer and Worker: A Story of Achievement*. New York: D. Appleton, 1909. 334 pp.

Moses writes a somewhat sentimental account of Alcott's life in this book. However, she also describes the life accurately, in part by quoting frequently from the author's poems and letters. Moses also makes the first attempt to study Alcott's writing in a scholarly manner.

28 Saxton, Martha. *Louisa May: A Modern Biography of Louisa May Alcott*. Boston: Houghton Mifflin, 1977. 428 pp.

This biographer makes a feminist analysis of Alcott's life and writings. However, in so doing she places too much emphasis on Bronson Alcott's role in Louisa's life.

29 Stern, Madeleine B. *Louisa May Alcott*. Norman: Univ. of Oklahoma Press, 1950. 424 pp.

Stern's book is scholarly, well detailed, and accurately documented. She remains an objective observer of Alcott's life in her narrative, which begins on the writer's third birthday and continues until her death.

30 Worthington, Marjorie M. *Miss Alcott of Concord*. New York: Doubleday Publishing, 1958. 330 pp.

Worthington's book concerns itself mainly with Alcott's family life and her friendships; her attempts at analyzing the writer's personality are not convincing. She quotes often from Alcott's journals but pays little attention to the other writings.

Alexander, Francesca   1837–1917

31   Alexander, Constance G. *Francesca Alexander: A "Hidden Servant."* Cambridge, Harvard Univ. Press, 1927. 233 pp.

Although this is the principal biography of Alexander, it is too sentimental to be of real value to a scholar. The book includes a useful foreword by George H. Palmer.

Allen, Florence E.   1884–1966

32   Tuve, Jeanette E. *First Lady of the Law: Florence Ellinwood Allen.* Washington, D.C.: Univ. Press of America, 1985. 220 pp.

Allen's career and private life are both described in this book. Tuve is especially concerned with her subject's relationships to her family and friends; by this approach she focuses on Allen's inner life.

Allen, Grace "Gracie"   1906–1964

33   Burns, George. *Gracie: A Love Story.* New York: G. P. Putnam's Sons, 1988. 319 pp.

In this book Burns pays tribute to his wife as a loving and intelligent woman. He begins with their meeting and marriage, then details all of their public and private lives together. He relies on many pertinent anecdotes to tell the story.

34   Burns, George, and Cynthia H. Lindsay. *I Love Her, That's Why! An Autobiography.* New York: Simon and Schuster, 1955. 267 pp.

Burns's autobiography focuses much attention on his wife's life and their marriage. He depicts her as an intelligent woman and repeats many anecdotes from their vaudeville career (some of which may be exaggerated).

Anderson, Marian   1902–

35   Vehanen, Kosti. *Marian Anderson: A Portrait.* New York: McGraw-Hill, 1941. 270 pp.

Vehanen, Anderson's accompanist for ten years, in this book chronicles the singer's career and her rise to fame. He gives fine details of the major concerts they played together; unfortunately, he admires her too much to write objectively.

Anderson, Mary   1873–1964

36 Daly, Sr. John Marie. "Mary Anderson, Pioneer Labor Leader." Dissertation. Georgetown Univ., 1968. 284 pp.

Anderson's life and public work are described in this dissertation, which begins in her sixteenth year. Her career as a labor leader is fully detailed for the years 1895 to 1944, including her work for the federal government.

Anthony, Susan B.   1820–1906

37 Anthony, Katharine S. *Susan B. Anthony: Her Personal History and Her Era*. New York: Doubleday Publishing, 1954. 521 pp.

Katharine Anthony, a descendant of the famous feminist, provides many details of Susan's life in this carefully researched book. She does particularly well in describing the family's ancestry in both England and America.

38 Barry, Kathleen L. *Susan B. Anthony: The Biography of a Singular Feminist*. New York: New York Univ. Press, 1988. 416 pp.

This is a complete and sympathetic approach to Anthony's development as a feminist; the influences on her are traced in detail, beginning in her childhood. Barry's discussion of Anthony's private adult life focuses on her being single rather than married. The book's most interesting feature is its account of how the U.S. press received Anthony.

39 Dorr, Rheta L. *Susan B. Anthony: The Woman Who Changed the Mind of a Nation*. New York: Frederick A. Stokes, 1928. 367 pp.

Dorr is biased in favor of Anthony and her work for women's rights. Dorr's book is also candid and highlights clearly women's life in the United States from 1848 to 1906.

40 Harper, Ida H. *The Life and Work of Susan B. Anthony*. Indianapolis: Hollenbeck Press, 1898–1908. 3 vols. 513 pp./605 pp./522 pp.

Harper's book is both highly detailed and mostly biased in Anthony's favor. These three volumes cover both her life and her public career. Harper believes the feminist was greatly influenced by her Quaker background.

41 Lutz, Alma. *Susan B. Anthony: Rebel, Crusader, Humanitarian*. Boston: Beacon Press, 1959. 340 pp.

Lutz provides all the basic data on Anthony's life but does not evaluate her career. She is best at detailing the political and ideological differences between Anthony and Elizabeth C. Stanton. The book contains an extensive bibliography.

Arbus, Diane   1923–1971

42 Bosworth, Patricia. *Diane Arbus: A Biography*. New York: Alfred A. Knopf, 1984. 366 pp.

Bosworth bases this book on numerous interviews with Arbus's family, friends, and colleagues. She draws a compassionate portrait of Arbus; she is especially apt at demonstrating how her subject's life and art interacted.

Arden, Elizabeth   1884–1966

43 Lewis, Alfred A., and Constance Woodworth. *Miss Elizabeth Arden*. New York: Coward, McCann and Geoghegan, 1972. 320 pp.

Lewis's biography, the first on Arden, is factually accurate. However, it is filled with many irrelevant details and much gossip.

Arnold, Margaret S.   1760–1804

44 Tillotson, Harry S. *Exquisite Exile: The Life and Fortunes of Mrs. Benedict Arnold*. Boston: D. Lothrop, 1932. 205 pp.

Tillotson's argument in this book is that Mrs. Arnold had no part in her husband's treason, although this cannot be proved for certain. The book's bibliography lists many nineteenth-century books on this couple.

Arnow, Harriette   1908–1986

45 Eckley, Wilton. *Harriette Arnow*. New York: Twayne Publishers, 1974. 144 pp.

See entry 26.

Astor, Nancy   1879–1964

46 Ayers, Phyllis L. "The Public Career of Lady Astor." Dissertation. Univ. of Pittsburgh, 1958. 159 pp.

Ayers's study begins with an account of Astor's early life up to 1906. The rest of the dissertation details her political career in England.

47 Collis, Maurice. *Nancy Astor: An Informal Biography*. New York: E. P. Dutton, 1960. 235 pp.

Collis, a friend to Mrs. Astor's son, admires her too much to draw an objective portrait. He discusses both her public career and her personal character, but his account relies too heavily on anecdotes and makes little analysis of its subject.

48   Langhorne, Elizabeth. *Nancy Astor and Her Friends*. New York: Praeger Publishers, 1974. 277 pp.

Astor's son cooperated with the author in this book, which is sympathetic to his mother. Her witty personality is described well here, as are all the aspects of her private life and political career. The book has an extensive bibliography.

49   Sykes, Christopher. *Nancy: The Life of Lady Astor*. New York: Harper and Row, 1972. 543 pp.

Sykes had access to many of his subject's family records; as a result, he describes all the stages of her life fully and candidly. He devotes considerable space to the activities of the Cliveden set.

Atherton, Gertrude   1857–1948

50   McClure, Charlotte S. *Gertrude Atherton*. Boston: Twayne Publishers, 1979. 163 pp.

See entry 26.

Audubon, Lucy G.   1788–1874

51   Delatte, Carolyn E. *Lucy Audubon: A Biography*. Baton Rouge: Louisiana State Univ. Press, 1982. 248 pp.

This is a well-documented biography of a life that left few records to posterity. It focuses on the years before 1830 and includes good footnotes.

Austen, Alice   1866–1952

52   Novotny, Ann. *Alice's World: The Life and Photography of an American Original, Alice Austen, 1866–1952*. New York: Chatham Press, 1976. 221 pp.

This well-written biography has a warm and appreciative tone. It reliably records the details of Austen's life, and it reprints many of her photographs. The book's sources, however, are not clearly documented.

Austin, Mary Hunter   1868–1934

53   Doyle, Helen M. *Mary Austin: Woman of Genius*. New York: Gotham House, 1939. 302 pp.

Doyle, a personal friend to Austin, offers some perceptive comments on her in this book. She covers all the stages of the life, often including intimate details. However, Doyle is overly sympathetic to her subject instead of remaining objective.

54 Pearce, Thomas M. *The Beloved House*. Caldwell, Idaho: Caxton Printers, 1940. 239 pp.

Pearce, a personal friend to Austin, praises her highly in this subjective memoir. He recalls her early years in Illinois, then focuses on life at her Santa Fe, New Mexico, home.

Ayer, Harriet H.   1849–1903

55 Ayer, Margaret H., and Isabella Taves. *The Three Lives of Harriet Hubbard Ayer*. Philadelphia: J. B. Lippincott, 1957. 284 pp.

This book is based mainly on the recollections of Ayer's daughter, covering the years 1864 to 1903. Some of the writing includes fictionalized elements that weaken the book's scholarship.

B

Bacall, Lauren   1924–

56   Greenberger, Howard. *Bogey's Baby*. New York: St. Martin's Press, 1978. 216 pp.

Greenberger compares and contrasts the lives of Bacall and Bogart. Unfortunately, his book is filled with gossip and anecdotes; he also relies too heavily on newspapers and magazines, from both of which he quotes at length.

57   Hymans, Joe. *Bogart and Bacall: A Love Story*. New York: David McKay, 1975. 245 pp.

Hymans, who knew both of his subjects, focuses on their courtship and married life. He briefly discusses Bacall's early years, then parallels her life to that of Bogart.

Bacon, Delia Salter   1811–1859

58   Bacon, Theodore. *Delia Bacon: A Biographical Sketch*. Boston: Houghton Mifflin, 1888. 322 pp.

This thorough biography, written by a nephew, allows the Bacon family to express their opinions on their eccentric relative. He supports Delia's controversial theory that Francis Bacon wrote Shakespeare's plays.

59   Hopkins, Vivian C. *Prodigal Puritan: A Life of Delia Bacon*. Cambridge: Harvard Univ. Press, 1959. 362 pp.

This book, the most complete and scholarly biography available on Bacon, also includes an extensive bibliography.

Baker, Josephine   1906–1975

60   Haney, Lynn. *Naked at the Feast: A Biography of Josephine Baker*. New York: Dodd, Mead, 1981. 338 pp.

Haney's book describes both Baker's entertainment career and her later life, when she did social and political work in France. This account is based both on facts and on anecdotes; unfortunately, the latter lend the text a gossipy tone.

61   Papich, Stephen. *Remembering Josephine*. New York: Bobbs-Merrill, 1976. 237 pp.

Papich, a choreographer and a close friend to Baker, is able to recall many personal incidents for his text. His book is thorough, although full of his admiration for Baker.

Balch, Emily G.   1867–1961

62   Randall, Mercedes M. *Improper Bostonian: Emily Greene Balch, Nobel Peace Laureate, 1946*. New York: Twayne Publishers, 1964. 475 pp.

Randall focuses on all six decades of Balch's public career in this factual and well-documented biography. The research for this book was based on Balch's private papers.

Ball, Lucille   1911–1989

63   Andrews, Bart, and Thomas J. Watson. *Loving Lucy: An Illustrated Tribute to Lucille Ball*. New York: St. Martin's Press, 1980. 226 pp.

The facts of Ball's life and career are presented accurately in this text, which neither exaggerates nor sensationalizes them. Gale Gordon, Ball's costar, wrote a foreword to this book.

64   Higham, Charles. *Lucy: The Real Life of Lucille Ball*. New York: St. Martin's Press, 1986. 261 pp.

Higham focuses on the hardships in Ball's life, such as her childhood in poverty and her failed marriage. He also includes new details about the investigation of Ball by the House Un-American Activities Committee in the 1950s.

65   Morella, Joe, and Edward Z. Epstein. *Forever Lucy: The Life of Lucille Ball*. Secaucus, N.J.: Lyle Stuart, 1986. 267 pp.

In this unauthorized biography the authors focus mainly on the sensational aspects of Ball's life; these include her failed marriage and her poor relationships with her two children.

Balsan, Consuelo V.   1877–1964

66   Brough, James. *Consuelo: Portrait of an American Heiress*. New York: Coward, McCann and Geoghegan, 1979. 266 pp.

This is a popular biography which dramatizes the main events in Balsan's life. Although the author does not document his sources carefully, he informs the reader that he has consulted Balsan's autobiography.

Bancroft, Anne   1931–

67 Holtzman, William. *Seesaw: A Dual Biography of Anne Bancroft and Mel Brooks*. New York: Doubleday Publishing, 1979. 300 pp.

This is a factual account of the couple that parallels both their lives and their careers. Bancroft's work on Broadway is discussed briefly and some telling theatrical anecdotes are provided.

Banister, Zilphia P. G.   1794–1874

68 Guilford, Lucinda T. *The Use of a Life: Memorials of Mrs. Z. P. G. Banister*. New York: American Tract Society, 1885. 368 pp.

This book, the only full-length biography available on Banister, includes extracts from many of her letters.

Bankhead, Tallulah   1903–1968

69 Brian, Denis. *Tallulah Darling: A Biography of Tallulah Bankhead*. New York: Macmillan Publishing, 1980. 292 pp.

Brian had access to some very personal data on Bankhead's life. He accomplished this by interviewing her shortly before her death and by carefully studying her autobiography.

70 Gill, Brendan. *Tallulah*. New York: Holt, Rinehart and Winston, 1972. 287 pp.

Gill is too sympathetic to his subject to write an objective account of her life. His portrait of Bankhead is also shallow and incomplete.

71 Israel, Lee. *Miss Tallulah Bankhead*. New York: G. P. Putnam's Sons, 1972. 384 pp.

This is an honest, objective biography that covers all of Bankhead's life, including her family background and details omitted from her autobiography. The author also analyzes the actress's character flaws, particularly those that hindered her career.

72 Tunney, Kieran. *Tallulah, Darling of the Gods: An Intimate Portrait*. New York: E. P. Dutton, 1973. 228 pp.

Tunney, a playwright, bases this book on much theatrical gossip. He sympathetically describes his friendship to the actress during the last two decades of her life.

Barnes, Djuna   1892–1982

73 Field, Andrew. *Djuna: The Life and Times of Djuna Barnes*. New York: G. P. Putnam's Sons, 1983. 288 pp.

Field provides no new insights or revelations about Barnes's life despite the fact that he interviewed her for this book. He relates events in her life to episodes in her writing, but because his approach is not chronological, it is confusing.

74 Scott, James B. *Djuna Barnes*. Boston: Twayne Publishers, 1976. 152 pp.
See entry 26.

Barnes, Margaret Ayer   1886–1967

75 Taylor, Lloyd C., Jr. *Margaret Ayer Barnes*. New York: Twayne Publishers, 1974. 152 pp.
See entry 26.

Barney, Natalie C.   1876–1972

76 Chalon, Jean. *Portrait of a Seductress: The World of Natalie Barney*. New York: Crown Publishers, 1979. 256 pp.

The author, who was a close friend to Barney in the last nine years of her life, is very biased in her favor. Chalon also had access to Barney's personal papers; as a result, she gives a frank account of Barney's sexual history.

77 Jay, Karla. *The Amazon and the Page: Natalie Clifford Barney and Renée Vivien*. Bloomington: Indiana Univ. Press, 1988. 168 pp.

Jay, who uses a feminist approach in this book, is very thorough in her analyses of these two women and their relationship to each other. Jay also includes some literary criticism in this text.

78 Secrest, Meryle. *Between Me and Life: A Biography of Romaine Brooks*. New York: Doubleday Publishing, 1974. 432 pp.
See under Brooks, Romaine.

79 Wickes, George. *The Amazon of Letters: The Life and Loves of Natalie Barney*. New York: G. P. Putnam's Sons, 1976. 286 pp.

Wickes's book, which is sympathetic to Barney, is also well-documented and frank. However, Barney's personality is described best by her friends, whose interviews Wickes reprints to close this book.

Barton, Clara H.   1821–1912

80   Barton, William E. *The Life of Clara Barton*. Boston: Houghton Mifflin, 1922. 2 vols. 348 pp./388 pp.

This laudatory, authorized biography is especially apt at describing Barton's years with the Red Cross. However, the book covers all her life thoroughly. The author is able to achieve this completeness because he had access to Barton's personal papers; in fact, he quotes at length from her letters.

81   Epler, Percy H. *The Life of Clara Barton*. New York: Macmillan Publishing, 1915. 438 pp.

Epler covers all of the stages of Barton's life by using her unpublished letters and diaries, as well as Red Cross records. He describes her personal life and devotes much of the book to her work during the Civil War.

82   Pryor, Elizabeth B. *Clara Barton: Professional Angel*. Philadelphia: Univ. of Pennsylvania Press, 1988. 444 pp.

This is a good, modern biography which makes use of Barton's recently discovered (ca. 1988) diaries. Although Pryor does not attempt to psychoanalyze Barton, she shows her to be a complex, troubled woman, who increasingly moved toward feminism as she matured.

83   Ross, Ishbel. *The Angel of the Battlefield: The Life of Clara Barton*. New York: Harper and Row, 1956. 305 pp.

In this book, which is competent and unsentimental, Ross devotes much space to the founding of the Red Cross. She has researched her subject very thoroughly.

84   Williams, Blanche C. *Clara Barton: Daughter of Destiny*. Philadelphia: J. B. Lippincott, 1941. 468 pp.

Williams's scholarly biography is especially good at describing Barton's career. She bases her narrative on newly found (ca. 1941) diaries and letters written by Barton.

Bates, Katharine Lee   1859–1929

85   Burgess, Dorothy. *Dream and Deed: The Story of Katharine Lee Bates*. Norman: Univ. of Oklahoma Press, 1952. 241 pp.

Burgess, Bates's niece, describes all aspects of her subject's personal life in this biography. Her admiring, yet accurate account is based on family papers.

Beach, Sylvia W.   1887–1962

86   Fitch, Noel R. *Sylvia Beach and the Lost Generation: A History of Literary Paris in the Twenties and Thirties*. New York: W. W. Norton, 1983. 447 pp.

Fitch covers all the stages of Beach's life, beginning with her childhood; he also provides new details on her relationship with James Joyce. This book is based on Beach's family papers and interviews with her friends.

Beals, Jessie Tarbox   1870–1942

87   Alland, Alexander. *Jessie Tarbox Beals: First Woman News Photographer*. New York: Cameragraphic Press, 1978. 191 pp.

This is an informative account that focuses on Beals's forty-year career rather than on her private life. Many of her photographs are reprinted in this book.

Beard, Mary Ritter   1876–1958

88   Lane, Ann J. *Mary Ritter Beard: A Sourcebook*. Boston: Northeastern Univ. Press, 1978. 252 pp.

Lane provides a good, extensive evaluation of Beard's life and career. The book also includes selections from Beard's best writing and a thorough bibliography of her works.

Beattie, Ann   1947–

89   Murphy, Christina. *Ann Beattie*. Boston: Twayne Publishers, 1986. 138 pp. See entry 26.

Beecher, Catharine E.   1800–1878

90   Harveson, Mae E. *Catharine Esther Beecher (Pioneer Educator)*. Philadelphia: Science Press Printing, 1932. 295 pp.

This is a scholarly book that describes all of Beecher's private life and her career; it also traces her intellectual growth. The biographer comments on Beecher's various writings, which are listed in the book's detailed bibliography. Other valuable features of this book are its appendices and footnotes.

91   Sklar, Kathryn K. *Catharine Beecher: A Study in American Domesticity*. New Haven: Yale Univ. Press, 1973. 356 pp.

This complete biography is scholarly, and its sources are documented well. The book clearly shows the paradoxes in Beecher's personality as it focuses on the major conflicts in her life.

Bell, Helen Choate   1830–1918

92   Drown, Paulina C. *Mrs. Bell*. Boston: Houghton Mifflin, 1932. 87 pp.

This personal tribute to Bell, written by her close friend, portrays her as a warm and witty woman.

Bell, Mabel   1859–1923

93   Toward, Lilias M. *Mabel Bell: Alexander's Silent Partner*. New York: Methuen Publishing, 1984. 220 pp.

Although Toward discusses the Bells' marriage at length, the focus remains on Mrs. Bell rather than on her famous husband. The book relies heavily on Mrs. Bell's letters to tell her story, and it includes extracts from her journals.

94   Waite, Helen E. *Make a Joyful Sound: The Romance of Mabel Hubbard and Alexander Graham Bell, an Authorized Biography*. Philadelphia: Macrae Smith, 1961. 284 pp.

This dual biography was authorized by the Bell family and uses their private papers. However, a more diverse view of the couple would have resulted had Waite used other sources of information.

Benedict, Ruth F.   1887–1948

95   Caffrey, Margaret M. *Ruth Benedict: Stranger in This Land*. Austin: Univ. of Texas Press, 1989. 464 pp.

Caffrey has written a major biography of this important woman intellectual. Her full life is described vividly, including her roles as anthropologist, poet, feminist, and, above all, leading scholar.

96   Mead, Margaret. *An Anthropologist at Work: Writings of Ruth Benedict*. Boston: Houghton Mifflin, 1959. 583 pp.

Mead produces an appreciative account of her friend and mentor, mainly by drawing on Benedict's published works and private papers. This book includes a useful section of bibliographical references.

97   ———. *Ruth Benedict: A Biography*. New York: Columbia Univ. Press, 1974. 180 pp.

Mead's book is intended as an introductory guide for the college student. It opens with a brief biography of Benedict, then reprints selections from her best writings.

98 Modell, Judith S. *Ruth Benedict: Patterns of a Life.* Philadelphia: Univ. of Pennsylvania Press, 1983. 355 pp.

Modell's well-researched book discusses both Benedict's private life and her career in an intertwining narrative. The text is somewhat repetitious because of this dual approach.

Bennett, Gwendolyn B.   1902–

99 Govan, Sandra Y. "Gwendolyn Bennett: Portrait of an Artist Lost." Dissertation. Emory Univ., 1980. 248 pp.

Govan relies on Bennett's oral memories to tell the story of her childhood and early career; this study then follows Bennett to the height of her artistic life. It also provides a thorough and insightful view of black American life in the 1920s.

Bernstein, Aline F.   1881–1955

100 Klein, Carole. *Aline.* New York: Harper and Row, 1979. 352 pp.

A large section of this biography is devoted to a discussion of Bernstein's relationship with Thomas Wolfe, which Klein describes fully and clearly. The book also includes a useful bibliography.

Berry, Martha M.   1866–1942

101 Byers, Tracy. *Martha Berry: The Sunday Lady of Possum Trot.* New York: G. P. Putnam's Sons, 1932. 268 pp.

This is a simple, straightforward narrative of Berry's career. The author retells warm anecdotes provided by Berry's pupils and their families. Nevertheless, the book does not overpraise her.

102 Kane, Harnett T., and Inez Henry. *Miracle in the Mountains: The Story of Martha Berry.* New York: Doubleday Publishing, 1956. 320 pp.

Henry, a secretary to Berry for many years, relies on her own personal recollections to tell Berry's life story. She devotes a small portion of the book to her subject's early years; the majority of the text is an enthusiastic, laudatory account of Berry and her school.

Bethune, Joanna G.   1770–1860

103 Bethune, George W. *Memories of Mrs. Joanna Bethune.* New York: Harper and Brothers, 1863. 250 pp.

This book is a tribute to the woman written by her son. An appendix contains selections from her writings.

Bethune, Mary McLeod   1875–1955

104 Holt, Rackham. *Mary McLeod Bethune: A Biography*. New York: Doubleday Publishing, 1964. 306 pp.
This is a detailed, yet romanticized book on all of Bethune's life. Its lack of documentation and bibliography will disappoint the serious student.

105 Peare, Catherine O. *Mary McLeod Bethune*. New York: Vanguard Press, 1951. 219 pp.
Peare has written a romanticized book that contains no scholarly apparatus. However, it does provide a thorough account of Bethune's work for the National Youth Administration (NYA).

106 Sterne, Emma G. *Mary McLeod Bethune*. New York: Alfred A. Knopf, 1957. 268 pp.
This biography, which romanticizes Bethune's life, is not always factually accurate.

Bevier, Isabel   1860–1942

107 Bane, (Juliet) Lita. *The Story of Isabel Bevier*. Peoria, Ill.: Bennett Publishing, 1955. 191 pp.
This uncritical biography consists largely of quotations from Bevier's writings. Bane, a former student and colleague of her subject, is overly admiring, but does offer some insights on Bevier.

Bickerdyke, Mary   1817–1901

108 Baker, Nina B. *Cyclone in Calico: The Story of Mary Ann Bickerdyke*. Boston: Little, Brown, 1952. 278 pp.
Baker's book, biased in favor of her subject, focuses much attention on this nurse's work during the Civil War, ignoring other aspects of her career. Useful, comprehensive notes list the sources of information for each chapter.

109 Chase, Julia A. *Mary A. Bickerdyke, "Mother."* Lawrence, Kans.: Journal Publishing House, 1896. 145 pp.

This biographer had interviewed Bickerdyke about her life experiences. She also bases her book on Bickerdyke's correspondence, original documents pertaining to her life, and case reports from her social work.

110 Kellogg, Florence S. *Mother Bickerdyke as I Knew Her*. Chicago: Unity Publishing, 1907. 176 pp.

Kellogg describes her subject well; she knew Bickerdyke during her years in nursing. The book also includes a bibliography and an introduction by Jenkin L. Jones.

Bishop, Elizabeth   1911–1979

111 Stevenson, Anne. *Elizabeth Bishop*. New York: Twayne Publishers, 1966. 143 pp.

See entry 26.

Black, Shirley T.   See **Temple, Shirley**

Blackwell, Antoinette B.   1825–1921

112 Cazden, Elizabeth. *Antoinette Brown Blackwell: A Biography*. Old Westbury, N.Y.: The Feminist Press, 1983. 315 pp.

Cazden, who quotes frequently from her subject's private papers in this text, analyzes Blackwell's character without exaggeration. The book contains useful endnotes, a chronology, and a genealogy chart.

113 Kerr, Laura N. *Lady in the Pulpit: Antoinette Blackwell*. New York: Woman's Press, 1951. 239 pp.

This is a popular biography written to entertain the general reader.

Blackwell, Elizabeth   1821–1910

114 Ross, Ishbel. *Child of Destiny: The Life Story of the First Woman Doctor*. New York: Harper and Brothers, 1949. 309 pp.

Ross's biography is especially informative concerning Blackwell's years in medical training and her life in Paris. The biographer also details the social and political causes that her subject supported.

115 Wilson, Dorothy C. *Lone Woman: The Story of Elizabeth Blackwell, the First Woman Doctor*. Boston: Little, Brown, 1970. 469 pp.

Although this book is based on unpublished archival materials, its scholarly uses are diminished due to its novelized writing style and lack of documentation. It does describe rather vividly Blackwell's years in the United States.

Blaine, Anita M.   1866–1954

116 Harrison, Gilbert A. *A Timeless Affair: The Life of Anita McCormick Blaine.* Chicago: Univ. of Chicago Press, 1979. 260 pp.

Harrison, Blaine's grandson by marriage, presents the family's version of Blaine's life. He begins with her childhood and pays particular attention to her family relationships and friendships. However, he does not evaluate her character.

Blake, Lillie D.   1833–1913

117 Blake, Katherine D., and Margaret L. Wallace. *Champion of Women: The Life of Lillie Devereux Blake.* New York: Fleming H. Revell, 1943. 224 pp.

Katherine Blake, Blake's daughter, quotes at length from her mother's diaries and letters in this book. It also provides a precise discussion of her mother's suffrage stances and of the problems within the movement itself.

Bloomer, Amelia Jenks   1818–1894

118 Bloomer, D. C. *The Life and Writings of Amelia Bloomer.* New York: Schocken Books, 1975. 387 pp.

This book was written by Bloomer's husband shortly after her death and is reissued here with an introduction by Susan J. Kleinberg. Bloomer's text quotes often from his wife's essays, speeches, and letters; he also includes eulogies from her friends and followers.

Bly, Nellie   1865–1922

119 Rittenhouse, Mignon. *The Amazing Nellie Bly.* New York: E. P. Dutton, 1956. 254 pp.

This book is intended to be simply entertaining, not scholarly. Its fictionalized sections recall Bly's career with much praise, while the biographer offers no analysis of her character or her journalism.

Bogan, Louise   1897–1970

120 Frank, Elizabeth. *Louise Bogan: A Portrait.* New York: Alfred A. Knopf, 1985. 460 pp.

Frank, a sympathetic biographer, describes well Bogan's complex personality and the interactions between her life and her art. This well-documented book is also good for its discussion of Bogan's life and career in the 1920s and 1930s.

121   Ridgeway, Jacqueline. *Louise Bogan.* Boston: Twayne Publishers, 1984. 146 pp.
See entry 26.

Bolton, Frances P.   1885–1977

122   Loth, David G. *A Long Way Forward: The Biography of Congresswoman Frances P. Bolton.* New York: Longmans, Green, 1957. 302 pp.
Loth covers all the stages of Bolton's life, with an emphasis on those personal qualities that suited her for a political career. Although the author admires his subject, his text remains factual and accurate.

Bonaparte, Elisabeth P.   1785–1879

123   Didier, Eugene L. *The Life and Letters of Madame Bonaparte.* New York: Charles Scribner's Sons, 1879. 376 pp.
Didier's book rests more on the legends about his subject than on the facts of her life. The book reprints letters written to her, but few composed by her.

124   Mitchell, Sidney. *A Family Lawsuit: The Story of Elisabeth Patterson and Jerome Bonaparte.* New York: Farrar, Straus, and Cudahy, 1958. 210 pp.
Mitchell first describes the meeting of this couple and their marriage in 1803. He then explains why the marriage was annulled by Napoleon and discusses Mrs. Bonaparte's resultant lawsuit. Mitchell employs period documents and pertinent letters to describe the lawsuit precisely.

125   Saffell, William. *The Bonaparte-Patterson Marriage.* Philadelphia: W. T. R. Saffell, 1873. 254 pp.
This early book on the couple bases its narrative on traditional stories, regardless of their veracity. It reprints letters written to Mrs. Bonaparte, but few from her own pen.

Bonner, Sherwood   1849–1883

126   Frank, William L. *Sherwood Bonner (Catherine McDowell).* Boston: Twayne Publishers, 1976. 158 pp.
See entry 26.

127 McAlexander, Hubert H. *The Prodigal Daughter: A Biography of Sherwood Bonner*. Baton Rouge: Louisiana State Univ. Press, 1981. 247 pp.

This is a well-researched biography that describes Bonner's life clearly and dynamically. McAlexander admires his subject as a brave individual, yet he discusses her influences on other writers without exaggeration.

Booth, Maud B. 1865–1948

128 Welty, Susan F. *Look Up and Hope! The Motto of the Volunteer Prison League: The Life of Maud Ballington Booth*. Nashville: Thomas Nelson, 1961. 284 pp.

Welty bases this complete biography on interviews with Booth and on previously published materials. The book includes a bibliography.

Borden, Lizzie A. 1860–1927

129 Radin, Edward D. *Lizzie Borden: The Untold Story*. New York: Simon and Schuster, 1961. 269 pp.

Radin opens his book with details of the Bordens' family life and their place in Fall River society. The author then re-creates the vicious murders; he concludes that the maid committed the crimes, but his proof of this hypothesis is weak.

130 Spiering, Frank. *Lizzie*. New York: Random House, 1984. 242 pp.

Spiering employs a fictionalized writing style to re-create the double murder. He concludes that Lizzie's sister Emma was the killer, but his evidence is inconclusive. In closing the book, he describes Lizzie's life after the trial.

Bosone, Reva Beck c. 1898–

131 Clopton, Beverly B. *Her Honor, the Judge*. Ames: Iowa State Univ. Press, 1980. 235 pp.

Clopton describes clearly three areas of Bosone's life: her early years, her private law practice in Utah, and her service in the U.S. House of Representatives.

Boudin, Katherine "Kathy" 1942–

132 Frankfort, Ellen. *Kathy Boudin and the Dance of Death*. Briarcliff Manor, N.Y.: Stein and Day, 1983. 192 pp.

Frankfort, whose approach is that of a feminist, focuses more on Boudin's political activities than on her private life, yet touches on both. This book provides only a surface view of its subject and her story; it could have been researched more deeply.

Bourke-White, Margaret   1904–1971

133   Goldberg, Vicki. *Margaret Bourke-White: A Biography.* New York: Harper and Row, 1986. 426 pp.

Goldberg has written an excellent, insightful biography. She begins with her subject's childhood and details her private life (including psychological problems) and career work (as it fit into her era).

Bow, Clara Gordon   1905–1965

134   Morella, Joe, and Edward Z. Epstein. *The "It" Girl: The Incredible Story of Clara Bow.* New York: Delacorte Press, 1976. 284 pp.

This popular biography contains many elements of fictionalized writing. The authors discuss Bow's acting ability, which they defend as being good.

135   Stenn, David. *Clara Bow: Runnin' Wild.* New York: Doubleday, 1988. 352 pp.

Stenn's book includes new information on Bow provided by her son. This biography dwells on all the sordid details of the actress's life, beginning with her childhood. At the same time, Stenn makes a firm attempt to disprove gossip about Bow.

Bowles, Jane Auer   1918–1973

136   Dillon, Millicent. *A Little Original Sin: The Life and Work of Jane Bowles.* New York: Holt, Rinehart, and Winston, 1981. 464 pp.

Dillon focuses on Bowles's life, beginning with childhood, rather than on her works. Many personal details are included while Dillon emphasizes the tragic elements in Bowles's life.

Boyd, Belle   1843–1900

137   Davis, Curtis C., ed. *Belle Boyd in Camp and Prison.* Cranbury, N.J.: Thomas Yoseloff, 1968. 448 pp.

This book is a reedition of Boyd's memoirs, first published in 1865 as authored by a ghostwriter, George A. H. Sala. Sala provided Boyd with unbelievably sophisticated speeches: for example, at her capture in 1863 at age nineteen.

138   Scarborough, Ruth. *Belle Boyd, Siren of the South.* Macon, Ga.: Mercer Univ. Press, 1983. 212 pp.

Scarborough heavily bases her account on Boyd's own memoirs, which were often exaggerated. This book remains a popular narrative with a weak scholarly apparatus.

139   Sigaud, Louis A. *Belle Boyd, Confederate Spy.* Richmond, Va.: Dietz Press, 1945. 254 pp.

Sigaud, who is very sympathetic to Boyd, has done considerable research and re-creates her personality vividly. However, he unequivocally accepts her own narrative of her work as a spy (much of which appears to have been exaggerated).

Boyd, Louise Arner   1887–1972

140   Olds, Elizabeth F. *Women of the Four Winds: The Adventures of Four of America's First Women Explorers.* Boston: Houghton Mifflin, 1985. 263 pp.

See under Akeley, Delia.

Boyle, Kay   1903–

141   Spanier, Sandra W. *Kay Boyle: Artist and Activist.* Carbondale: Southern Illinois Univ. Press, 1986. 261 pp.

Spanier's work is a fine critical biography that describes in detail both Boyle's life and work. The biographer, who had Boyle's assistance in researching this book, seems to have gained insight into her subject's personal character as well as into her development as a writer.

Bradley, Marion Z.   1930–

142   Arbur, Rosemarie. *Marion Zimmer Bradley.* Mercer Island, Wash.: Starmont House, 1985. 138 pp.

Arbur's book contains both a biographical sketch of Bradley and an analysis of her career as a science-fiction writer. The study also includes annotated bibliographies, both primary and secondary.

Bradstreet, Anne   1612–1672

143   Caldwell, Luther. *An Account of Anne Bradstreet, the Puritan Poetess and Kindred Topics.* Boston: Damrell and Upham, 1898. 64 pp.

Caldwell covers all of Bradstreet's life and career in this brief book. However, he has written not a straightforward factual account, but a tribute to her.

144   Campbell, Helen. *Anne Bradstreet and Her Time.* Boston: D. Lothrop, 1891. 373 pp.

Campbell's full treatment of Bradstreet has somewhat sentimentalized the poet's life. Unfortunately, Campbell also spends much of her narrative on the American colonial era in general, instead of on Bradstreet in particular.

145 Piercy, Josephine K. *Anne Bradstreet*. New York: Twayne Publishers, 1965. 144 pp.

See entry 26.

146 White, Elizabeth W. *Anne Bradstreet: "The Tenth Muse."* New York: Oxford Univ. Press, 1971. 410 pp.

White provides a very complete biography of Bradstreet, especially considering that few records of her life exist. The biography includes her genealogy, her childhood in Puritanical America, and her early experiences in a colonial society. In covering Bradstreet's later life, White focuses on her personal tragedies.

Breckinridge, Madeline M.   1872–1920

147 Breckinridge, Sophonisba P. *Madeline McDowell Breckinridge: A Leader in the New South*. Urbana: Univ. of Illinois Press, 1921. 275 pp.

This text is the main source on Breckinridge's life. Although the work of an admiring sister-in-law, it is a detailed and accurate biography.

Brice, Fanny   1891–1951

148 Katkov, Norman. *Fabulous Fanny: The Story of Fanny Brice*. New York: Alfred A. Knopf, 1952. 337 pp.

Katkov uses Brice's unpublished autobiography as one of his sources. He is better at providing a clear picture of Brice's personality than he is at relating the facts of her life and career.

Bridgman, Laura D.   1829–1889

149 Elliott, Maud H., and Florence H. Hall. *Laura Bridgman: Dr. Howe's Famous Pupil and What He Taught Her*. Boston: Little, Brown, 1903. 384 pp.

The authors, the daughters of Dr. Howe, knew Bridgman personally and observed her education. They quote extensively from the Howe family's letters and diaries to relate the details of Bridgman's life.

150 Lamson, Mary S. *The Life and Education of Laura Dewey Bridgman: The Deaf, Dumb and Blind Girl*. Boston: New England Publishing, 1878. 373 pp.

Lamson was one of Bridgman's teachers at the Perkins Institute for the Blind in Boston. She provides an intimate, detailed look at her pupil's life and training.

Bright Eyes   1854–1903

151 Wilson, Dorothy C. *Bright Eyes: The Story of Susette La Flesche, an Omaha Indian.* New York: McGraw-Hill, 1974. 396 pp.

Although this is a popular biography written in the style of a historical romance, its facts are correct. Wilson is sympathetic to Bright Eyes and her tribe.

Brooks, Gwendolyn   1917–

152 Kent, George E. *A Life of Gwendolyn Brooks.* Lexington: Univ. Press of Kentucky, 1988. 304 pp.

Kent, a prominent black literary critic, writes the first book-length biography covering all of Brooks's life and career.

153 Shaw, Harry B. *Gwendolyn Brooks.* Boston: Twayne Publishers, 1980. 200 pp.

See entry 26.

Brooks, Juanita   1898–

154 Peterson, Levi S. *Juanita Brooks: Mormon Woman Historian.* Salt Lake City: Univ. of Utah Press, 1988. 528 pp.

Peterson covers all of Brooks's life, but focuses chiefly on her role as a Utah historian and her opposition to the Mormon Church, which resulted from her work.

Brooks, Louise   1906–1985

155 Jaccard, Roland, ed. *Louise Brooks: Portrait of an Anti-star.* Trans. Gideon Schein. New York: Zoetrope, 1986. 160 pp.

This book describes both the public career and the private life of this silent-movie star. It also describes in full detail her controversial 1929 film, *Lulu.*

Brooks, Romaine   1874–1970

156 Secrest, Meryle. *Between Me and Life: A Biography of Romaine Brooks.* New York: Doubleday Publishing, 1974. 432 pp.

Secrest's focus is on Brooks's adult years and her love affairs, especially on her fifty-year relationship with Natalie Barney; the biographer is always detailed and frank in discussing Brooks's sexual history. Secrest is so thorough that if an episode in Brooks's life has conflicting versions, she relates them all.

Brown, Alice   1856–1948

157 Walker, Dorothea. *Alice Brown.* New York: Twayne Publishers, 1974. 181 pp.
See entry 26.

Brown, Rachel Fuller   1898–1980

158 Baldwin, Richard S. *The Fungus Fighters: Two Women Scientists and Their Discovery.* Ithaca: Cornell Univ. Press, 1981. 212 pp.
Baldwin's book focuses on the work these two women accomplished together, yet shows little of their personal lives or character traits in the process. Baldwin's handling of his material is disproportionate, giving too much space to nonessential facts.

Bryant, Louise Stevens   1890–1936

159 Beam, Lura. *Bequest from a Life: A Biography of Louise Stevens Bryant.* Baltimore: Waverly Press, 1963. 194 pp.
Beam, a friend and lover to Bryant, writes a book that is rich in detail and effusive in its tribute to this subject.

160 Gelb, Barbara. *So Short a Time: A Biography of John Reed and Louise Bryant.* New York: W. W. Norton, 1973. 394 pp.
This is a competent biography that accurately records the facts about these two people, with an emphasis on the years that they lived together. In order to personalize her account of the couple, Gelb quotes from their poetry and love letters.

Buck, Pearl S.   1892–1973

161 Doyle, Paul A. *Pearl S. Buck.* New York: Twayne Publishers, 1965. 175 pp.
See entry 26.

162 Harris, Theodore F. *Pearl S. Buck: A Biography.* New York: John Day, 1969, 1971. 2 vols. 381 pp./372 pp.
Harris has written a very thorough biography of Buck, based in part on his conversations with her. He remains fairly objective as he depicts much of her personal life, beginning with her childhood; he even analyzes various aspects of

her personality. Volume two is a compilation of quotations from Buck's essays, letters, and speeches.

163   Spencer, Cornelia. *The Exile's Daughter: A Biography of Pearl S. Buck.* New York: Coward-McCann, 1944. 228 pp.

Spencer, Buck's sister, covers the writer's life from childhood up to the time this book was written. Because they are what she knows best, Spencer emphasizes details of their family life together.

164   Stirling, Nora. *Pearl Buck: A Woman in Conflict.* Piscataway, N.J.: New Century, 1983. 352 pp.

Stirling gives her reader a less than traditional view of Buck by focusing on her love affairs. This book's analysis of Buck's personal character is also controversial.

Burnett, Frances H.   1849–1924

165   Burnett, Vivian. *Romantick Lady (Frances Hodgson Burnett): The Life Story of an Imagination.* New York: Charles Scribner's Sons, 1927. 423 pp.

Vivian Burnett is the writer's son. Basing his book on his mother's correspondence, he does not provide a very intimate look at her personal life. He concentrates mainly on describing how the events of her life affected her writing.

166   Thwaite, Ann. *Waiting for the Party: The Life of Frances Hodgson Burnett, 1849–1924.* New York: Charles Scribner's Sons, 1974. 274 pp.

Thwaite, who views her subject as a liberated woman, provides a fairly intimate biography of her. Thwaite also details some of Burnett's friendships with famous people of her era.

Burr, Theodosia   1783–1813

167   Pidgin, Charles F. *Theodosia: The First Gentlewoman of Her Time.* Boston: C. M. Clark Publishing, 1907. 484 pp.

At times this biographer errs in the details of this account, which mainly reprints the major documents extant from Burr's life. He does best when describing her family background and relating the many stories about her death.

Butler, Mother Marie Joseph   1860–1940

168   Burton, Katherine K. *Mother Butler of Marymount.* New York: Longmans, Green, 1944. 290 pp.

Burton's account is totally biased in her subject's favor; it is an overly laudatory tribute to Mother Butler.

Byrne, Jane Burke   1934–

169 FitzGerald, Kathleen W. *Brass: Jane Byrne and the Pursuit of Power*. Chicago: Contemporary Books, 1981. 231 pp.

FitzGerald presents a fairly deep analytical approach to Byrne's personal and political motivations, although she dwells too much on Byrne's first marriage. The book closes on the Chicago election in 1979.

170 Granger, Bill, and Lori Granger. *Fighting Jane: Mayor Jane Byrne and the Chicago Machine*. New York: Dial Press, 1980. 244 pp.

The Grangers describe Byrne's family background and her formative years, then concentrate their account on her various roles in Chicago politics over the years. They are especially apt at demonstrating some of the influences on Byrne.

C

"Calamity Jane"   See **Canary, Martha B.**

Caldwell, (Janet) Taylor   1900–

171   Stearn, Jess. *In Search of Taylor Caldwell.* Briarcliff Manor, N.Y.: Stein and Day, 1981. 172 pp.

Stearn, a friend to Caldwell since 1962, unfortunately mixes gossip with facts in this book, providing an incomplete and confused portrait of Caldwell.

172   ———. *The Search for a Soul: Taylor Caldwell's Psychic Lives.* New York: Doubleday Publishing, 1973. 312 pp.

Stearn, a writer on psychic topics, believes Caldwell has had previous lives due to reincarnation. In this book he describes these earlier existences to Caldwell, who is (as her epilogue to this book states) an unbeliever.

Callas, Maria   1923–1977

173   Callas, Evangelia, and Lawrence G. Blochman. *My Daughter, Maria Callas.* New York: Fleet Press, 1960. 186 pp.

Although the author is Callas's mother, she does not write this complete biography with any affection for her subject. Rather, in detailing their mother-daughter relationship, she includes highly personal facts unflattering to the singer.

174   Galatopoulos, Stelios. *Callas, La Divina: Art That Conceals Art.* Elmsford, N.Y.: London House and Maxwell, 1970. 218 pp.

This biographer writes both of Callas's life and her singing, but he seems to lack the proper background in music to evaluate her performances. However, he does describe clearly her contributions to the major operas in which she appeared.

175   Jellinek, George. *Callas: Portrait of a Prima Donna.* New York: Ziff-Davis Publishing, 1961. 354 pp.

Jellinek interviewed many people to complete this book: a grade-school teacher of Callas's, colleagues in music, and members of her early Greek audiences. He provides a richly detailed portrait of the singer that is mainly objective. However, he offers no deep analysis of her personality or insights into her motivations.

176   Linakis, Steven. *Diva: The Life and Death of Maria Callas*. Englewood Cliffs, N.J.: Prentice-Hall, 1980. 169 pp.

Linakis is a cousin with whom Callas quarreled; the result is that he writes a book hostile to her. He provides only a discussion of the highlights of her career without any thorough evaluation of her art or her character.

177   Meneghini, Giovanni B., and Renzo Allegri. *My Wife Maria Callas*. Trans. Henry Wisneski. New York: Farrar, Straus, Giroux, 1982. 331 pp.

This is a factual rather than interpretive account of the singer's life and career by her former husband and manager. Though Meneghini's book is based on his own reminiscences and correspondence, he effectively employs footnotes to inform the reader.

178   Stancioff, Nadia. *Maria: Callas Remembered*. New York: E. P. Dutton, 1987. 258 pp.

Stancioff provides only a sketch of the singer and her personality, not a full biography. She gives some brief facts of Callas's early life, then details the years they were friends, 1969 to 1977. Most of what she relates about the singer's private life is controversial and portrays Callas in a bad light.

179   Stassinopoulos, Arianna. *Maria Callas: The Woman behind the Legend*. New York: Simon and Schuster, 1981. 383 pp.

This biographer emphasizes the complexities and infelicities of Callas's personality to such an extent that little else is said about her. There are a few detailed explanations about her major roles, but the author lacks a complete knowledge of music, which shows in these sections.

180   Wisneski, Henry. *Maria Callas: The Art behind the Legend*. New York: Doubleday Publishing, 1975. 422 pp.

Wisneski's book focuses mainly on Callas's career, providing only an overview of her basic biography. The text is filled with photographs and selected reviews of Callas's performances.

Cameron, Donaldina M.   1869–1968

181   Martin, Mildred C. *Chinatown's Angry Angel: The Story of Donaldina Cameron*. Palo Alto, Calif.: Pacific Books, 1977. 308 pp.

Although Martin did much research for this book among Cameron's private papers, her sources are not well documented. She attempts, fairly successfully, to explain her subject's complex personality. The last chapters describe Cameron's life after 1942.

182   Wilson, Carol G. *Chinatown Quest*. Stanford: Stanford Univ. Press, 1931. 263 pp.

This is an unscholarly biography that does not document its sources. Since Wilson wrote the book just as Cameron retired from her career, not enough time elapsed to put her work into proper perspective.

Canary, Martha B. "Calamity Jane"   1852–1903

183   Clairmonte, Glenn. *Calamity Was the Name for Jane*. Denver: Sage Books, 1959. 215 pp.

Clairmonte makes use of documents revealed to the public in 1941 by Mrs. Jane McCormick, who claimed to be Canary's daughter by Bill Hickok. She possessed a certificate purporting to prove the two had been married.

184   Mumey, Nolie. *Calamity Jane, 1852–1903: A History of Her Life and Adventures in the West*. Denver: Range Press, 1950. 146 pp.

Mumey's book is useful to researchers because it includes two small pamphlets that Canary herself wrote about her life. This book also contains a map and bibliographical footnotes.

185   Sollid, Roberta B. *Calamity Jane: A Study in Historical Criticism*. Montana: Western Press, 1958. 147 pp.

This is a well-documented and thorough study of Canary. Sollid discusses clearly the various myths about her subject. The book also includes an extensive bibliography.

Cannon, Harriet Starr   1823–1896

186   Dix, Morgan. *Memoir of Harriet Starr Cannon: First Mother Superior of the Sisterhood of St. Mary*. New York: Longmans, Green, 1897. 149 pp.

Dix's account of this woman focuses on her good works and leadership in her religious community. The section dealing with Cannon's efforts during a yellow-fever epidemic in Memphis in 1878 is especially well written.

Carroll, Anna E.   1815–1893

187   Greenbie, Sydney, and Marjorie L. Greenbie. *Anna Ella Carroll and Abraham Lincoln*. Tampa, Fla.: Univ. of Tampa Press, 1952. 539 pp.

This biography contains fictionalization, including imaginary conversations. The authors are overly enthusiastic about their subject and therefore not objective.

Carson, Rachel Louise   1907–1964

188   Brooks, Paul. *The House of Life: Rachel Carson at Work*. Boston: Houghton Mifflin, 1972. 350 pp.

A good sourcebook based primarily on Carson's private papers. Brooks's sympathetic narrative focuses more on her work than on her private life and therefore describes Carson's career effectively.

189   Gartner, Carol B. *Rachel Carson*. New York: Frederick Ungar Publishing, 1983. 161 pp.

This is one in a series of books on modern American writers that serve as introductory volumes to each author and her work. Each book opens with at least one chapter of biographical information, followed by a few chapters that analyze the author's canon. Also included in each book are useful endnotes and bibliographical materials (which are not annotated). Each volume in this series is written with a beginning college student in mind.

Carter, Rosalynn S.   1927–

190   Norton, Howard. *Rosalynn: A Portrait*. Plainfield, N.J.: Logos International, 1978. 220 pp.

Norton's mawkish approach provides neither a clear nor an objective profile of Mrs. Carter.

Carver, Ada Jack   1890–1972

191   Ford, Oliver J. "Ada Jack Carver: A Critical Biography." Dissertation. Univ. of Connecticut, 1975. 186 pp.

Ford reviews Carver's entire writing career, but focuses on the 1920s and after. He describes the events of her personal life and the societal influences that made her cease writing.

Cary, Alice   1820–1871

192   Clemmer, Mary A. *A Memorial of Alice and Phoebe Cary*. New York: Hurd and Houghton, 1873. 351 pp.

Since Clemmer was a friend to Alice Cary, her approach to these two women is sympathetic. The book is well written, although the overly sentimental tone affects its credibility and seriousness.

Cary, Phoebe   1824–1871

193   Clemmer, Mary A. *A Memorial of Alice and Phoebe Cary*. New York: Hurd and Houghton, 1873. 351 pp.
See under Cary, Alice.

Cassatt, Mary   1844–1926

194   Carson, Julia M. H. *Mary Cassatt*. New York: David McKay, 1966. 193 pp.
Although factually correct, this basic biography merely summarizes Cassatt's life, making no analysis of her character. Her art is not discussed at great length, though her art consultations to the wealthy are.

195   Hale, Nancy. *Mary Cassatt*. New York: Doubleday Publishing, 1975. 333 pp.
Hale is especially good at placing Cassatt's later life in proper perspective. She provides the reader with insights as to how the artist worked; in addition, she discusses Cassatt's psychological states.

196   Love, Richard H. *Cassatt: The Independent*. Chicago: Milton H. Kreines, 1980. 270 pp.
Love's competent, understanding approach to Cassatt covers both her life and art. He explains how her background influenced her work and describes what he terms the American aspects of her work. The book contains an extensive bibliography.

197   Mathews, Nancy M. *Mary Cassatt*. New York: Harry N. Abrams, 1987. 160 pp.
This brief life of Cassatt covers all her years, but is best for 1860 to 1876. The author defines her subject's character well and describes some of the social and political influences on her art.

198   Pollock, Griselda. *Mary Cassatt*. New York: Harper and Row, 1980. 119 pp.
Pollock approaches Cassatt's life and art from a feminist viewpoint. The major weakness of her book is a lack of knowledge of U.S. art. The text is well illustrated with Cassatt's paintings.

199   Sweet, Frederick A. *Miss Mary Cassatt, Impressionist from Pennsylvania*. Norman: Univ. of Oklahoma Press. 1966. 242 pp.

This book is scholarly, thoroughly documented, and has a complete bibliography. Sweet covers all the facts of Cassatt's life with care. He quotes frequently from her correspondence to describe her family background and early years.

Cather, Willa S.   1873–1947

200   Bennett, Mildred R. *The World of Willa Cather*. New York: Dodd, Mead, 1951. 226 pp.

Bennett's focus is on Cather's childhood in Nebraska and the novelist's use of its people and setting in her fiction. The biographer interviewed numerous people who knew Cather in order to draw a portrait of her.

201   Bonham, Barbara. *Willa Cather*. Radnor, Penn.: Chilton Books, 1970. 120 pp.

Bonham, who evaluates Cather's life and literary achievements, is sympathetic to her. The first one-quarter of the book deals with Cather's life in Nebraska; the remainder focuses on her writing career.

202   Brown, Edward K., and Leon Edel. *Willa Cather: A Critical Biography*. New York: Alfred A. Knopf, 1953. 351 pp.

Brown presents clearly all the facts of Cather's life, but he does not attempt to evaluate her character. He had the cooperation of Edith Lewis in gaining access to some special materials, yet others were denied him. Leon Edel, who completed this book after Brown's death, writes an introduction to the text.

203   Byrne, Kathleen D., and Richard C. Snyder. *Chrysalis: Willa Cather in Pittsburgh, 1896–1906*. Pittsburgh: Historical Society of Western Pennsylvania, 1980. 125 pp.

This excellent book reveals many new details on this one decade in Cather's life. The text is well documented and clearly written, and includes a good scholarly apparatus.

204   Gerber, Philip. *Willa Cather*. Boston: Twayne Publishers, 1975. 187 pp. See entry 26.

205   Lewis, Edith. *Willa Cather Living: A Personal Record*. New York: Alfred A. Knopf, 1952. 197 pp.

Lewis, an intimate friend to Cather, provides an account of their domestic life together as well as Cather's daily duties and private habits. Although this book is written as a memoir, it is as detailed as a full biography.

206 McFarland, Dorothy T. *Willa Cather*. New York: Frederick Ungar Publishing, 1972. 154 pp.
See entry 189.

207 Moorhead, Elizabeth. *These Two Were Here: Louise Homer and Willa Cather*. Pittsburgh: Univ. of Pittsburgh Press, 1950. 62 pp.
This small volume details the lives of these two artists during their Pittsburgh years. Cather's stay at the McClung home from 1901 to 1906 is described.

208 O'Brien, Sharon. *Willa Cather: The Emerging Voice*. New York: Oxford Univ. Press, 1986. 576 pp.
This scholarly biography gives the reader an accurate, detailed account of Cather's entire life; it supersedes earlier, less thorough biographies. O'Brien, whose approach is that of a feminist, is honest in discussing Cather's sexuality and creative struggles.

209 Rapin, Rene. *Willa Cather*. New York: Robert M. McBride, 1930. 115 pp.
Rapin's early study highlights the major events of Cather's career. This book also includes a brief appreciation of Cather's talent and traces its development.

210 Robinson, Phyllis C. *Willa: The Life of Willa Cather*. New York: Doubleday Publishing, 1983. 321 pp.
Robinson, who admires Cather very much, has written an adequate introductory book for a general reader. She writes best when describing the first half of Cather's life; unfortunately, too much speculation mars the rest of this biography.

211 Sergeant, Elizabeth S. *Willa Cather: A Memoir*. Philadelphia: J. B. Lippincott, 1953. 288 pp.
Sergeant, a longtime friend to Cather, describes their literary relationship in this memoir. She sketches in some personal details about Cather, especially for the years 1910 to 1931. Overall, the book is informal and unscholarly; it also lacks an index.

212 Woodress, James. *Willa Cather: A Literary Life*. Lincoln: Univ. of Nebraska Press, 1987. 583 pp.
Woodress's second book on Cather is filled with many new details about her life. He discusses her sexuality frankly, but without any sensationalizing. He also describes the more eccentric aspects of her personality, although he does not use them to psychoanalyze her.

213 ———. *Willa Cather: Her Life and Art*. New York: Pegasus Publishing, 1970. 288 pp.

Woodress bases his thorough and scholarly biography on newly found (ca. 1970) letters dealing with Cather.

Catt, Carrie Chapman   1859–1947

214 Fowler, Robert B. *Carrie Catt: Feminist Politician*. Boston: Northeastern Univ. Press, 1986. 226 pp.

Fowler's purpose in this biography is to restore Catt to her original place at the center of the suffragist movement. His first three chapters discuss her life's milestones, then he analyzes her career as a brilliant political leader. The book is well documented throughout.

215 Peck, Mary G. *Carrie Chapman Catt: A Biography*. New York: H. W. Wilson, 1944. 495 pp.

Peck's book is mainly concerned with Catt's role as a suffrage-movement leader; it gives few details about her private life. Peck, who was a friend to Catt, admires her and praises the accomplishments of her career.

216 Van Voris, Jacqueline. *Carrie Chapman Catt: A Public Life*. Old Westbury, N.Y.: The Feminist Press, 1987. 300 pp.

Van Voris deals only briefly with Catt's personal life in this book. Instead, she details Catt's public work for the cause of peace. The author also depicts Catt as an international leader of women.

Chadwick, Elizabeth B.   1857–1907

217 Crosbie, John. *The Incredible Mrs. Chadwick: The Most Notorious Woman of Her Age*. New York: McGraw-Hill, 1975. 240 pp.

Crosbie produces a well-written book on Chadwick. He bases his text mainly on newspaper files of her era and a study written about her life in 1905.

Chase, Kate   1840–1899

218 Belden, Thomas G., and Marva R. Belden. *So Fell the Angels*. Boston: Little, Brown, 1956. 401 pp.

The Beldens view Chase as a proud, aggressive, and very political woman. They dwell on the sensational aspects of her life, in particular her frenetic attempt to win her father the U.S. presidency.

219   Phelps, Mary M. *Kate Chase, Dominant Daughter: The Life Story of a Brilliant Woman and Her Famous Father*. New York: Thomas Y. Crowell, 1935. 316 pp.

This is a popular biography that dwells more on Mr. Chase than on his daughter; however, the author does explain Kate's role in her father's political career. Phelps quotes from the family's diaries and letters, particularly when they explain tragic events.

220   Ross, Ishbel. *Proud Kate: Portrait of an Ambitious Woman*. New York: Harper and Brothers, 1952. 309 pp.

This biography relies on fictionalization and overuse of superlative adjectives to tell its story. Although Ross is sympathetic to Chase, she does not sufficiently describe her complex personality.

221   Sokoloff, Alice H. *Kate Chase for the Defense*. New York: Dodd, Mead, 1971. 315 pp.

Sokoloff researched her book thoroughly and makes good use of Chase's diaries and letters. Describing her as less ambitious than do other biographers, Sokoloff also explains how unhappy Chase was in her marriage.

Chase, Mary Ellen   1887–1973

222   Chase, Evelyn H. *Feminist Convert: A Portrait of Mary Ellen Chase*. Santa Barbara, Calif.: John Daniel, 1988. 192 pp.

The biographer, a sister-in-law to her subject, does not successfully explain how Chase became a feminist. The writer is also less than candid about Chase's complex sexuality.

223   Westbrook, Perry D. *Mary Ellen Chase*. New York: Twayne Publishers, 1965. 176 pp.

See entry 26.

Chesnut, Mary B.   1823–1886

224   Muhlenfeld, Elisabeth. *Mary Boykin Chesnut: A Biography*. Baton Rouge: Louisiana State Univ. Press, 1981. 271 pp.

Muhlenfeld used Chesnut's private papers to write this biography, which details the diarist's life, beginning in her childhood. Some emphasis is given to the last two decades of this woman's life, when she flourished as a writer.

Child, Lydia Maria   1802–1880

225 Baer, Helene G. *The Heart Is Like Heaven: The Life of Lydia Maria Child.* Philadelphia: Univ. of Pennsylvania Press, 1964. 339 pp.

Baer describes both Child's private life and her career as a reformist. She explains clearly both Child's marriage and her various friendships. An extensive bibliography is included.

226 Meltzer, Milton. *Tongues of Flame: The Life of Lydia Maria Child.* New York: Thomas Y. Crowell, 1965. 210 pp.

This is a popular biography that summarizes Child's life and career concisely; it depicts her personal traits especially well. Meltzer bases his book on much primary research, particularly contemporary letters to and by Child.

227 Osborne, William S. *Lydia Maria Child.* Boston: Twayne Publishers, 1980. ca. 150 pp.

See entry 26.

Chopin, Kate O.   1851–1904

228 Ewell, Barbara C. *Kate Chopin.* New York: Frederick Ungar Publishing, 1986. 208 pp.

See entry 189.

229 Rankin, Daniel S. *Kate Chopin and Her Creole Stories.* Philadelphia: Press of the Univ. of Pennsylvania, 1932. 313 pp.

While Rankin discusses all of Chopin's life here, his real focus is on her short stories (eleven of which are reprinted in this book). He also provides a nicely detailed chronology of her writings.

230 Seyersted, Per. *Kate Chopin: A Critical Biography.* Baton Rouge: Louisiana State Univ. Press, 1970. 246 pp.

Seyersted focuses in this book on how Chopin's writing was influenced by her personal life. He analyzes her personality fairly well by a deliberate use of psychoanalytic techniques. Most of his text discusses her literature.

231 Skaggs, Peggy. *Kate Chopin.* Boston: Twayne Publishers, 1985. 144 pp.

See entry 26.

Churchill, Jennie Jerome   1850–1921

232 Churchill, Peregrine, and Julian Mitchell. *Jennie, Lady Randolph Churchill: A Portrait with Letters.* New York: St. Martin's Press, 1975. 285 pp.

This is a superficial depiction of Mrs. Churchill based on her private correspondence. The reader gets only a brief glimpse of her life and that of her husband; no new details surface.

233   Kraus, Rene. *Young Lady Randolph: The Life and Times of Jennie Jerome, American Mother of Winston Churchill*. New York: G. P. Putnam's Sons, 1943. 372 pp.

The opening six chapters of this book describe Jennie's early life. The next seventeen chapters concentrate on her married life, her literary efforts, and her relationships to her sons.

234   Leslie, Anita. *Lady Randolph Churchill: The Story of Jennie Jerome*. New York: Charles Scribner's Sons, 1969. 416 pp.

Leslie, a grandniece to her subject, describes her entire life with sympathy. Two weaknesses of this book are its informal writing style and its reliance on gossip.

235   Martin, Ralph G. *Jennie: The Life of Lady Randolph Churchill, the Romantic Years, 1854–1895*. Englewood Cliffs, N.J.: Prentice-Hall, 1969. Vol 1. 404 pp.

Martin's book is not scholarly; he does not provide the necessary evidence for some of the claims he makes on his subject's behalf. This volume ends when Jennie becomes a widow.

236   ———. *Jennie: The Life of Lady Randolph Churchill, the Dramatic Years, 1895–1921*. Englewood Cliffs, N.J.: Prentice-Hall, 1971. Vol 2. 498 pp.

Martin's second volume on Mrs. Churchill uses her own letters, in part, to describe her widowed years; the reader receives a vivid impression of her personality in this manner. This volume covers her two later marriages and her aid to her son Winston's political career.

Claflin, Tennessee C.   1846–1923

237   Brough, James. *The Vixens: A Biography of Victoria and Tennessee Claflin*. New York: Simon and Schuster, 1981. 288 pp.

Brough's book leaves much to be desired. He does not document the sources of his quotations, his views of these two women are stereotyped, and he does not explain their political ideas.

Clark, Kate F.   1875–1957

238   Tucker, Cynthia G. *Kate Freeman Clark: A Painter Rediscovered*. Jackson: Univ. Press of Mississippi, 1981. 104 pp.

This study emphasizes Clark's personal life and her role as a teacher. However, there is also some evaluation of her art. The entire book is based on archival materials, and the text is well illustrated with color reproductions of her art.

Clark, Marguerite   1887–1940

239 Nunn, William C. *Marguerite Clark: America's Darling of Broadway and the Silent Screen*. Fort Worth: Texas Christian Univ. Press, 1981. 189 pp.

Nunn bases his biography on theatrical memoirs from Clark's era, as well as on reviews of her work. Although his book is objective and well documented, it is too brief to do its subject justice.

Clay, Laura   1849–1941

240 Fuller, Paul E. *Laura Clay and the Woman's Rights Movement*. Lexington: Univ. Press of Kentucky, 1975. 216 pp.

Fuller's book, the result of much research, focuses on Clay's intellectual composition rather than on her personal life. Fuller also describes Clay's suffrage work, first in Kentucky and then at the national level.

241 Goodman, Clavia. *Bitter Harvest: Laura Clay's Suffrage Work*. Lexington, Ky.: Bur Press, 1946. 72 pp.

Although this study emphasizes Clay's work for female suffrage, it also treats her ancestry, childhood, and early years.

Clemens, Jane L.   1803–1890

242 Varble, Rachel M. *Jane Clemens: The Story of Mark Twain's Mother*. New York: Doubleday Publishing, 1964. 374 pp.

Varble covers all of Clemens's life, beginning with her birth. Her book, which is based on the Clemens family's letters, is well documented and contains many domestic details.

Clemmer, Mary E.   1831–1884

243 Hudson, Edmund. *A Memorial of Mary Clemmer: An American Woman's Life and Work*. Boston: Ticknor, 1886. 243 pp.

This biography, written by Clemmer's husband, is a sympathetic account of her life and career.

Colbert, Claudette   1905–

244 Quirk, Lawrence J. *Claudette Colbert: An Illustrated Biography*. New York: Crown Publishers, 1985. 212 pp.

Colbert's career is the focus of this book. Quirk discusses the highlights of her acting career, beginning with silent films. He provides a good view of the Hollywood background of her era.

Collson, Mary   1870–1953

245 Tucker, Cynthia G. *A Woman's Ministry: Mary Collson's Search for Reform as a Unitarian Minister, Hull House Social Worker, and a Christian Science Practitioner*. Philadelphia: Temple Univ. Press, 1984. 216 pp.

This well-written book deals more with Collson's career than with her private life, since little information is available on the latter. Her public activities were broad-ranging and this account follows them all.

Cone, Claribel   1864–1929

246 Pollack, Barbara. *The Collectors: Dr. Claribel and Miss Etta Cone*. New York: Bobbs-Merrill, 1961. 320 pp.

Gertrude Stein looms large in this portrait of two sisters. She was their friend and wrote her sketch, "Two Women," about them. (It is reprinted here.) The book also reprints a section of Etta's will concerning their art collection.

Cone, Etta   1870–1949

247 Pollack, Barbara. *The Collectors: Dr. Claribel and Miss Etta Cone*. New York: Bobbs-Merrill, 1961. 320 pp.

See under Cone, Claribel.

Connelly, Cornelia   1809–1879

248 Bisgood, Mother Marie T. *Cornelia Connelly: A Study in Fidelity*. Westminster, Md.: The Newman Press, 1963. 326 pp.

This accurate biography is based chiefly on church documents and archival materials. More details of Connelly's early life are provided here than in other books about her. The controversial aspects of her life are not avoided, yet the emphasis is always on Connelly's extraordinary virtue.

249   A Religious of the Society of the Holy Child Jesus. *Cornelia Connelly, 1809–1879: Foundress of the Society of the Holy Child Jesus.* New York: Longmans, Green, 1922. 263 pp.

This biography was actually begun in one of her convents shortly after Connelly's death; it was intended to record the facts of her life for reading by the religious of her community. The book briefly treats her early life, then becomes more detailed after her conversion to Roman Catholicism. The emphasis is always on her religious works, powerful spirituality, and dedication to her vocation.

250   Wadham, Juliana. *The Case for Cornelia Connelly.* New York: Pantheon Books, 1957. 276 pp.

The "case" of this book's title refers to Connelly's case for sainthood in the Catholic church, which is Wadham's primary concern. The author could be more precise in some of the details of this life, which includes some complex, controversial episodes.

Coolbrith, Ina   1841–1928

251   Rhodehamel, Josephine D., and Raymund F. Wood. *Ina Coolbrith: Librarian and Laureate of California.* Provo, Utah: Brigham Young Univ. Press, 1973. 531 pp.

This biography is concerned with three major elements of Coolbrith's life: the personal, the literary, and her career as a librarian. Although the book is well researched, the subject is described only in a simplified manner, with no faults or complexities to her nature.

Coolidge, Grace G.   1879–1957

252   Ross, Ishbel. *Grace Coolidge and Her Era: The Story of a President's Wife.* New York: Dodd, Mead, 1962. 370 pp.

Ross covers all the stages of this first lady's life, but she also pads this book with many details of the major events in her era. Much space is also devoted to Calvin Coolidge and his famous remarks.

Cooper, Anna J.   1859–1964

253   Gabel, Leona C. *From Slavery to the Sorbonne and Beyond: The Life and Writings of Anna J. Cooper.* Northampton, Mass.: Smith College Press, 1982. 104 pp.

Gabel's study of Cooper, actually written before the one by Hutchinson (see below), is less detailed, but contains a good introduction by Sidney Kaplan and a useful bibliography.

254 Hutchinson, Louise D. *Anna J. Cooper: A Voice from the South.* Washington, D.C.: Smithsonian Press, 1981. 201 pp.

Hutchinson describes both Cooper's personal and family life in this book, as well as her distinguished career in education. Her achievements are carefully noted, and she is seen very vividly in the perspective of her era. Hutchinson also discusses Cooper's writing.

Corbin, Margaret C.   1751–1800

255 Hall, Edward H. *Margaret Corbin, Heroine of the Battle of Fort Washington, 16 November 1776.* New York: American Scenic and Historic Preservation Society, 1932. 47 pp.

This brief, nicely illustrated monograph discusses the veracity of Corbin's service record and accepts her military feats as genuine.

Cornell, Katharine   1898–1974

256 Mosel, Tad, and Gertrude Macy. *Leading Lady: The World and Theatre of Katharine Cornell.* Boston: Little, Brown, 1978. 534 pp.

Macy, Cornell's manager and friend, provides many intimate details about her private life and acting career. The book continually praises Cornell; it is also informative on American theater history. Unfortunately, the authors do not adequately document their sources.

Cowles, Anne Roosevelt   1855–1931

257 Rixey, Lilian. *Bamie: Theodore Roosevelt's Remarkable Sister.* New York: David McKay, 1963. 308 pp.

For the most part, this book is an honest and unsentimental biography. It makes use of Mrs. Cowles's unpublished memoirs, which she wrote for her son.

Crabtree, Lotta   1847–1924

258 Dempsey, David, and Raymond P. Baldwin. *The Triumphs and Trials of Lotta Crabtree.* New York: William Morrow, 1968. 341 pp.

The authors describe Crabtree's theatrical career effectively. However, this book is best on detailing the posthumous legal arguments that ensued when Crabtree's will was contested.

259 Rourke, Constance M. *Troupers of the Gold Coast; or, The Rise of Lotta Crabtree.* New York: Harcourt, Brace, 1928. 262 pp.

Rourke's book is the result of thorough research on California's history and records of its early theaters. She has also uncovered many domestic details of the star's life and her relationship to her mother. However, Crabtree herself is not a vivid figure in this book.

Crandall, Prudence   1803–1889

260   Fuller, Edmund. *Prudence Crandall: An Incident of Racism in Nineteenth Century Connecticut.* Middletown, Conn.: Wesleyan Univ. Press, 1971. 113 pp.
Fuller's book provides the fullest account of Crandall's school for black girls in early Connecticut and her community's reactions to it. Other events in her life are not covered in any detail here.

Crandon, Mina S.   1890?–1941

261   Tietze, Thomas R. *Margery.* New York: Harper and Row, 1973. 201 pp.
This is a scholarly and detailed book. Crandon appears vividly in the biographer's narrative.

Crane, Cora H.   1868–1910

262   Gilkes, Lillian B. *Cora Crane: A Biography of Mrs. Stephen Crane.* Bloomington: Indiana Univ. Press, 1959. 416 pp.
This is a scholarly, well-written, and adequately documented biography, based on Cora Crane's private papers. The book re-creates her personality clearly as Gilkes addresses the scandalous elements of her life and tries to resolve them.

Crapsey, Adelaide   1878–1914

263   Alkalay-Gut, Karen. *Alone in the Dawn: The Life of Adelaide Crapsey.* Athens: Univ. of Georgia Press, 1988. 286 pp.
This first full-length modern biography of Crapsey describes her personal life in more detail than has previously been available. The book is well illustrated.

264   Butscher, Edward. *Adelaide Crapsey.* Boston: Twayne Publishers, 1979. 129 pp.
See entry 26.

265   Osborn, Mary E. *Adelaide Crapsey.* Boston: Bruce Humphries, 1933. 119 pp.

Osborn wrote this brief memoir in appreciation of Crapsey after her death. Her account is mainly sympathetic and makes good use of details.

Cratty, Mabel   1868–1928

266 Burton, Margaret E. *Mabel Cratty: Leader in the Art of Leadership*. New York: Woman's Press, 1929. 248 pp.

Burton, a colleague of Cratty, re-creates her character and her leadership abilities in this book. This volume opens with a biographical sketch, then reprints portions of Cratty's notebooks, letters, and speeches.

Crawford, Joan   1908–1977

267 Crawford, Christina. *Mommie Dearest*. New York: William Morrow, 1978. 286 pp.

In this book Christina paints a grim portrait of her mother, depicting her as a child abuser. However, the author does not display bitterness in her account; rather, she calmly relates the facts of her unhappy childhood.

268 Thomas, Bob. *Joan Crawford: A Biography*. New York: Simon and Schuster, 1978. 315 pp.

Thomas's biography relies too much on movie magazines (from which he quotes often) to tell of Crawford's life. He relates many of her poor qualities, some of which coincide with those discussed in Christina Crawford's book (see above).

269 Walker, Alexander. *Joan Crawford: The Ultimate Star*. New York: Harper and Row, 1983. 192 pp.

This biography, which is based on the MGM studio files, describes Crawford's life at the height of her career. Few details of her personal problems are revealed, and the book is weak on the years after 1943.

Crosby, Fanny   1820–1915

270 Jackson, Samuel T. *Fanny Crosby's Story of Ninety-four Years*. New York: Fleming H. Revell, 1915. ca. 180 pp.

This book, which was written shortly after the composer's death, relies heavily on Crosby's personal reminiscences to tell the story. Her own two autobiographies are more richly detailed than is this biography.

271 Ruffin, Bernard. *Fanny Crosby*. New York: United Church Press, 1976. 257 pp.

This is a complete, well-researched, and properly documented book on Crosby's life and work. Ruffin bases his study on Crosby's private papers and on interviews with her friends and relatives. He defines her musical accomplishments and evaluates her role in American hymnal music.

Crothers, Rachel   1878–1958

272 Gottlieb, Lois C. *Rachel Crothers*. Boston: Twayne Publishers, 1979. 170 pp.
See entry 26.

Cunningham, Imogen   1883–1976

273 Dater, Judy. *Imogen Cunningham: A Portrait*. Boston: New York Graphic Society, 1979. 188 pp.
Dater's text relates the basic facts of Cunningham's long life. She also includes interviews with friends and colleagues of her subject, who describe her personality effectively. Many Cunningham photographs are reprinted in this book.

Curzon, Mary Leiter   1870–1906

274 Nicolson, Nigel. *Mary Curzon*. New York: Harper and Row, 1978. 227 pp.
Nicolson was commissioned by Curzon's daughter to write this book; as a result, his approach is highly sympathetic. He quotes from his subject's diaries, which were written in India, to provide a personal view of her life there.

Cushman, Charlotte S.   1816–1876

275 Clement, Clara E. *Charlotte Cushman*. Boston: James R. Osgood, 1882. 193 pp.
Although this biography covers Cushman's life and career in some detail, it eulogizes her too much. When Clement discusses the actress's personal character, it is merely to praise her. The book also relies on lengthy, favorable reviews to describe Cushman's acting talent.

276 Leach, Joseph. *Bright Particular Star: The Life and Times of Charlotte Cushman*. New Haven: Yale Univ. Press, 1970. 453 pp.
This well-researched biography includes many informative details on Cushman's life. It also describes actors she knew and their era in the theater. Leach's notes to the book are helpful to a serious student.

277 Stebbins, Emma. *Charlotte Cushman: Her Letters and Memories of Her Life*. Boston: Houghton Mifflin, 1899. 308 pp.

Stebbins, a friend to Cushman, relies on her subject's correspondence to relate much of her life. Stebbins had also interviewed Cushman in order to record her own remembrances. The book closes with various tributes written to the actress.

Cushman, Pauline   1833–1893

278 Sarmiento, F. L. *The Life of Pauline Cushman*. Philadelphia: J. E. Potter, 1865. 374 pp.

Sarmiento's is a popular, laudatory account of the spy's career. The facts he supplies here are verified in the files of the U.S. federal government.

D

Davidson, Margaret M.   1823–1838

279   Irving, Washington. *The Biography of the Late Margaret Miller Davidson.* Ed. Elsie L. West. Boston: Twayne Publishers, 1978. 654 pp.

This biography of a young poet who died at age fifteen is printed in one volume along with Irving's biography of Oliver Goldsmith. In writing of Davidson, Irving uses notes given to him by the girl's mother.

Davies, Marion C.   1897–1961

280   Guiles, Fred L. *Marion Davies: A Biography.* New York: McGraw-Hill, 1972. 419 pp.

Although Davies is the main subject of this book, Guiles spends a good amount of space discussing her love affair with William R. Hearst. The biographer also praises Davies's talents as an actress.

Davis, Angela Y.   1944–

281   Nadelson, Regina. *Who Is Angela Davis? The Biography of a Revolutionary.* New York: Wyden Publishing House, 1972. 208 pp.

This is a popular and sympathetic book on Davis. Nadelson is especially apt at detailing her subject's early years and personal development. There is little information about Davis's trial here.

282   Parker, J. A. *Angela Davis: The Making of a Revolutionary.* Arlington, Va.: Arlington House, 1973. 272 pp.

Parker's coverage of Davis's early life is scant, filling only twenty pages of this book. The emphasis is on her adult years, her political views, and her teaching career.

Davis, Bette   1908–1989

283   Higham, Charles. *Bette: The Life of Bette Davis.* New York: Macmillan Publishing, 1981. 361 pp.

Higham focuses more attention on Davis's personal life than he does on her film career. His account opens with the star's childhood and narrates all the events of her life; he relies heavily on gossip and sensational items to tell her story.

284   Hyman, Barbara D. *My Mother's Keeper*. New York: William Morrow, 1985. 348 pp.

Hyman, Davis's daughter, examines their troubled relationship. She describes her mother in a negative light throughout the book.

285   Stine, Whitney. *Mother Goddam: The Story of the Career of Bette Davis*. New York: Hawthorn Books, 1974. 374 pp.

Stine focuses on the various stages of Davis's career, including in his text very little of her personal life. An informative feature of the book is the actress's own interspersed comments on and corrections to the text.

286   Vermilye, Jerry. *Bette Davis*. New York: Pyramid Publishers, 1973. 159 pp.

This is one in a series of books on noted actresses called "The Pyramid Illustrated History of the Movies." Each book serves as an introduction to the actress's life and career (film-by-film evaluations are given), and many are written by teachers of cinema studies. Also included in each of these volumes are a filmography and a bibliography, which add to their value as reference tools.

287   Walker, Alexander. *Bette Davis: A Celebration*. Boston: Little, Brown, 1986. 192 pp.

Walker includes all the basic facts of Davis's life in this book. He also makes a critical evaluation of her career. Although this book has a filmography, it lacks an index.

Davis, Rebecca B.   1831–1910

288   Langford, Gerald. *The Richard Harding Davis Years: A Biography of a Mother and Son*. New York: Holt, Rinehart and Winston, 1961. 336 pp.

Langford provides a candid account of this close mother-son relationship. He had access to the personal papers of both writers; therefore, he is able to quote from their letters (which he does judiciously).

Davis, Varina Howell   1826–1906

289   Ross, Ishbel. *First Lady of the South: The Life of Mrs. Jefferson Davis*. New York: Harper and Brothers, 1957. 475 pp.

Ross is sympathetic to Davis in this simple biography, which emphasizes Davis's marriage rather than the politics of the era. The biographer details this woman's private life, but provides no analysis of her character.

290   Rowland, Eron O. *Varina Howell, Wife of Jefferson Davis.* New York: Macmillan Publishing, 1927. Vol 1. 499 pp.

In this volume, full of domestic details, Rowland covers Mrs. Davis's life up to the time her husband assumes the Confederate Presidency. Throughout, the book has high praise for its subject, whom the author views in a sentimental light.

291   ———. *Varina Howell, Wife of Jefferson Davis.* New York: Macmillan Publishing, 1931. Vol 2. 583 pp.

In this second volume Rowland chronicles his subject's life from the start of the Confederacy until her death. He explains much of the political background of her era and makes an interesting evaluation of her character.

292   Van der Heuvel, Gerry. *Crowns of Thorns and Glory: Mary Todd Lincoln and Varina Howell Davis, the Two First Ladies of the Civil War.* New York: E. P. Dutton, 1988. 352 pp.

The author has not succeeded in integrating these two biographies into one narrative. She does explain the parallel experiences of both women, particularly their victimization at the hands of their husbands' opponents.

Day, Dorothy   1897–1980

293   Forest, Jim. *Love Is the Measure: A Biography of Dorothy Day.* Mahwah, N. J.: The Paulist Press, 1987. 224 pp.

Forest, while providing the basic facts of Day's life, delineates her character clearly. He focuses on her career with the *Catholic Worker*, where he was also an editor.

294   Miller, William D. *Dorothy Day: A Biography.* New York: Harper and Row, 1982. 527 pp.

Although Miller constantly praises Day in this book, he uses candid details from her private papers to describe her life precisely. This is the better of his two books on Day (see below).

295   ———. *A Harsh and Dreadful Love: Dorothy Day and the Catholic Worker Movement.* New York: Doubleday Publishing, 1974. 356 pp.

Two chapters of this book are strictly biographical and are based on Day's own writings. After the year 1932, Miller discusses only Day's work for her movement and not her private life.

de Havilland, Olivia   1916–

296 Higham, Charles. *Sisters: The Story of Olivia de Havilland and Joan Fontaine*. New York: Coward, McCann and Geoghegan, 1984. 257 pp.

This dual biography compares the actresses' lives and careers, highlighting the jealousy that exists between them. The author makes some factual errors.

Deland, Margaret   1857–1945

297 Reep, Diana C. *Margaret Deland*. Boston: Twayne Publishers, 1985. 152 pp.

See entry 26.

Demorest, Ellen C.   1825–1898

298 Ross, Ishbel. *Crusades and Crinolines: The Life and Times of Ellen Curtis Demorest and William Jennings Demorest*. New York: Harper and Row, 1963. 275 pp.

Many famous people appear in this book, not just the two in the title. Although too much unnecessary detail of the social history of their era fills this biography, when Ross does discuss the couple, she vividly describes their magazine publishing.

Denton, Mary F.   1857–1947

299 Clapp, Frances B. *Mary Florence Denton and the Doshisha*. Kyoto, Japan: Doshisha Univ. Press, 1955. 439 pp.

Clapp, a missionary who worked with Denton, writes a complete biography of her colleague's life and her work at Doshisha Women's College in Japan.

DeWolfe, Elsie   1865–1950

300 Smith, Jane S. *Elsie de Wolfe: A Life in High Style*. New York: Atheneum Publishers, 1982. 366 pp.

Smith's meticulously researched book is not only descriptive of her subject's career, but is also illuminating on the history of interior design. However, this account does not reveal DeWolfe's personality clearly.

Dickey, Sarah Ann   1838–1904

301 Griffith, Helen. *Dauntless in Mississippi: The Life of Sarah A. Dickey, 1838–1904*. South Hadley, Mass.: Dinosaur Press, 1965. 170 pp.

Griffith's book is based on exhaustive research from archival material, as well as interviews with Dickey's former students. She describes well Dickey's own years as a college student.

Dickinson, Emily   1830–1886

302   Bianchi, Martha D. *Emily Dickinson Face to Face: Unpublished Letters with Notes and Reminiscences.* Boston: Houghton Mifflin, 1932. 282 pp.

Bianchi, the poet's niece, recalls life among the Dickinson family in this book. She describes particularly vividly her childhood reactions to the poet. More than one hundred pages of this volume reprint Dickinson's letters to Bianchi's mother.

303   ——. *The Life and Letters of Emily Dickinson.* Boston: Houghton Mifflin, 1924. 386 pp.

This early biography of the poet was written by her niece. The biographer is swayed by the legend of her aunt as a mysterious and dramatic personality in Amherst.

304   Bingham, Millicent T. *Emily Dickinson: A Revelation.* New York: Harper and Brothers, 1954. 109 pp.

Bingham describes the poet's deeply felt emotional regard for Judge Otis Lord in her later years. The book reprints drafts of the letters the poet wrote to Lord in the late 1870s and early 1880s.

305   Chase, Richard V. *Emily Dickinson.* New York: William Sloane Associates, 1951. 328 pp.

The first half of this book describes the poet's life up to 1862. The rest of the book contains an analysis of her poetry, and closes with a discussion of her last years.

306   Cody, John. *After Great Pain: The Inner Life of Emily Dickinson.* Cambridge: Harvard Univ. Press, 1971. 538 pp.

Cody, a psychiatrist, analyzes Dickinson through a study of her poems. His is a controversial book that feminist scholars oppose.

307   Ferlazzo, Paul J. *Emily Dickinson.* Boston: Twayne Publishers, 1976. 168 pp.

See entry 26.

308   Garbowsky, Maryanne M. *The House without the Door: Emily Dickinson and the Illness of Agoraphobia.* Madison, N. J.: Fairleigh Dickinson Univ. Press, 1988. 189 pp.

Garbowsky believes that the poet's reclusiveness was the result of agoraphobia; she describes how the illness affected Dickinson's life and work. The biographer also refutes earlier theories about Dickinson's withdrawal into her home.

309 Gelpi, Albert J. *Emily Dickinson: The Mind of the Poet*. Cambridge: Harvard Univ. Press, 1965. 201 pp.

By studying essential sections of Dickinson's poetry and prose, Gelpi fairly successfully re-creates her inner life.

310 Higgins, David. *Portrait of Emily Dickinson: The Poet and Her Prose*. New Brunswick, N. J.: Rutgers Univ. Press, 1967. 266 pp.

Higgins re-creates the poet's life by reading the facts and emotions in her letters. He also devotes much of the text to describing how her family and friends influenced her. He identifies "Master" as Samuel Bowles.

311 Jenkins, MacGregor. *Emily Dickinson: Friend and Neighbor*. Boston: Little, Brown, 1939. 150 pp.

Jenkins was a neighbor whose house faced that of the Dickinsons; here he recalls his impressions of the poet and her family. Since Jenkins was born in 1869, he cannot reveal much about the poet's early years.

312 Johnson, Thomas H. *Emily Dickinson: An Interpretive Biography*. Cambridge: Harvard Univ. Press, 1955. 276 pp.

Johnson's book describes both Dickinson's life and her art. The biographical elements, which focus on the poet's life among her family and friends, were based on newly found data (ca. 1955).

313 Leyda, Jay. *The Years and Hours of Emily Dickinson*. New Haven: Yale Univ. Press, 1960. 2 vols. 400 pp./528 pp.

Leyda's is the most detailed and comprehensive book on Dickinson's entire life; all of his sources are well documented. Volume one covers the years 1828 to 1860, and volume two discusses the final years of the poet's life.

314 Longsworth, Polly. *Emily Dickinson: Her Letter to the World*. New York: Thomas Y. Crowell, 1965. 170 pp.

Longsworth emphasizes the poet's upbringing in Amherst. She writes in clear detail of life there in the middle of the 1800s.

315 Miller, Ruth. *The Poetry of Emily Dickinson*. Middletown, Conn.: Wesleyan Univ. Press, 1968. 480 pp.

The opening chapters of this book highlight elements of the poet's personal life that most affected her art: Austin Dickinson's love affair, Emily's letters to Thomas Higginson, and her friendship with Samuel Bowles.

316 Mossberg, Barbara A. C. *Emily Dickinson: When a Writer Is a Daughter.* Bloomington: Indiana Univ. Press, 1983. 214 pp.

Mossberg studies the poet's early life, particularly her relationships to both her parents, in order to understand her personality. Mossberg employs a feminist approach in this book, which is based on good scholarship.

317 Patterson, Rebecca. *The Riddle of Emily Dickinson.* Boston: Houghton Mifflin, 1951. 434 pp.

Patterson's theory is that the poet's disappointment in love came about when she was hurt by a female lover. However, the author gives too little evidence to substantiate her claim.

318 Pickard, John B. *Emily Dickinson: An Introduction and Interpretation.* New York: Holt, Rinehart and Winston, 1967. 140 pp.

This short introductory book combines biography with literary criticism. It is best for use by a beginning college student.

319 Pollitt, Josephine. *Emily Dickinson: The Human Background of Her Poetry.* New York: Harper and Brothers, 1930. 350 pp.

This life of the poet focuses on the influences of New England on her intellect and career. Pollitt believes that Dickinson's private love was for Major Edward Hunt.

320 Sewall, Richard B. *The Life of Emily Dickinson.* New York: Farrar, Straus and Giroux, 1974. 2 vols.

This is a comprehensive biography that includes all the known facts about and discusses all the theories on Dickinson. Sewall places her precisely in the context of her social environs and her family relationships. Volume one describes her time and place; volume two details her individual life.

321 Shurr, William H. *The Marriage of Emily Dickinson.* Lexington: Univ. Press of Kentucky, 1983. 240 pp.

Shurr's book, which remains objective, presents the theory that the poet had a spiritual love affair with the Reverend Charles Wadsworth, to whom much of her poetry is addressed.

322 Taggard, Genevieve. *The Life and Mind of Emily Dickinson.* New York: Alfred A. Knopf, 1930. 378 pp.

Taggard's sympathetic biography theorizes that the poet was in love with the Reverend George H. Gould, of whom her father disapproved.

323 Walsh, John E. *The Hidden Side of Emily Dickinson.* New York: Simon and Schuster, 1971. 286 pp.

Walsh speculates (without enough evidence) on the reasons why the poet became a recluse. He includes an imaginative (not scholarly) discussion of her relationships to men. He is clear and accurate only on her friendship with Judge Otis Lord.

324 Ward, Theodora V. *The Capsule of the Mind: Chapters in the Life of Emily Dickinson.* Cambridge: Harvard Univ. Press, 1961. 205 pp.

Ward's book is a collection of six of her essays on the poet: one on her inner life, one on her mid-life emotional trauma, one on her spiritual life after 1865, and three on her important friendships.

325 Whicher, George F. *This Was a Poet: A Critical Biography of Emily Dickinson.* New York: Charles Scribner's Sons, 1939. 337 pp.

This is an accurate and fairly thorough biography. Whicher emphasizes the New England mores and culture in which the poet was raised.

326 Wolff, Cynthia G. *Emily Dickinson.* New York: Alfred A. Knopf, 1986. 641 pp.

This book is more concerned with the poet's career than with her personal life. Those parts of the account that are biographical deal with too many general details about nineteenth-century life and not with the poet specifically.

Didion, Joan 1934–

327 Henderson, Katherine U. *Joan Didion.* New York: Frederick Ungar Publishing, 1981. 164 pp.

See entry 189.

328 Winchell, Mark R. *Joan Didion.* Boston: Twayne Publishers, 1980. 185 pp.

See entry 26.

Didrikson, Mildred "Babe"   See **Zaharias, Mildred "Babe"**

Dix, Beulah M.   1876–1970

329 Scott, Evelyn F. *Hollywood When Silents Were Golden.* New York: McGraw-Hill, 1972. 256 pp.

In this nostalgic book, Scott describes the life of her mother, a Hollywood screenwriter; she focuses on Dix's friendship with the DeMille family.

Dix, Dorothea Lynde   1802–1887

330 Marshall, Helen E. *Dorothea Dix: Forgotten Samaritan.* Chapel Hill: Univ. of North Carolina Press, 1937. 298 pp.

This basic, informative biography of Dix, which is carefully researched and clearly documented, discusses her personal life as well as her career.

331 Tiffany, Frances. *The Life of Dorothea Lynde Dix.* Boston: Houghton Mifflin, 1890. 392 pp.

This complete biography of Dix covers all the eras of her life, beginning with her genealogy. In a closing section, Tiffany analyzes Dix's character and the contributions she made to U.S. society.

332 Wilson, Dorothy C. *Stranger and Traveler: The Story of Dorothea Dix, American Reformer.* Boston: Little, Brown, 1975. 360 pp.

This study of Dix is primarily a popularized and superficial account of her life and career. Wilson does not document her sources of information.

Dix, Dorothy   1870–1951

333 Kane, Harnett T., and Ella B. Arthur. *Dear Dorothy Dix: The Story of a Compassionate Woman.* New York: Doubleday Publishing, 1952. 314 pp.

This overly sympathetic biography of Dix, which focuses on her years as a journalist, offers only a shallow portrait of its subject.

Dixon, Jeane P.   1918–

334 Montgomery, Ruth. *A Gift of Prophecy: The Phenomenal Jeane Dixon.* New York: William Morrow, 1965. 192 pp.

This is a popular biography that does not discuss Dixon's life in adequate detail. It includes an explanation of her prediction of the JFK assassination.

Dodge, Grace H.   1856–1914

335 Graham, Abbie. *Grace H. Dodge: Merchant of Dreams*. New York: Woman's Press, 1926. 329 pp.
Dodge's entire career and work methods are detailed in this book. This is her official biography, which was sanctioned by the YWCA.

Doolittle, Hilda (H.D.)   1886–1961

336 Guest, Barbara. *Herself Defined: The Poet H.D. and Her World*. New York: Doubleday Publishing, 1984. 360 pp.
This is an authorized biography prepared with the cooperation of H.D.'s daughter. Guest mainly writes objectively of her subject and provides new domestic and family information about her. She quotes often in her text from the poet's letters.

337 Quinn, Vincent. *Hilda Doolittle (H. D.)*. New York: Twayne Publishers, 1967. 160 pp.
See entry 26.

338 Robinson, Janice S. *H.D.: The Life and Work of an American Poet*. Boston: Houghton Mifflin, 1982. 490 pp.
About one-quarter of this book is biographical and the rest is literary criticism. Robinson discusses all of the periods of the poet's life while focusing on her relationships to men.

Douglas, Harriet   1790–1872

339 Davidson, Angus. *Miss Douglas of New York: A Biography*. New York: Viking Press, 1953. 255 pp.
Written by a distant relative, this well-researched biography is the only one available on Douglas. Davidson places her well in the literary society of the New York of her era.

Draper, Dorothy   1889–1969

340 Varney, Carleton. *The Draper Touch: The High Life and High Style of Dorothy Draper*. Englewood Cliffs, N.J.: Prentice-Hall, 1988. 320 pp.
Varney, who now heads the Dorothy Draper Company, writes on its founder's life and career. His account is full of anecdotes and sensational details.

Draper, Ruth   1884–1956

341 Zabel, Morton D. *The Art of Ruth Draper: Her Dramas and Characters.* New York: Doubleday Publishing, 1960. 114 pp.

This book consists of Zabel's biographical memoir of Draper and a section that reprints the scripts of thirty-five of her monologues.

Dulles, Eleanor L.   1895–

342 Mosley, Leonard. *Dulles: A Biography of Eleanor, Allen, and John Foster Dulles and Their Family Network.* New York: Dial Press, 1978. 530 pp.

Mosley relies on episodic tales and anecdotes to tell the Dulles story in this book, which makes some factual errors. The author is especially sympathetic to Eleanor.

Dunbar-Nelson, Alice   1875–1935

343 Williams, Ruby O. "An In-Depth Portrait of Alice Dunbar-Nelson." Dissertation. Univ. of California at Irvine, 1974. 265 pp.

Williams's study focuses on her subject's four decades in public life. She discusses the nature of Dunbar-Nelson's personality and details her work for social causes, as well as her writing career.

Duncan, Isadora   1877–1927

344 Blair, Fredrika. *Isadora: Portrait of the Artist as a Woman.* New York: McGraw-Hill, 1986. 470 pp.

This well-documented book offers many interesting details about Duncan, her family, and her intimate friends. The author is mainly objective in her approach.

345 Desti, Mary. *Untold Story: The Life of Isadora Duncan, 1921–1927.* New York: Horace Liveright, 1929. 281 pp.

Desti, a close friend to Duncan, describes the last six years of her life (those not covered in the autobiography). This book includes a frank account of the dancer's marriage to the Russian poet Esenin.

346 Duncan, Irma, and Allan R. Macdougall. *Isadora Duncan's Russian Days and Her Last Years in France.* London: Victor Gollancz, 1929. 384 pp.

The authors of this biography are Duncan's adopted daughter and Duncan's secretary, respectively. They offer many intimate details of her later life.

347 Macdougall, Allan R. *Isadora: A Revolutionary in Art and Love.* Nashville: Thomas Nelson, 1959. 296 pp.

The author, Duncan's secretary in 1916 and 1917, gives the details of her life in this book, but emphasizes her career. He is especially good at describing how the press of her era received Duncan.

348 McVay, Gordon. *Isadora and Esenin.* Ann Arbor: Ardis Publishers, 1980. 335 pp.

McVay, Sergei Esenin's biographer, describes the brief love affair and marriage of the celebrated couple. McVay has done much careful research; as a result, his book is thorough and scholarly.

349 Schneider, Ilya I. *Isadora Duncan: The Russian Years.* Trans. David Magarshack. New York: Harcourt, Brace and World, 1969. 221 pp.

This biography covers the years 1921 to 1926. The author, a friend to Duncan, is rather frank about the dancer's marriage to Esenin.

350 Seroff, Victor. *The Real Isadora.* New York: Dial Press, 1971. 441 pp.

Seroff is apt at separating the truth about Duncan from the legends about her. He covers all of her life and career in documented detail; however, he is best at describing her late career, when he knew her personally.

351 Stokes, Sewell. *Isadora Duncan: An Intimate Portrait.* New York: Bretano's, 1928. 208 pp.

Stokes provides an emotional account of Duncan, whom he knew in the last years of her life.

352 Terry, Walter. *Isadora Duncan: Her Life, Her Art, Her Legacy.* New York: Dodd, Mead, 1964. 174 pp.

Terry's book has two major sections: the first describes Duncan's life and career, and the second analyzes her achievements in dance. He also includes a discussion of her theory of dance.

Dunham, Katherine   1910–

353 Beckford, Ruth. *Katherine Dunham: A Biography.* New York: Marcel Dekker, 1979. 146 pp.

Beckford, a friend to Dunham, writes an admiring account of her personal life and career. A useful glossary is included.

354   Haskins, James. *Katherine Dunham*. New York: Coward, McCann and Geoghegan, 1982. 158 pp.

Haskins's book strikes a fine balance between Dunham's personal life and her dance career. He describes particularly well her role as a black American artist.

Duniway, Abigail Scott   1834–1915

355   Moynihan, Ruth B. *Rebel for Rights, Abigail Scott Duniway*. New Haven: Yale Univ. Press, 1983. 273 pp.

This is a complete biography of Duniway's private life and public career. Based mainly on her family papers, it begins with her birth and traces the influences that caused her to work for women's rights. Moynihan also discusses her subject's political views in some detail.

E

Eagels, Jeanne   1894–1929

356   Doherty, Edward J. *Rain Girl: The Tragic Story of Jeanne Eagels*. Philadelphia: Macrae Smith, 1931. 313 pp.

Although Doherty has researched his subject fairly well, he has not documented his sources. His account appears to be accurate, but some scenes and conversations are fictionalized.

Earhart, Amelia M.   1898–1937

357   Briand, Paul L. *Daughter of the Sky: The Story of Amelia Earhart*. New York: Duell, Sloan and Pearce, 1960. 230 pp.

Briand, an admirer of Earhart and himself a pilot, is best at describing her flying abilities and missions. He does not detail her personal life too clearly, except for an objective discussion of her marriage.

358   Burke, John. *Winged Legend: The Story of Amelia Earhart*. New York: G. P. Putnam's Sons, 1970. 256 pp.

Burke has nothing but praise for his subject. His book covers both Earhart's life and her career. He offers a good perspective on her family background when he discusses her grandparents' lives.

359   Morrissey, Muriel E. *Courage Is the Price*. Wichita, Kans.: McCormick-Armstrong, 1963. 221 pp.

Morrissey covers her sister's life fully, beginning with her childhood. She writes affectionately yet candidly of Earhart. She seems to understand her older sister's nature completely, and she has sympathy for her work in aviation. (In 1987 this book was reissued as *Amelia: My Courageous Sister*.)

360   Putnam, George P. *Soaring Wings: A Biography of Amelia Earhart*. New York: Harcourt, Brace, 1939. 294 pp.

Putnam, Earhart's husband, describes her personality vividly while he focuses on her career in aviation. His well-written book also relates enough about her early life to make this a complete biography.

Eaton, Margaret "Peggy"   1799–1879

361 Phillips, Leon. *That Eaton Woman: In Defense of Peggy O'Neale Eaton*. Barre, Mass.: Barre/Westover, 1974. 184 pp.

Phillips covers all of Eaton's life, but devotes much of the book to the controversies she created, particularly the famous incident involving Andrew Jackson's cabinet. Too many trivial details that add little to her biography are included.

362 Pollock, Queena. *Peggy Eaton, Democracy's Mistress*. New York: Minton, Balch, 1931. 295 pp.

This is a popular biography which romanticizes Eaton's life while it takes her side in the scandal that centered on her. The book relies heavily on quotations from newspapers and letters to tell her story.

Eddy, Mary Baker   1821–1910

363 Bates, Ernest S., and John V. Dittemore. *Mary Baker Eddy: The Truth and the Tradition*. New York: Alfred A. Knopf, 1932. 510 pp.

This is a well-documented book that attempts to clear away mistaken ideas about Eddy and her theology. Dittemore was a dissenter from Christian Science; therefore, he is not always favorable to Eddy.

364 Beasley, Norman. *Mary Baker Eddy*. New York: Duell, Sloan and Pearce, 1962. 371 pp.

Beasley reiterates all the known facts of Eddy's life but provides only a superficial view of the woman. He covers nothing controversial in this book.

365 Dakin, Edwin F. *Mrs. Eddy: The Biography of a Virginal Mind*. New York: Charles Scribner's Sons, 1929. 553 pp.

After having done careful research, Dakin presents the facts of Eddy's life and teachings. His account of her life is full and objective, including a vivid view of her late years. The book is well documented and has a ten-page bibliography.

366 D'Humy, Fernand E. *Mary Baker Eddy in a New Light*. New York: Library Publishers, 1952. 181 pp.

Although the author is sympathetic to Eddy, he does not seem to understand the fine details of Christian Science. He offers no new facts or an analysis of her life.

367 Kennedy, Hugh A. S. *Mrs. Eddy: Her Life, Her Work, and Her Place in History*. San Francisco: Farallon Press, 1947. 507 pp.

Kennedy, a loyal follower of Eddy, attempts to write a sincere and complete account of her life without exaggeration. However, he does not discuss the controversial aspects of her career.

368 Milmine, Georgine. *The Life of Mary Baker G. Eddy and the History of Christian Science*. New York: Doubleday, Page, 1909. 495 pp.

Milmine's book attempts to expose any misconduct by Eddy and her church. The author was able to interview many people who knew Eddy in her early life and career.

369 Peel, Robert. *Mary Baker Eddy: The Years of Discovery*. New York: Holt, Rinehart and Winston, 1966. Vol 1. 372 pp.

Peel's, the best biography of Eddy available in recent years, is scholarly and thorough. He writes to clarify legends about her and to replace them with the facts he found in the church archives (which house new data on her life). This first volume closes in 1875.

370 ———. *Mary Baker Eddy: The Years of Trial*. New York: Holt, Rinehart and Winston, 1972. Vol 2. 391 pp.

Peel, who has thoroughly researched Eddy, includes some new materials on her in this volume of his biography, which covers the years 1876 to 1891. This book offers a frank and balanced view of the woman and her work.

371 ———. *Mary Baker Eddy: The Years of Authority*. New York: Holt, Rinehart and Winston, 1977. Vol 3. 528 pp.

Peel focuses both on Eddy's domestic life and on her teachings in this volume, which covers the years 1892 to 1910. He reveals here that he considers her to be a genius, yet his approach remains mostly objective.

372 Powell, Lyman P. *Mary Baker Eddy: A Life Size Portrait*. New York: Macmillan Publishing, 1930. 364 pp.

Powell is completely biased in favor of Eddy and her teachings. The biography is incomplete since he omits any details unfavorable to his subject.

373 Ramsay, E. Mary. *Christian Science and Its Discoverer*. Boston: The Christian Science Publishing Society, 1955. 137 pp.

Ramsay, an enthusiastic supporter of Eddy and her church, writes a competent but biased biography. Ramsay herself was a major leader of the Christian Science movement in Scotland and so is only positive about its founder.

374   Silberger, Julius. *Mary Baker Eddy: An Interpretive Biography of the Founder of Christian Science.* Boston: Little, Brown, 1980. 274 pp.

This book provides a basic and objective biography of Eddy. Silberger is a psychoanalyst, yet his evaluation of her character remains simplistic.

375   Springer, Fleta C. *According to the Flesh: A Biography of Mary Baker Eddy.* New York: Coward-McCann, 1930. 497 pp.

Springer focuses on Eddy's personal character rather than on her career in this book. The author is especially good at describing Eddy's childhood.

376   Tomlinson, Irving C. *Twelve Years with Mary Baker Eddy: Recollections and Experiences.* Boston: The Christian Science Publishing Society, 1945. 227 pp.

Tomlinson's account of Eddy is most detailed for the years 1908 to 1910, when he was a secretary living in her household. He employs his own notes and recollections of those years to describe Eddy's conversations with him.

377   Wilbur, Sibyl. *The Life of Mary Baker Eddy.* Boston: The Christian Science Publishing Society, 1938. 423 pp.

This, one of the earliest biographies of Eddy, is written by a biased Christian Scientist. It is a thorough book that begins by describing Eddy's genealogy. After the subject's childhood and education are discussed briefly, Wilbur devotes twenty chapters to the adult years. She continually attempts in her writing to clear Eddy of any scandal.

Edwards, Sarah P.   1710–1758

378   Dodds, Elisabeth D. *Marriage to a Difficult Man: The "Uncommon Union" of Jonathan and Sarah Edwards.* Philadelphia: Westminster Press, 1971. 224 pp.

Dodds's emphasis is on the Edwards's marriage, and her account includes many details of their domestic life. Dodds is sympathetic to Sarah and describes her personality vividly, but without any psychological depth.

Eisenhower, Mamie Doud   1896–1979

379   Brandon, Dorothy B. *Mamie Doud Eisenhower: A Portrait of a First Lady.* New York: Charles Scribner's Sons, 1954. 307 pp.

This is an informal portrait of the first lady that provides no analysis of her character. Brandon begins with the initial meeting of the young couple and closes with Eisenhower's first inauguration.

380   David, Lester, and Irene David. *Ike and Mamie: The Story of the General and His Lady.* New York: G. P. Putnam's Sons, 1981. 288 pp.

This biography begins when Ike and Mamie meet, and proceeds to describe their married life, especially the White House years. Too many trivial details are included in this book.

381   Hatch, Alden. *Red Carpet for Mamie.* New York: Henry Holt, 1954. 277 pp.

Hatch's book is best for its detailed description of Mamie's family background. He views her as a down-to-earth woman.

Elliott, Maxine   1873–1940

382   Forbes-Robertson, Diana. *My Aunt Maxine: The Story of Maxine Elliott.* New York: Viking Press, 1964. 306 pp.

The author, Elliott's niece, did much research for this book, including reading the family diaries; she writes candidly on any problems in this full account of the actress's life. She covers each era of Elliott's life, but emphasizes her early years in Maine.

Elliott, Sarah B.   1848–1928

383   Mackenzie, Clara C. *Sarah Barnwell Elliott.* Boston: Twayne Publishers, 1980. 183 pp.

See entry 26.

384   ———. "Sarah Barnwell Elliott: A Biography." Dissertation. Case Western Reserve Univ., 1971. 281 pp.

Elliott's entire public life is described clearly in this study. The author is particularly interested in how Elliott's early life was reflected in her writing; she also details the writer's work for women's suffrage.

Emerson, Ellen T.   1809?–1831

385   Pommer, Henry F. *Emerson's First Marriage.* Carbondale: Southern Illinois Univ. Press, 1967. 126 pp.

Emerson's first marriage of eighteen months is described in this book. As his main source, Pommer presents some newly discovered letters (ca. 1967) written by Ellen; he quotes from them, but not at length.

Emerson, Lidian J.   1802–1892

386 Emerson, Ellen T. *The Life of Lidian Jackson Emerson*. Boston: Twayne Publishers, 1981. 269 pp.

This biography, written by Lidian's daughter, describes rather vividly their family life. She relies mainly on anecdotes to tell of Emerson's second marriage.

Emery, Sarah E. V.   1838–1895

387 Adams, Pauline, and Emma S. Thornton. *A Populist Assault: Sarah E. Van de Vort Emery on American Democracy, 1862–1895*. Bowling Green, Ohio: Bowling Green Univ. Press, 1982. 146 pp.

Since few details of Emery's private life exist, Adams describes her era in the Midwest to round out the account. This biography contains a useful, lengthy bibliography.

Ephron, Phoebe W.   1916–1971

388 Ephron, Henry. *We Thought We Could Do Anything*. New York: W. W. Norton, 1977. 211 pp.

Ephron bases his remembrances of his and his wife's scriptwriting career on meaningful anecdotes. In an epilogue to this book, Nora Ephron writes a eulogy for her mother.

F

Fahs, Sophia Lyon   1876–1978

389   Hunter, Edith F. *Sophia Lyon Fahs: A Biography*. Boston: Beacon Press, 1966. 276 pp.

Hunter, a colleague of Fahs, is able to capture her personality precisely in this book. She also discusses the influences that formed Fahs's character and intellect.

Farmer, Frances   1914–1970

390   Arnold, William. *Shadowland*. New York: McGraw-Hill, 1978. 260 pp.

Arnold focuses on the hardships and controversial aspects of Farmer's life that led to her being institutionalized. He is extremely sympathetic to her in this biography.

Felton, Katherine C.   1873–1940

391   Burton, Jean. *Katherine Felton and Her Social Work in San Francisco*. Stanford: Stanford Univ. Press, 1948. 274 pp.

Burton's biography covers all of Felton's life; however, the book describes especially well her career from 1899 to 1940, including Felton's working methods.

Felton, Rebecca L.   1835–1930

392   Talmadge, John E. *Rebecca Latimer Felton: Nine Stormy Decades*. Athens: Univ. of Georgia Press, 1960. 187 pp.

This biography covers all of Felton's life; it was researched from her private papers and contains an informative bibliography.

Ferber, Edna   1887–1968

393   Gilbert, Julie G. *Ferber: A Biography*. New York: Doubleday Publishing, 1978. 445 pp.

Gilbert, a grandniece to Ferber, had access to the writer's personal papers, from which she quotes in this biography. Gilbert's theory is that Ferber's unmarried state troubled her greatly; she also reveals her aunt's character flaws.

Ferguson, Miriam A.   1875–1961

394 Nalle, Ouida F. *The Fergusons of Texas: Two Governors for the Price of One*. San Antonio: Naylor, 1946. 272 pp.

Nalle, the Fergusons' daughter, writes a favorably biased account of her parents' political and private lives.

Ferraro, Geraldine   1935–

395 Breslin, Rosemary, and Joshua Hammer. *Gerry! A Woman Making History*. New York: Pinnacle Books, 1984. 162 pp.

Gloria Steinem writes an introduction to this book that discusses Ferraro's role as a female politician on a presidential ticket. The text of the biography deals equally with Ferraro's background and early life and her political career.

396 Katz, Lee M. *My Name Is Geraldine Ferraro: An Unauthorized Biography*. New York: New American Library, 1984. 224 pp.

Katz's basic biography of Ferraro opens with her forebears' immigration to America and her own early life, courtship, and marriage. The second half of the book deals with her congressional record and her political views.

Field, Kate   1838–1896

397 Whiting, Lilian. *Kate Field: A Record*. Boston: Little, Brown, 1899. 610 pp.

Whiting's book, though detailed and accurate, is biased on behalf of Field. She quotes generously from Field's personal papers, many of which are now lost.

Fields, Annie A.   1834–1915

398 Howe, M. A. DeWolfe. *Memories of a Hostess: A Chronicle of Eminent Friendships*. Boston: The Atlantic Monthly Press, 1922. 312 pp.

Howe was willed Fields's personal papers; he uses them carefully and quotes from them effectively in this book. He depicts Fields and her literary friends exceedingly well.

399 Rotundo, Barbara R. "Mrs. James T. Fields, Hostess and Biographer." Dissertation. Syracuse Univ., 1968. 213 pp.

Rotundo focuses on Fields during her married years, especially emphasizing the literary salon she kept in the 1860s and 1870s. Rotundo evaluates how Fields's personal traits contributed to make her a success.

Fisher, Dorothy Canfield   1879–1958

400   Washington, Ida H. *Dorothy Canfield Fisher: A Biography*. Shelburne, Vt.: New England Press, 1982. 258 pp.

This is both a biography and a critical study of Fisher as an author. Washington describes informatively Fisher's life, including her family background and her New England values; she also quotes from her subject's letters.

Fiske, Fidelia   1816–1864

401   Fiske, Daniel T. *Faith Working by Love, As Exemplified in the Life of Fidelia Fiske*. Boston: Congregational Sabbath School and Publishing Co., 1868. 416 pp.

This early biography was written to set up Fiske's life as an example for young people to follow. It provides a good account of her life, career, and character.

Fiske, Minnie M.   1865–1932

402   Binns, Archie, and Olive Kooken. *Mrs. Fiske and the American Theatre*. New York: Crown Publishers, 1955. 436 pp.

The authors consulted Fiske's private papers in order to re-create her seven decades in the theatre. Their book is full of colorful details and covers the basic facts of her personal life and career, but without evaluating them.

Fitzgerald, Ella   1918–

403   Colin, Sid. *Ella: The Life and Times of Ella Fitzgerald*. North Pomfret, Vt.: David and Charles, 1987. 151 pp.

This brief biography captures Fitzgerald's personality effectively. Colin discusses some of the influences on her life and art, but the reader wishes for more personal details.

Fitzgerald, Zelda Sayre   1900–1948

404   Mayfield, Sara. *Exiles from Paradise: Zelda and Scott Fitzgerald*. New York: Delacorte Press, 1971. 309 pp.

Mayfield, a girlhood friend to Zelda, is very sympathetic to her in this book. She deletes any material that appears too scandalous, and she denies that Zelda was crazy (as other writers depict her to be).

405   Mellow, James R. *Invented Lives: F. Scott and Zelda Fitzgerald*. Boston: Houghton Mifflin, 1984. 569 pp.

Both Fitzgeralds receive equal and detailed treatment in this dual biography. Mellow describes perceptively the interactions between their private lives and the fiction each wrote.

406 Milford, Nancy. *Zelda: A Biography*. New York: Harper and Row, 1970. 424 pp.
Milford's insightful and comprehensive biography reveals many new details about Zelda's life. She understands her subject exceedingly well and sensitively describes the many hardships of her life, particularly her mental illness.

Flanagan, Hallie   1890–1969

407 Bentley, Joanne. *Hallie Flanagan: A Life in the American Theatre*. New York: Alfred A. Knopf, 1988. 436 pp.
Bentley, a stepdaughter to Flanagan, bases her book on the director's diaries and on the existing records of the Federal Theatre Project. Bentley provides highly personal explanations of her subject's life, which she views as divided uncomfortably between her family and her career.

Fletcher, Alice C.   1838–1923

408 Mark, Joan. *A Stranger in Her Native Land: Alice Fletcher and the American Indians*. Lincoln: Univ. of Nebraska Press, 1988. ca. 464 pp.
This is the first full-length study of Fletcher's life and her anthropological career, both of which Mark discusses in ample detail. Mark's approach to her subject is that of a feminist, which works exceptionally well in this book.

Flexner, Helen T.   See **Thomas, Helen**

Flynn, Elizabeth G.   1890–1964

409 Baxandall, Rosalyn F. *Words on Fire: The Life and Writings of Elizabeth Gurley Flynn*. New Brunswick, N.J.: Rutgers Univ. Press, 1988. 302 pp.
This book contains both a biography and a collection of Flynn's writings about women. The biographical sections, which open and close the book, deal with her personal life and her political views.

Fonda, Jane   1937–

410 Brough, James. *The Fabulous Fondas*. New York: David McKay, 1973. 296 pp.

This anecdotal, informal view of the Fondas (Peter, Henry, and Jane) covers their personal lives and their film careers. Brough devotes some space to a discussion of Jane's radical politics.

411 Guiles, Fred L. *Jane Fonda: The Actress in Her Time*. New York: Doubleday Publishing, 1982. 298 pp.

Guiles's biography focuses primarily on Fonda's career years. He is not too clear in his discussion of her psychology and her politics (both of which he oversimplifies).

412 Kiernan, Thomas. *Jane: An Intimate Biography of Jane Fonda*. New York: G. P. Putnam's Sons, 1973. 358 pp.

Although this book purports to be a biography of Jane, it also includes much material on her father and her brother (at her expense). Kiernan provides details of Jane's family background and growing-up years as well as her career and politics; however, he offers no insights into her character.

413 Springer, John. *The Fondas: The Films and Careers of Henry, Jane and Peter Fonda*. Secaucus, N.J.: Citadel Press, 1970. 279 pp.

Springer's book is actually about Henry Fonda, with a small portion devoted to his children. Most of the text consists of synopses and reviews of their films; as a result, the biographical material on them is rather brief.

414 Vadim, Roger. *Bardot, Deneuve, Fonda*. Trans. Melinda C. Porter. New York: Simon and Schuster, 1986. 328 pp.

Vadim, once married to Jane Fonda, relies on gossip and sensational detail to tell his story of their life together. He depicts her as very dedicated to both her career and her political causes.

Fontaine, Joan   1917–

415 Higham, Charles. *Sisters: The Story of Olivia de Havilland and Joan Fontaine*. New York: Coward, McCann and Geoghegan, 1984. 257 pp.

See under de Havilland, Olivia.

Foote, Mary Hallock   1847–1938

416 Johnson, Lee Ann. *Mary Hallock Foote*. Boston: Twayne Publishers, 1980. 180 pp.

See entry 26.

Ford, Elizabeth "Betty"   1918–

417 Feinman, Jeffrey. *Betty Ford.* New York: Award Books, 1976. 171 pp.

This biography was published to coincide with the 1976 presidential election. It is a popular account of Mrs. Ford with some discussion of her early life, but the most emphasis is on her marriage and time in the White House. The book includes a list of bibliographical references.

418 Weidenfeld, Sheila R. *First Lady's Lady: With the Fords at the White House.* New York: G. P. Putnam's Sons, 1979. 419 pp.

Weidenfeld, who formerly served as Mrs. Ford's press secretary, writes a sympathetic account of their years together in the White House. In her opinion, Mrs. Ford is a rather typical American wife and mother.

Forsberg, Vivian   fl. 1940s

419 Fell, Doris. *Lady of the Tboli.* Chappaqua, N.Y.: Christian Herald Books, 1979. 201 pp.

Fell describes all of Forsberg's life, but she concentrates most heavily on her twenty-five years of missionary work. While this book is not a eulogy, it never shows Forsberg in an unfavorable light.

Fox, Katherine "Kate"   1839–1894

420 Jackson, Herbert G., Jr. *The Spirit Rappers.* New York: Doubleday Publishing, 1972. 240 pp.

Jackson focuses more on Margaret than on Kate in this book. He believes both sisters were clever frauds.

421 Taylor, William G. L. *Katie Fox: Epochmaking Medium and the Making of the Fox-Taylor Record.* New York: G. P. Putnam's Sons, 1933. 326 pp.

Taylor, a friend to Kate Fox, shows his great admiration for her in this sympathetic account of her life and work. The book includes a written record of twenty-three years of her seances.

Fox, Margaret   1836–1893

422 Fornell, Earl W. *The Unhappy Medium: Spiritualism and the Life of Margaret Fox.* Austin: Univ. of Texas Press, 1964. 204 pp.

Fornell's book is too brief to adequately describe Fox's life and career. He actually focuses more attention on her cult followers than on Fox herself.

423   Jackson, Herbert G., Jr. *The Spirit Rappers*. New York: Doubleday Publishing, 1972. 240 pp.

See under Fox, Katherine "Kate."

Frankenthaler, Helen   1928–

424   Rose, Barbara. *Frankenthaler*. New York: Harry N. Abrams, 1970. 272 pp.

Rose writes an overview of the artist's life and career in this book. This monograph also includes lists of Frankenthaler's reviews and exhibitions; many color reproductions of her works accompany the text.

Frazier, Brenda D.   1921–1982

425   Diliberto, Gioia. *Debutante: The Story of Brenda Frazier*. New York: Alfred A. Knopf, 1987. 331 pp.

Diliberto has researched her subject thoroughly, and she accurately presents all the facts in this book. She focuses on Frazier's rise to celebrity, then follows her decline.

Frederick, Pauline   1885–1938

426   Elwood, Muriel. *Pauline Frederick On and Off Stage*. Chicago: A. Kroch, 1939. 225 pp.

This biography, suitable for a general reader, offers a complete account of Frederick's life. The author writes with admiration for her subject.

Freeman, Mary E. Wilkins   1852–1930

427   Foster, Edward. *Mary E. Wilkins Freeman*. New York: Hendricks House, 1956. 238 pp.

Foster is best at describing Freeman's early life and family background in this comprehensive biography. He remains sympathetic to his subject throughout the text; he also clearly depicts her life in her community.

428   Glasser, Leah B. " 'In a Closet Hidden': The Life and Work of Mary Wilkins Freeman." Dissertation. Brown Univ., 1982. 260 pp.

Glasser analyzes Freeman's canon in detail in order to show how its themes reflect her life's major conflicts.

429   Westbrook, Perry D. *Mary Wilkins Freeman*. New York: Twayne Publishers, 1967. 191 pp.
See entry 26.

Fremont, Jessie Benton   1824–1902

430   Herr, Pamela. *Jessie Benton Fremont: A Biography*. New York: Franklin Watts, 1987. 512 pp.
Herr has done much meticulous research on her subject. The result is a biography that covers fully all of Fremont's life.

431   Phillips, Catherine C. *Jessie Benton Fremont: A Woman Who Made History*. San Francisco: John Henry Nash, 1936. 361 pp.
Phillips's emphasis is on the Fremonts' marriage and their work together. She uses newly found letters (ca. 1936) that are especially detailed on the couple's life from 1880 to 1902. This book also contains a partial bibliography of Mrs. Fremont's writings.

French, Alice   See Thanet, Octave

Fuller, (Sarah) Margaret   1810–1850

432   Anthony, Katharine S. *Margaret Fuller: A Psychological Biography*. New York: Harcourt, Brace, 1920. 223 pp.
Anthony's book relies too heavily on Freudian psychology (and misses other influences and factors) in trying to explain Fuller's life. She explains most clearly her subject's role as an early feminist.

433   Bell, Margaret. *Margaret Fuller*. New York: Boni Books, 1930. 320 pp.
Bell's novelized biography presents the basic facts of Fuller's life accurately. However, she neglects to explain much about her subject's intellectual life or her influence on American culture.

434   Blanchard, Paula. *Margaret Fuller: From Transcendentalism to Revolution*. New York: Delacorte Press, 1978. 370 pp.
Blanchard, writing from a feminist perspective, reanalyzes Fuller's life and accomplishments. This thoroughly researched biography details efficiently all of the influences that shaped Fuller.

435 Brown, Arthur. *Margaret Fuller*. New York: Twayne Publishers, 1964. 159 pp.

See entry 26.

436 Channing, William H., Ralph W. Emerson, and James F. Clarke. *Memoirs of Margaret Fuller Ossoli*. Boston: Roberts Brothers, 1852. 2 vols.

The three men who wrote this first biography of Fuller all knew her personally. They greatly admire and praise both her work for social causes and her literary ability.

437 Chipperfield, Faith. *In Quest of Love: The Life and Death of Margaret Fuller*. New York: Coward-McCann, 1957. 311 pp.

Chipperfield theorizes that Fuller was a suicide, a claim that she fails to substantiate. She also dwells on her subject's psychological problems, which she believes are the result of her upbringing as an intellectual woman.

438 Deiss, Jay. *The Roman Years of Margaret Fuller*. New York: Thomas Y. Crowell, 1971. 338 pp.

Deiss bases his book about the years 1847 to 1850 on newly found (ca. 1971) correspondence of Fuller and her husband. His account is highly detailed on Fuller's life in Rome and on her husband's family.

439 Higginson, Thomas W. *Margaret Fuller Ossoli*. Boston: Houghton Mifflin, 1884. 323 pp.

Higginson covers all of Fuller's life beginning with her ancestry. He uses her own letters and writings as his sources, from which he quotes frequently. He analyzes her personality graciously, revealing few of her psychological problems.

440 Howe, Julia W. *Margaret Fuller (Marchesa Ossoli)*. Boston: Roberts Brothers, 1896. 398 pp.

Howe's book begins with Fuller's childhood and covers the stages of her life in detail. Howe envisions her subject as a pioneering, intellectual woman, and she pays tribute to her courage. A final chapter evaluates Fuller's literary accomplishments.

441 Stern, Madeleine B. *The Life of Margaret Fuller*. New York: E. P. Dutton, 1942. 549 pp.

Although this is a fairly well researched and accurate biography, it includes fictionalized elements that render it less than scholarly. Stern focuses mainly on Fuller's personal life, not on her public career.

442   Szymanski, Karen A. "Margaret Fuller: The New York Years." Dissertation. Syracuse Univ., 1980. 405 pp.

This study opens and closes with brief reviews of Fuller's early and late years, respectively. The body of this dissertation focuses on the years 1844 to 1846, when Fuller worked for the *New York Tribune*.

443   Wade, Mason. *Margaret Fuller, Whetstone of Genius*. New York: Viking Press, 1940. 304 pp.

Wade is mainly objective in this well-balanced book on Fuller's life. He is a careful researcher who provides many interesting facts about her life in Europe.

G

Gág, Wanda   1893–1946

444   Scott, Alma O. *Wanda Gág: The Story of an Artist*. Minneapolis: Univ. of Minnesota Press, 1949. 235 pp.

Scott, a friend to Gág, admires her too much to write objectively about her. She does describe all of Gág's life and career and documents her sources clearly.

Gale, Zona   1874–1938

445   Derleth, August. *Still Small Voice: The Biography of Zona Gale*. New York: Appleton-Century, 1940. 319 pp.

Derleth examines Gale's life in fine detail; he praises her highly and describes her personality effectively. This book also contains Gale's unfinished autobiography.

Gardner, Ava   1922–

446   Daniell, John. *Ava Gardner*. London: Comet, 1982. 224 pp.

This biography depicts Gardner the private person as well as Gardner the film star. The author discusses her on-screen personality at some length.

447   Flamini, Roland. *Ava: A Biography*. New York: Coward, McCann and Geoghegan, 1982. 269 pp.

This is an undocumented, poorly written book that focuses on Gardner's various love affairs. The author believes that her acting career is without distinction.

448   Higham, Charles. *Ava: A Life Story*. New York: Delacorte Press, 1974. 208 pp.

Higham bases his book on many interviews, but none with the subject herself. The result is an anecdotal record of her life that is of uneven quality.

449   Kass, Judith M. *Ava Gardner*. New York: Pyramid Publishers, 1977. 158 pp.

See entry 286.

Gardner, Isabella S.   1840–1924

450 Carter, Morris. *Isabella Stewart Gardner and Fenway Court*. Boston: Houghton Mifflin, 1925. 254 pp.

Carter highlights the major events of Gardner's life, which he has selected judiciously. He is especially apt at discussing the essential aspects of her character.

451 Tharp, Louise H. *Mrs. Jack: A Biography of Isabella Stewart Gardner*. Boston: Little, Brown, 1965. 365 pp.

Tharp's is an excellent, well-documented biography. She is particularly careful to separate the facts from the legends about Gardner; she uses contemporary quotations to achieve this.

Garland, Judy   1922–1969

452 Dahl, David, and Barry Kehoe. *Young Judy*. New York: Mason/Charter, 1975. 250 pp.

The authors describe Garland's early life and career through 1935. They also attempt to psychoanalyze her by exploring her childhood experiences, but they simplify matters too much to be effective.

453 Deans, Mickey, and Ann Pinchot. *Weep No More, My Lady*. New York: Hawthorn Books, 1972. 256 pp.

Deans, Garland's widower, has nothing new to offer about her life, character, or career in this book.

454 DiOrio, Al. *Little Girl Lost: The Life and Hard Times of Judy Garland*. New Rochelle, N.Y.: Arlington House, 1974. 300 pp.

This book is a basic and judicious biography of Garland. The author quotes frequently from reviews of the singer's performances and from magazine articles about her. The book also contains a very thorough discography.

455 Edwards, Anne. *Judy Garland: A Biography*. New York: Simon and Schuster, 1975. 349 pp.

Edwards's book is unique in that it reprints poetry written by Garland. Her depiction of the singer's childhood is too brief; otherwise, this is a complete account of Garland's life.

456 Finch, Christopher. *Rainbow: The Stormy Life of Judy Garland*. New York: Grosset and Dunlap, 1975. 255 pp.

Finch's sources for this book are earlier biographies of Garland. This account is filled with gossip, anecdotes, and unsubstantiated speculations; the illustrations are profuse, while the text is brief.

457   Frank, Gerold. *Judy*. New York: Harper and Row, 1975. 654 pp.

This biography was authorized by Garland's family; as a result, Frank had access to her personal papers. He clearly describes her complex and troubled personality; however, he includes too many trivial details that do not help explain Garland's life.

458   Juneau, James. *Judy Garland*. New York: Pyramid Publishers, 1974. 159 pp.

See entry 286.

459   Meyer, John. *Heartbreaker*. New York: Doubleday Publishing, 1983. 322 pp.

Meyer, a musician, claims to have been Garland's lover for two months in 1968. His account of their affair is sordid and vulgar.

460   Morella, Joe, and Edward Z. Epstein. *Judy: The Films and Career of Judy Garland*. Secaucus, N.J.: Citadel Press, 1969. 216 pp.

This book opens as Garland begins her film career at age fourteen; the authors then cover the next thirty years of her career and life. Reminiscences by her colleagues round out her story in this well-organized book.

461   Spada, James, and Karen Swenson. *Judy and Liza*. New York: Doubleday Publishing, 1983. 216 pp.

The authors explore the mother-daughter relationship of these two entertainers. They first review the facts of Garland's early years, then focus on her life after Liza's birth. Liza's career is also described in this book.

462   Tormé, Mel. *The Other Side of the Rainbow: With Judy Garland on the Dawn Patrol*. New York: William Morrow, 1970. 241 pp.

Tormé describes his work on Garland's television program in 1963 and 1964, focusing on himself rather than on her. Although he admires the woman, his account of her personal problems is candid.

463   Watson, T. J., and B. Chapman. *Judy: Portrait of an American Legend*. New York: McGraw-Hill, 1986. 160 pp.

This overview of Garland's life covers both the high spots and the low points of her personal history. The authors are always sympathetic to her in their text.

Garrett, Eileen J.   1893–1970

464 Angoff, Allan. *Eileen Garrett and the World beyond the Senses.* New York: William Morrow, 1974. 256 pp.

Angoff, an associate of Garrett's, provides only a sketch of her in this book. He offers some brief anecdotes about her early life and then repeats the details of her many successful seances.

Gellhorn, Martha E.   1908–

465 Kert, Bernice. *The Hemingway Women.* New York: W. W. Norton, 1983. 555 pp.

See under Hemingway, Grace.

466 Orsagh, Jacqueline E. "A Critical Biography of Martha Gellhorn." Dissertation. Michigan State Univ., 1978. 468 pp.

This study, which begins by describing Gellhorn's childhood, emphasizes how she developed into an author. Orsagh discusses all the stages of her life and her adult character.

Gilbreth, Lillian M.   1878–1972

467 Yost, Edna. *Frank and Lillian Gilbreth, Partners for Life.* New Brunswick, N.J.: Rutgers Univ. Press, 1949. 372 pp.

Yost, a friend to this couple, writes a book that is too admiring of them to be objective. She concentrates on their careers and also describes Mrs. Gilbreth's work as a widow.

Gilman, Charlotte P.   1860–1935

468 Hill, Mary A. *Charlotte Perkins Gilman: The Making of a Radical Feminist, 1860–1896.* Philadelphia: Temple Univ. Press, 1980. 362 pp.

Hill describes well Gilman's complex personality and her personal relationships, particularly those to her first husband and to her mother. The author also produces a fine analysis of Gilman's unpublished diaries.

469   Scharnhorst, Gary. *Charlotte Perkins Gilman*. Boston: Twayne Publishers, 1985. 160 pp.
See entry 26.

Gilpin, Laura   1891–1979

470   Sandweiss, Martha A. *Laura Gilpin: An Enduring Grace*. Austin: Univ. of Texas Press, 1986. 336 pp.
Rather than a critical biography, this is a book sympathetic to Gilpin. The author explains how her subject, not always successfully, pursued a career in a man's field. This book contains 170 Gilpin photographs.

Gish, Dorothy   1898–1968

471   Gish, Lillian, and James E. Frasher, ed. *Dorothy and Lillian Gish*. New York: Charles Scribner's Sons, 1973. 311 pp.
Gish merely outlines her life and that of her sister. She mostly reminisces in this book and relates humorous anecdotes about their two careers.

Gish, Lillian   1896–

472   Paine, Albert B. *Life and Lillian Gish*. New York: Macmillan Publishing, 1932. 303 pp.
Paine writes with deep admiration for his subject and her career. Therefore, his is neither an objective nor a balanced portrait of Gish.

Glasgow, Ellen   1873–1945

473   Godbold, E. Stanly. *Ellen Glasgow and the Woman Within*. Baton Rouge: Louisiana State Univ. Press, 1972. 322 pp.
Godbold's depiction of the various aspects (personal and literary) of Glasgow's life is evenly proportioned; he is especially vivid when describing her final years. He has based his book on meticulous research.

474   Raper, J. R. *Without Shelter: The Early Career of Ellen Glasgow*. Baton Rouge: Louisiana State Univ. Press, 1971. 273 pp.
This is an intellectual and psychological biography of the novelist up to 1906. Raper includes many interesting details on Glasgow's daily life.

475   Rouse, Blair. *Ellen Glasgow*. New York: Twayne Publishers, 1962. 160 pp.
See entry 26.

476   Thiebaux, Marcelle. *Ellen Glasgow*. New York: Frederick Ungar Publishing, 1982. 222 pp.
See entry 189.

477   Wagner, Linda W. *Ellen Glasgow: Beyond Convention*. Austin: Univ. of Texas Press, 1982. 150 pp.
Wagner analyzes both Glasgow's writings and her personal life, especially where the two overlap. She believes that her subject is undervalued as a writer because of her sex.

Glaspell, Susan   1882–1948

478   Waterman, Arthur. *Susan Glaspell*. New York: Twayne Publishers, 1966. 144 pp.
See entry 26.

Goddard, Paulette   1911–

479   Morella, Joe, and Edward Z. Epstein. *Paulette: The Adventurous Life of Paulette Goddard*. New York: St. Martin's Press, 1985. 240 pp.
This is a popular biography of Goddard that relies too much on gossip. The authors have especially highlighted her marriages to famous men.

Goldman, Emma   1869–1940

480   Drinnon, Richard. *Rebel in Paradise: A Biography of Emma Goldman*. Chicago: Univ. of Chicago Press, 1962. 349 pp.
Although this book is sympathetic to Goldman, it is also objective in discussing her life and politics. The author's use of details is thorough and accurate.

481   Falk, Candace. *Love, Anarchy and Emma Goldman*. New York: Harcourt, Rinehart, Winston, 1984. 603 pp.
Falk bases her book heavily on Goldman's correspondence with Ben Reitman, and highlights their relationship. However, all stages and aspects of Goldman's life are covered here, including her feminism.

482   Solomon, Martha. *Emma Goldman*. Boston: Twayne Publishers, 1987. 182 pp.
See entry 26.

483   Wexler, Alice. *Emma Goldman: An Intimate Life*. New York: Pantheon Books, 1984. 339 pp.

Wexler describes accurately Goldman's complex personality and her political philosophy. She also writes candidly of Goldman's private life and shows how it interacted with her public career. The book closes in 1919 when Goldman was deported from America.

Goodrich, Annie W.   1866–1954

484   Koch, Harriett R. *Militant Angel*. New York: Macmillan Publishing, 1951. 167 pp.

This is a well-documented book in which Koch has high praise for her subject. Goodrich's years at Yale are described best.

485   Werminghaus, Esther A. *Annie W. Goodrich: Her Journey to Yale*. New York: Macmillan Publishing, 1950. 104 pp.

Werminghaus's book opens in 1890 when Goodrich begins nurse's training. The next three decades of her career are then discussed, ending at the time she becomes dean of the Yale University School of Nursing.

Gordon, Caroline   1895–1981

486   Makowsky, Veronica A. *Caroline Gordon: A Biography*. New York: Oxford Univ. Press, 1989. 288 pp.

This sympathetic biography includes more details on Gordon's life than have previously been published. Makowsky focuses on Gordon's various life roles and analyzes how she maintained them all.

487   Stuckey, William J. *Caroline Gordon*. New York: Twayne Publishers, 1972. 159 pp.

See entry 26.

488   Waldron, Ann. *Close Connections: Caroline Gordon and the Southern Renaissance*. New York: G. P. Putnam's Sons, 1987. 416 pp.

Waldron, in this well-written biography, takes a feminist approach to Gordon, focusing more on her personal life and character than on her literary career. Her marriage to Allen Tate is discussed in detail, as are her relationships to other major writers who were her friends.

Gould, Helen   1868–1938

489   Seton, Celeste A. *Helen Gould Was My Mother-in-Law (as told to Clark Andrews)*. New York: Thomas Y. Crowell, 1953. 277 pp.

Seton writes affectionately of Gould while supplying interesting family anecdotes about her. This actually is a delineation of Gould's character rather than a full biography.

490   Snow, Alice N., and Henry N. Snow. *The Story of Helen Gould: Daughter of Jay Gould, Great American*. New York: Fleming H. Revell, 1943. 340 pp.

Mrs. Snow, a niece to Gould, is able to relate many intimate family anecdotes in this book. She focuses on her subject's relationship to her father, Jay Gould.

Grable, Betty   1916–1973

491   Pastos, Spero. *Pin-up: The Tragedy of Betty Grable*. New York: G. P. Putnam's Sons, 1986. 175 pp.

Pastos's book is primarily concerned with the failures and scandals of Grable's life; therefore, this is not a balanced biography of the actress.

492   Warren, Doug. *Betty Grable: The Reluctant Movie Queen*. New York: St. Martin's Press, 1981. 237 pp.

Warren begins with Grable's childhood and covers all of her life and career. His book is fairly objective in tone, although he admires his subject.

Graham, Katharine M.   1917–

493   Davis, Deborah. *Katharine the Great: Katharine Graham and the Washington Post*. New York: Harcourt, Brace, Jovanovich, 1979. 267 pp.

Graham seldom appears in this book. When she does, Davis's facts on her are inaccurate. The author makes assumptions about Graham for which there is little evidence.

Graham, Martha   1893–

494   Leatherman, LeRoy. *Martha Graham: Portrait of the Lady as an Artist*. New York: Alfred A. Knopf, 1966. 179 pp.

Since Graham wishes her personal life to remain private, almost no details of it are given in this book. Instead, Leatherman, her longtime associate, focuses on the dancer's character and her career.

495 McDonagh, Don. *Martha Graham: A Biography.* New York: Praeger Publishers, 1973. 341 pp.

This unauthorized biography is objective about Graham and her career. The author presents an overview of the entire career, with few details included. A complete list of the dancer's performances appears in the book.

496 Stodelle, Ernestine. *Deep Song: The Dance Story of Martha Graham.* New York: Shirmer Books, 1984. 300 pp.

Stodelle, a friend to Graham, writes a sympathetic account of her life and art; the book is also perceptive and intelligent.

497 Terry, Walter. *Frontiers of Dance: The Life of Martha Graham.* New York: Thomas Y. Crowell, 1975. 178 pp.

Terry, a friend to Graham, describes her personality and her creativity vividly in this book, which includes a chronology of Graham's choreographies to 1975.

Grant, Julia Dent   1826–1902

498 Ross, Ishbel. *General's Wife: The Life of Mrs. Ulysses S. Grant.* New York: Dodd, Mead, 1959. 372 pp.

Ross's book focuses on Mrs. Grant's domestic role and her relationship with her husband. It includes many details on their life in the White House, based largely on their own diaries and letters.

Gratz, Rebecca   1781–1869

499 Osterweis, Rollin G. *Rebecca Gratz: A Study in Charm.* New York: G. P. Putnam's Sons, 1935. 244 pp.

This book depicts Gratz in relationship to her life in early Philadelphia. The author covers all the eras of his subject's life and quotes from her many letters.

Grau, Shirley Ann   1929–

500 Schlueter, Paul. *Shirley Ann Grau.* Boston: Twayne Publishers, 1981. 158 pp.
See entry 26.

Green, Hetty   1834–1916

501 Sparkes, Boyden, and Samuel T. Moore. *Hetty Green: A Woman Who Loved Money.* New York: Doubleday Publishing, 1930. 338 pp.

The authors produce a thorough biography of Green, which separates the facts from the legends about her. They provide several anecdotes to explain her personality, and they analyze her character completely.

Greenhow, Rose O.   ca. 1815–1864

502 Ross, Ishbel. *Rebel Rose: The Life of Rose O'Neal Greenhow, Confederate Spy.* New York: Harper and Brothers, 1954. 294 pp.

Although this book is based on research Ross conducted in both England and the United States, few new ideas about Greenhow are provided here.

Grimké, Angelina E.   1805–1879

503 Birney, Catherine H. *The Grimké Sisters, Sarah and Angelina: The First American Women Advocates of Abolition and Woman's Rights.* New York: C. T. Dillingham, 1885. 319 pp.

This is a highly detailed and sympathetic account of the lives and careers of both sisters. This biography is based on the family's letters and diaries; it includes quotations from Angelina's diary. The book has no index, but its table of contents is detailed.

504 Lerner, Gerda. *The Grimké Sisters from South Carolina: Rebels against Slavery.* Boston: Houghton Mifflin, 1968. 479 pp.

Lerner's book discusses both sisters and describes the influences that moved them to work for social reforms. Necessarily, much of the social and political background of their era is discussed in detail. Angelina's speeches are reprinted in an appendix to this book.

505 Lumpkin, Katharine D. *The Emancipation of Angelina Grimké.* Chapel Hill: Univ. of North Carolina Press, 1974. 265 pp.

Lumpkin concentrates on her subject's complex relationships to her husband and to her sister. She draws a vivid portrait of Angelina and explains her retirement from public works in a new light.

506 Stubbs, Carolyn A. "Angelina Weld Grimké: Washington Poet and Playwright." Dissertation. George Washington Univ., 1978. 255 pp.

Stubb's first chapter deals with the poet's family background, education, and early career. The remaining chapters discuss the thirty years in which she wrote and analyze her poetic talents.

507 Weld, Theodore D. *In Memory: Angelina Grimké Weld*. Boston: George H. Ellis, 1880. 81 pp.

Weld wrote this book as a tribute to his wife shortly after her death; he focuses on her abolitionist activities in this text. The book also includes a sketch of Sarah Grimké.

Grimké, Sarah M.   1792–1873

508 Birney, Catherine H. *The Grimké Sisters, Sarah and Angelina: The First American Women Advocates of Abolition and Woman's Rights*. New York: C. T. Dillingham, 1885. 319 pp.

See under Grimké, Angelina.

509 Lerner, Gerda. *The Grimké Sisters from South Carolina: Rebels against Slavery*. Boston: Houghton Mifflin, 1968. 479 pp.

See under Grimké, Angelina.

510 Weld, Theodore D. *In Memory: Angelina Grimké Weld*. Boston: George H. Ellis, 1880. 81 pp.

See under Grimké, Angelina.

Grossinger, Jennie   1892–1972

511 Pomerantz, Joel. *Jennie and the Story of Grossinger's*. New York: Grosset and Dunlap, 1970. 325 pp.

This biography was authorized by the Grossinger family; it is a warm and affectionate view of this businesswoman.

Guggenheim, Marguerite "Peggy"   1898–1979

512 Weld, Jacqueline B. *Peggy: The Wayward Guggenheim*. New York: E. P. Dutton, 1986. 493 pp.

In order to prepare this authorized biography, Weld researched Guggenheim's personal papers. By using ideas found in them, Weld is able to describe her subject's eccentricities clearly and to trace their development from her childhood.

Guggenheimer, Minnie   1882–1966

513 Untermeyer, Sophie G., and Alix Williamson. *Mother Is Minnie*. New York: Doubleday Publishing, 1960. 213 pp.

This is a humorous, popular biography of an eccentric woman written by her daughter. Although some serious topics are discussed in this book, the authors' approach is mainly light and anecdotal.

Guiney, Louise I.   1861–1920

514 Brown, Alice. *Louise Imogene Guiney*. New York: Macmillan Publishing, 1921. 111 pp.

Brown was a friend and admirer of Guiney, to whom she pays tribute in this book. Selections from Guiney's writings appear here and receive too much praise from Brown.

515 Fairbanks, Henry G. *Louise Imogene Guiney: Laureate of the Lost*. Albany, N.Y.: Magi Books, 1972. 315 pp.

Fairbanks describes both Guiney's life and her books in this biography. Because he admires her greatly, he renders his account too subjective for scholarly purposes.

516 Hart, Sr. Mary A. *Soul Ordained To Fail: Louise Imogene Guiney, 1861–1920*. New York: Pageant Press, 1962. 178 pp.

This biographer covers the milestones of Guiney's life in the book's opening section, then discusses the events of her subject's literary career. An excellent comprehensive bibliography of Guiney's canon is included.

517 Tenison, E. M. *Louise Imogene Guiney: Her Life and Works, 1861–1920*. New York: Macmillan Publishing, 1923. 348 pp.

Tenison, a close friend to Guiney, pays tribute to her life and writing in this book. The biographer tells her life story by quoting from her own works; he understands his subject well.

H

Hackley, E(mma) Azalia   1867–1922

518 Davenport, M. Marguerite. *Azalia: The Life of Madame E. Azalia Hackley*. Boston: Chapman and Grimes, 1947. 196 pp.
This is the only full-length biography of Hackley's life and career, but it does not adequately cover its subject.

Hafen, Ann W.   1893–1970

519 Hafen, Leroy R. *The Joyous Journey of Leroy R. and Ann W. Hafen: An Autobiography*. Glendale, Calif.: A. H. Clark, 1973. 334 pp.
This candid book mainly focuses on the Hafens' life and work as a couple. The author reprints selections from both of their diaries and from some of their letters.

Hale, Sarah Josepha   1788–1879

520 Entrikin, Isabelle W. *Sarah Josepha Hale and "Godey's Lady's Book."* Privately printed, 1946. 160 pp.
This carefully written biography is good on details and includes a useful bibliography. However, it does not evaluate its subject to enough extent.

521 Finley, Ruth E. *The Lady of Godey's: Sarah Josepha Hale*. Philadelphia: J. B. Lippincott, 1931. 318 pp.
This is a popular biography of Hale that focuses mainly on her work as an editor. The biographer writes a critical evaluation of Hale's place in American social history.

522 Fryatt, Norma R. *Sarah Josepha Hale: The Life and Times of a Nineteenth-Century Woman*. New York: Hawthorn Books, 1975. 152 pp.
Although all the aspects of Hale's life and career are discussed in detail in this book, her complex personality remains unclear. Fryatt often quotes from primary materials, and she documents her sources well.

523 Rogers, Sherbrooke. *Sarah Josepha Hale: A New England Pioneer, 1788–1879*. Hamden, Conn.: Shoe String Press, 1985. 135 pp.

Rogers has written a good, concise biography for the general reader. His book includes comprehensive bibliographies of primary and secondary sources.

Hall, Sharlot M.   1870–1943

524   Maxwell, Margaret F. *A Passion for Freedom: The Life of Sharlot Hall.* Tucson: Univ. of Arizona Press, 1982. 234 pp.

Much research went into this biography. The book has a dual focus: it describes Hall's work as a historian and relates the struggles she faced in her personal life.

Hamilton, Alice   1869–1970

525   Sicherman, Barbara. *Alice Hamilton: A Life in Letters.* Cambridge: Harvard Univ. Press, 1984. 460 pp.

Sicherman studies Hamilton's life in full. Her method is to reprint letters from each period and to write an informative introductory essay for each set of letters. The result is actually a portrait of Hamilton rather than a complete biography.

Hamilton, Edith   1867–1963

526   Reid, Doris F. *Edith Hamilton: An Intimate Portrait.* New York: W. W. Norton, 1967. 174 pp.

Although Reid was a close friend to Hamilton, she has not written a sentimental account. Rather, she provides a vivid portrait of the scholar's life. In closing the book, Reid discusses Hamilton's writings.

Hanks, Nancy   1927–1983

527   Straight, Michael. *Nancy Hanks, An Intimate Portrait: The Creation of a National Commitment to the Arts.* Durham, N.C.: Duke Univ. Press, 1988. 429 pp.

A colleague of Hanks, Straight describes not only her life and career, but also her contribution to the arts in the United States. Straight also describes her complex personality in detail.

Hansberry, Lorraine   1930–1965

528   Cheney, Anne. *Lorraine Hansberry.* Boston: Twayne Publishers, 1984. 174 pp.

See entry 26.

Hardey, Mary A. 1809–1886

529 Garvey, Mary. *Mary Aloysia Hardey*. New York: America Press, 1910. 405 pp.

The best feature of this lengthy book is that it reprints a number of Mother Hardey's letters, the originals of which have since been lost.

530 Williams, Margaret. *Second Sowing: The Life of Mary Aloysia Hardey*. New York: Sheed and Ward, 1942. 495 pp.

Williams details all of Hardey's life in this laudatory biography. In some periods of her life, especially the early years, fictionalized scenes embellish the plain facts; the adult life is covered in a more straightforward manner.

Harkness, Rebekah 1915–1982

531 Unger, Craig. *Blue Blood*. New York: William Morrow, 1988. 432 pp.

Unger discusses all of Harkness's private life in candid detail, but he concentrates on her founding and management of the Harkness Ballet. He makes many suppositions about her emotional life, most of which he cannot substantiate.

Harlow, Jean 1911–1937

532 Davies, Dentner. *Jean Harlow: Hollywood Comet*. London: Constable, 1937. 153 pp.

Dentner Davies is a pseudonym for David Sentner. He wrote this book shortly after Harlow died to pay tribute to her and to detail her brief acting career.

533 Morella, Joe, and Edward Z. Epstein. *Gable and Lombard and Powell and Harlow*. New York: Dell Publishing, 1976. 204 pp.

Lombard and her relationship to Gable are covered more fully in this book than is Harlow's relationship to Powell. This popular account shows each actress in both her private life and her career.

534 Shulman, Irving. *Harlow: An Intimate Biography*. New York: Bernard Geis Associates, 1964. 408 pp.

Shulman bases this biography on questionable sources. He also stereotypes Harlow's character in this sensationalized account of her life.

Harris, Corra May 1869–1935

535 Talmadge, John E. *Corra Harris, Lady of Purpose*. Athens: Univ. of Georgia Press, 1969. 179 pp.

This is an adequate biography that is based on Harris's personal papers. It includes a detailed bibliography of her works.

Harris, Jean Witt   1924–

536 Alexander, Shana. *Very Much a Lady: The Untold Story of Jean Harris and Dr. Herman Tarnower*. Boston: Little, Brown, 1983. 316 pp.
Alexander's thoroughly researched book opens with an account of Harris's childhood, emphasizing a complex father-daughter relationship. All of her adult life is covered, with an emphasis on the relationship to Dr. Tarnower. Even Harris's prison life is described.

Harrison, Marguerite   1879–1970

537 Olds, Elizabeth F. *Women of the Four Winds: The Adventures of Four of America's First Women Explorers*. Boston: Houghton Mifflin, 1985. 263 pp.
See under Akeley, Delia.

Haven, Alice B.   1827–1863

538 Richards, Cornelia B. *Cousin Alice: A Memoir of Alice B. Haven*. New York: D. Appleton, 1865. 392 pp.
This personal remembrance, written by Haven's cousin, also includes extracts from Haven's journal.

Haviland, Laura S.   1808–1898

539 Danforth, Mildred E. *A Quaker Pioneer: Laura Haviland, Superintendent of the Underground*. New York: Exposition Press, 1961. 259 pp.
Danforth's book is a popular account, not suitable for a serious student. She bases her book on Haviland's autobiography of 1881, among other sources.

Hawes, Elizabeth   1903–1971

540 Berch, Bettina. *Radical by Design: The Life and Style of Elizabeth Hawes*. New York: E. P. Dutton, 1988. ca. 256 pp.
Berch takes a feminist approach to Hawes in this well-researched book. She concentrates mainly on Hawes's fashion career, as well as on her journalism and labor organizing. The book is somewhat repetitive.

Hawthorne, Sophia P.   1809–1871

541 Hawthorne, Julian. *Hawthorne and His Wife*. Boston: Houghton Mifflin, 1884. 2 vols. 505 pp./464 pp.

Julian Hawthorne deals more with his father's life and career in this biography than with his mother's. However, many domestic and familiar scenes are described that focus on Mrs. Hawthorne and her children.

542 Lathrop, Rose H. *Memories of Hawthorne*. Boston: Houghton Mifflin, 1897. 482 pp.

Lathrop's book describes her mother's life, beginning in 1838 with her courtship by Hawthorne (the book ends with his death in 1864). Lathrop uses her mother's diaries judiciously to describe her life.

543 Tharp, Louise H. *The Peabody Sisters of Salem*. Boston: Little, Brown, 1950. 372 pp.

Tharp, an excellent biographer, describes the sisters' lives by detailing one episode at a time for each. The book is thoroughly researched and well written. Although Tharp discusses all three sisters, Elizabeth receives the most coverage.

Hayes, Helen   1900–

544 Barrow, Kenneth. *Helen Hayes: First Lady of the American Theatre*. New York: Doubleday Publishing, 1985. 216 pp.

This is not an objective biography of Hayes, for its purpose is to pay tribute to her as an actress and as a person.

545 Robbins, Jhan. *Front Page Marriage: Helen Hayes and Charles Mac-Arthur*. New York: G. P. Putnam's Sons, 1982. 224 pp.

Robbins, who greatly admires Hayes, shows her early life briefly, then details her 1928 meeting of MacArthur, their marriage, family life, and two careers. The book relies heavily on anecdotes, some of which may be untrue.

Hayes, Lucy Webb   1831–1889

546 Geer, Emily A. *First Lady: The Life of Lucy Webb Hayes*. Kent, Ohio: Kent State Univ. Press, 1984. 330 pp.

Geer has written a very scholarly biography of Hayes. She researched her subject's extensive collection of personal papers, which cover the years 1841 to 1890. The biographer has good insights into the first lady's life.

Hayward, Susan   1919–1975

547   Andersen, Christopher P. *A Star, Is a Star, Is a Star! The Lives and Loves of Susan Hayward.* New York: Doubleday Publishing, 1980. 269 pp.

Andersen focuses on the scandals and tragedies of Hayward's personal life; his approach is melodramatic throughout the text.

548   LaGuardia, Robert, and Gene Arceri. *Red: The Tempestuous Life of Susan Hayward.* New York: Macmillan Publishing, 1985. 288 pp.

This is a fairly well researched book that covers all of Hayward's life, concentrating on her career years. However, even the problems and illnesses of her last years are described fully.

549   Linet, Beverly. *Susan Hayward: Portrait of a Survivor.* New York: Atheneum Publishers, 1980. 337 pp.

Linet appears to have not researched her subject adequately, as some of the facts in her book are inaccurate. She does cover all of the actress's life, from childhood to death, but in so doing relies too heavily on gossip.

550   McClelland, Doug. *The Complete Life Story of Susan Hayward.* New York: Pinnacle Books, 1975. 213 pp.

McClelland focuses his attention more on Hayward's film career than on her private life. He analyzes her acting abilities rather competently.

Hayworth, Rita   1918–1987

551   Hill, James. *Rita Hayworth: A Memoir.* New York: Simon and Schuster, 1983. 238 pp.

Hill, who was once married to Hayworth, constantly reiterates in his text all the mistakes he made in their marriage. He never provides the reader with a clear view of Hayworth's personality.

552   Kobal, John. *Rita Hayworth: The Time, the Place and the Woman.* New York: W. W. Norton, 1978. 328 pp.

Kobal is generously sympathetic to the actress in this biography. He describes her personal life in fair detail, but he also includes unnecessary summaries of many of the films in which she starred.

553   Morella, Joe, and Edward Z. Epstein. *Rita: The Life of Rita Hayworth.* New York: Delacorte Press, 1983. 261 pp.

The authors provide all the basic data on the star's life in this popular biography. They emphasize her private life over her career and include many sensational details.

Hazen, Elizabeth Lee   1885–1975

554 Baldwin, Richard S. *The Fungus Fighters: Two Women Scientists and Their Discovery.* Ithaca: Cornell Univ. Press, 1981. 212 pp.
See under Brown, Rachel.

Hearst, Patricia C.   1954–

555 Weed, Steven, and Scott Swanton. *My Search for Patty Hearst.* New York: Crown Publishers, 1976. 343 pp.
Weed, Hearst's fiancé at the time of her kidnapping, provides intimate details of his life with her. He then explains how he and her family worked to find her and gain her release.

Hearst, Phoebe A.   1842–1919

556 Black, Winifred. *The Life and Personality of Phoebe Apperson Hearst.* San Francisco: Privately printed, 1928. 155 pp.
Although this is the most complete account of Hearst's life that is available, it is too adulatory to be objective. It was written by a journalist employed by the Hearst family.

H.D.   See **Doolittle, Hilda**

Hellman, Lillian   1905–1984

557 Falk, Doris V. *Lillian Hellman.* New York: Frederick Ungar Publishing, 1978. 180 pp.
See entry 189.

558 Feibleman, Peter. *Lilly: Reminiscences of Lillian Hellman.* New York: William Morrow, 1988. 364 pp.
Feibleman, who was Hellman's companion during her last years, includes in his book many unflattering details of her private habits and personality traits. Nevertheless, he is also able to provide some insightful comments on her problems and career.

559 Lederer, Katherine. *Lillian Hellman*. Boston: Twayne Publishers, 1980. 159 pp.
See entry 26.

560 Moody, Richard. *Lillian Hellman, Playwright*. New York: Bobbs-Merrill, 1972. 384 pp.
Moody covers the main facts of Hellman's life, but does not go into detail on anything but her play writing. He demonstrates how her works are autobiographical, but he also seems to accept too readily Hellman's fabrications about her life.

561 Newman, Robert P. *The Cold War Romance of Lillian Hellman and John Melby*. Chapel Hill: Univ. of North Carolina Press, 1988. 376 pp.
Newman chronicles a period of Hellman's life not covered in her memoirs, her thirty-year romance and friendship with John Melby. The biographer uses the couples' letters as well as FBI files to describe their relationship and their political interests.

562 Rollyson, Carl. *Lillian Hellman: Her Legend and Her Legacy*. New York: St. Martin's Press, 1988. 613 pp.
Rollyson writes in opposition to the accounts of Hellman's life that she invented in her writing. He uses FBI files and the memoirs of Arthur Kober, her ex-husband, to provide the facts about her.

563 Whitesides, G. Edward. "Lillian Hellman: A Biographical and Critical Study." Dissertation. Florida State Univ., 1968. 318 pp.
This study opens with a chapter on Hellman's background and early years, focusing on the influences that caused her to become a writer; this first chapter reviews her life up to the time of her first play on Broadway. The remaining chapters show how her private life affected her literary output.

564 Wright, William. *Lillian Hellman: The Image, the Woman*. New York: Simon and Schuster, 1986. 507 pp.
Wright adequately covers all of Hellman's life in this finely detailed and well-documented book. He describes at some length the fabrications she made in her autobiographical writing.

Hemingway, Grace Hall   1872–1951

565 Kert, Bernice. *The Hemingway Women*. New York: W. W. Norton, 1983. 555 pp.

Kert's book is written from a feminist viewpoint. She opens with a section on Ernest Hemingway's mother, and then details his relationships to each of his four wives. This book is based on considerable research and is sympathetic to these women; it includes a good discussion of Martha Gellhorn's early years as a writer.

Hemingway, Hadley   1891–1979

566 Kert, Bernice. *The Hemingway Women.* New York: W. W. Norton, 1983. 555 pp.
See under Hemingway, Grace Hall.

567 Sokoloff, Alice H. *Hadley: The First Mrs. Hemingway.* New York: Dodd, Mead, 1973. 208 pp.
Sokoloff concerns herself mainly with the years that Hadley was married to Ernest. The book lacks depth and offers only a few new details from Hadley's letters and Sokoloff's interviews with her. No scholarly apparatus is included.

Hemingway, Mary Welsh   1908–

568 Kert, Bernice. *The Hemingway Women.* New York: W. W. Norton, 1983. 555 pp.
See under Hemingway, Grace Hall.

Hemingway, Pauline Pfeiffer   1895–1951

569 Kert, Bernice. *The Hemingway Women.* New York: W. W. Norton, 1983. 555 pp.
See under Hemingway, Grace Hall.

Henry, Sarah Winston   1710–1784

570 Hartless, Eva C. *Sarah Winston Syme Henry: Mother of Patrick Henry.* Boston: Branden Press, 1977. 138 pp.
Detailed genealogy tables are one excellent feature of this book, which is only one-half about Mrs. Henry. The other half discusses her son, on whose life more facts are available.

Hepburn, Katharine   1909–

571 Andersen, Christopher P. *Young Kate: The Remarkable Hepburn and the Childhood That Shaped an American Legend.* New York: Holt, Rinehart and Winston, 1988. 270 pp.

Andersen reaches back into Hepburn's childhood to show how, because of family influences, she developed into an actress. He begins with her parents' marriage and details their lives, as well as Kate's as a child. The material in this book derives from the author's interviews with Hepburn.

572   Carey, Gary. *Katharine Hepburn: A Hollywood Yankee.* New York: St. Martin's Press, 1983. 284 pp.

Carey devoted only two chapters to Hepburn's early life and college years. The rest of the book is filled with details on her career years, which he describes well. His account is balanced between her private and her public lives.

573   Edwards, Anne. *A Remarkable Woman: A Biography of Katharine Hepburn.* New York: William Morrow, 1985. 511 pp.

This is a very comprehensive book on both the actress's career and her personal life. Edwards paints an in-depth portrait of her subject that details her personality and her political views.

574   Freedland, Michael. *Katharine Hepburn.* London: W. H. Allen, 1984. 250 pp.

Freedland writes candidly in this biography, which focuses on the actress's career. He is honest about her failures and her romances.

575   Higham, Charles. *Kate: The Life of Katharine Hepburn.* New York: W. W. Norton, 1975. 244 pp.

Higham's interviews with friends and colleagues of the actress sometimes result in opposite opinions of her; instead of resolving such differences, he merely prints them all. He does describe her entire acting career, including her television roles.

576   Kanin, Garson. *Tracy and Hepburn: An Intimate Memoir.* New York: Viking Press, 1971. 307 pp.

Kanin, who knew these two stars, focuses his attention mainly on Hepburn and on himself at the same time. He bases his book, which follows an awkward chronology, mostly on personal anecdotes.

577   Marill, Alvin H. *Katharine Hepburn.* New York: Pyramid Publishers, 1973. 159 pp.

See entry 286.

578   Morley, Sheridan. *Katharine Hepburn.* Boston: Little, Brown, 1984. 190 pp.

Morley, a great admirer of Hepburn, tempers his praise adequately in this book. He describes her personality vividly and evaluates her acting style, as well as the achievements of her career.

Herbst, Josephine Frey   1897–1969

579 Bevilacqua, W. F. *Josephine Herbst*. Boston: Twayne Publishers, 1985. 131 pp. See entry 26.

580 Kempthorne, Dion Q. "Josephine Herbst: A Critical Introduction." Dissertation. Univ. of Wisconsin, 1973. 261 pp.
The lengthy opening chapter of this study relates Herbst's biography. Kempthorne, who considers the writer to be a feminist, especially focuses on her literary friendships, both here and abroad.

581 Langer, Elinor. *Josephine Herbst*. Boston: Little, Brown, 1984. 374 pp.
Langer, whose focus is on Herbst's personal life, mentions details of her literary career as well. The source for this book was the recently opened (ca. 1984) private papers of Herbst. By using them, Langer precisely details her subject's emotional and intellectual states.

Hickok, Lorena A.   1892–1968

582 Faber, Doris. *The Life of Lorena Hickok: E. R.'s Friend*. New York: William Morrow, 1980. 384 pp.
Faber covers Hickok's life in detail, but concentrates on the personal aspects, especially her thirty-year friendship with Eleanor Roosevelt. Faber bases her account on the newly released (ca. 1980) letters of the two women.

Hill, Grace L.   1865–1947

583 Karr, Jean. *Grace Livingston Hill: Her Story and Her Writings*. Sykesville, Md.: Greenberg Publishing, 1948. 134 pp.
A brief introduction to this book presents Hill's biography. The majority of the text weakly analyzes her writing; no negative comments are made. The book also includes a comprehensive bibliography of Hill's works.

Hill, Joan R.   1931–1969

584 Thompson, Thomas. *Blood and Money*. New York: Doubleday Publishing, 1976. 450 pp.

This biography of Joan Hill begins in her infancy and tells her life story in detail. Thompson focuses more attention on the year 1969, when Hill was murdered, and the resulting trial of her husband for that crime. Thompson uses novelized elements in his narrative.

Hobson, Mary Quinn   1857–1892+

585 Draper, Mabel H. *Though Long the Trail*. New York: Rinehart, 1946. 313 pp.
Draper describes Hobson's life to age thirty-six, which includes her time in the Western frontier. Draper, Hobson's daughter, writes the book in the first person and bases it mainly on conversations with her mother.

Holiday, Billie   1915–1959

586 Chilton, John. *Billie's Blues: A Survey of Billie Holiday's Career, 1933–1959*. Briarcliff Manor, N.Y.: Stein and Day, 1975. 264 pp.
Chilton's account of Holiday's life focuses on her career years, yet he details the personal problems of her adult life. He does well at clearing away the legends perpetrated by her autobiography.

587 DeVeaux, Alexis. *Don't Explain: A Song of Billie Holiday*. New York: Harper and Row, 1980. 151 pp.
This is an honest, candid account of all the problems Holiday faced in life, as well as the struggles of her career. It details every stage of her life.

588 James, Burnett. *Billie Holiday*. New York: Hippocrene Books, 1984. 95 pp.
This is a basic and concise monograph on both the singer's life and career. Its discography is comprehensive and correct up to ca. 1984.

Holley, Marietta   1836–1926

589 Blyley, Katherine G. "Marietta Holley." Dissertation. Univ. of Pittsburgh, 1937. 151 pp.
This is an accurately detailed, scholarly study—the first on Holley. Blyley completed it in 1925.

590 Winter, Kate H. *Marietta Holley: Life with "Josiah Allen's Wife."* Syracuse: Syracuse Univ. Press, 1984. 182 pp.

Winter concentrates mainly on Holley's life and less so on her writings. She describes clearly the domestic and social aspects of this life, but does not analyze her subject's character.

Holley, Mary Austin   1784–1846

591 Hatcher, Mattie A. *Mary Austin Holley*. Dallas: Southwest Press, 1933. 216 pp.

Hatcher's book reprints newly found letters (ca. 1933) that Holley wrote to her daughter; these, along with Hatcher's comments, provide intimate details of her subject's life. Holley's "History of Texas" is also included in this book.

592 Lee, Rebecca. *Mary Austin Holley: A Biography*. Austin: Univ. of Texas Press, 1962. 447 pp.

This is a basic, informative biography that also contains maps, genealogy tables, and a rather extensive bibliography.

Holley, Sallie   1818–1893

593 Chadwick, John W., ed. *A Life for Liberty: Anti-slavery and Other Letters of Sallie Holley*. New York: G. P. Putnam's Sons, 1899. n.p.

This is a sympathetic biography of Holley. The text includes, in edited form, many of her letters.

Holliday, Judy   1922–1965

594 Carey, Gary. *Judy Holliday: An Intimate Life Story*. New York: Seaview Books, 1982. 271 pp.

Carey's text is comprised of the basic biographical facts and some anecdotes on Holliday's career. He attempts to analyze her, with only partial success, and does not offer any insights into her character.

595 Holtzman, Will. *Judy Holliday*. New York: G. P. Putnam's Sons, 1982. 306 pp.

Holtzman covers all the stages of his subject's life, beginning in her childhood. Unfortunately, his book relies too much on gossip (especially by Holliday's friend Yetta Cohn) to be useful to a serious student.

Hollingworth, Leta S.   1886–1939

596 Hollingworth, Harry L. *Leta Stetter Hollingworth: A Biography*. Lincoln: Univ. of Nebraska Press, 1943. 204 pp.

Hollingworth's husband produces a good sourcebook on her. It includes her basic biography, numerous quotations from her letters, and a bibliography of her entire canon.

Holman, Libby   1906–1971

597 Bradshaw, Jon. *Dreams That Money Can Buy: The Tragic Life of Libby Holman*. New York: William Morrow, 1985. 431 pp.

Bradshaw's is a vivid book that describes all of Holman's life, but focuses on her alleged crime. He also describes her life after her husband's death.

Holtzmann, Fanny E.   1903–

598 Berkman, Ted. *The Lady and the Law: The Remarkable Life of Fanny Holtzmann*. Boston: Little, Brown, 1976. 403 pp.

Berkman, Holtzmann's nephew, presents a highly detailed account of her life in which her personality shows forth. He also concentrates on her political work during and after World War II.

Homer, Louise   1871–1947

599 Homer, Anne. *Louise Homer and the Golden Age of Opera*. New York: William Morrow, 1974. 439 pp.

Anne Homer, the singer's daughter, writes in admiration of her mother as a person, as a wife, and as a singer. She vividly describes her parents' marriage in this well-documented book.

600 Homer, Sidney. *My Wife and I: The Story of Louise and Sidney Homer*. New York: Macmillan Publishing, 1939. 269 pp.

Homer describes with humor and enthusiasm his wife's career. He is best in the early chapters when he discusses their marriage and her career difficulties.

601 Moorhead, Elizabeth. *These Too Were Here: Louise Homer and Willa Cather*. Pittsburgh: Univ. of Pittsburgh Press, 1950. 62 pp.

See under Cather, Willa.

Hooks, Julia Ann   1852–1942

602 Lewis, Selma S., and Marjean G. Kremer. *The Angel of Beale Street: A Biography of Julia Ann Hooks*. Memphis: St. Luke's Press, 1986. 293 pp.

This account covers Hooks's life up to her fortieth year. Unfortunately, because many of the facts are unavailable, the biographers must interpolate imaginary scenes.

Hopper, Hedda   1885–1966

603   Eells, George. *Hedda and Louella*. New York: G. P. Putnam's Sons, 1972. 360 pp.

Eells's well-researched book offers alternating chapters on the lives of these two women, whom he evaluates wisely. He focuses mainly on the career years of each writer.

Horne, Lena   1917–

604   Arstein, Helen, and Carlton Moss. *In Person—Lena Horne*. Sykesville, Md.: Greenberg Publishing, 1950. 249 pp.

The authors describe Horne's early life, then focus on her career years. They depict the struggles she faced as a black performer.

605   Haskins, James, and Kathleen Benson. *Lena: A Personal and Professional Biography of Lena Horne*. Briarcliff Manor, N.Y.: Stein and Day, 1984. 226 pp.

Haskins describes Horne's early life, concentrating on the hardships she faced as a black woman. He then concentrates most of his book on her career and describes her personal growth. Some unsubstantiated speculations mar his commentary.

Houston, Margaret L.   1819–1867

606   Seale, William. *Sam Houston's Wife: A Biography of Margaret Lea Houston*. Norman: Univ. of Oklahoma Press, 1972. 287 pp.

Seale employs many domestic details to tell the story of Houston's third wife in this well-documented book. He emphasizes throughout the text her unwavering devotion to her family.

Howe, Julia Ward   1819–1910

607   Clifford, Deborah P. *Mine Eyes Have Seen the Glory: A Biography of Julia Ward Howe*. Boston: Little, Brown, 1979. 313 pp.

Clifford is the first modern author to write a life of Howe; it is a scholarly study with illustrations and a good bibliography. She judges Howe's literary talents for the reader, demonstrating the brilliance of the lectures in comparison to the poetry. She also includes an interesting discussion of Howe's difficulties with her marriage.

608   Elliott, Maud H. *The Eleventh Hour in the Life of Julia Ward Howe.* Boston: Little, Brown, 1911. 74 pp.

Howe's daughter wrote this small volume immediately after her mother's death to read to family friends. It gives insight into the old age of a remarkably spry and solidly intelligent woman who faced her final years with unusual vigor and courage. It also emphasizes Howe's keen wit and her need to give of herself for worthy causes.

609   Hall, Florence M. H. *Memories Grave and Gay.* New York: Harper and Brothers, 1918. 341 pp.

The eldest surviving daughter of Julia Ward Howe gives the reader an intimate portrait of her mother in her reminiscences. Hall includes chapters on the anti-slavery movement, the Civil War, and her mother's work on behalf of soldiers and women. She also pays tribute to her mother in closing this book.

610   Richards, Laura E., and Elliott, Maud H. *Julia Ward Howe, 1819–1910.* Boston: Houghton Mifflin, 1916. 2 vols.

Howe's two daughters won a Pulitzer Prize for this excellent study of their mother. They relied on many of Howe's own letters to tell her fascinating story. Her personal life as well as her public life is recounted in this lively narrative.

611   Tharp, Louise H. *Three Saints and a Sinner: Julia Ward Howe, Louisa, Annie and Sam Ward.* Boston: Little, Brown, 1956. 406 pp.

In a very well researched book with a good bibliography, the author keeps the reader eager for more of her engrossing and well-paced narrative. She is good at presenting the essential interactions among the Ward siblings, as she places them in the social background of nineteenth-century New York, Boston, and Europe.

Howells, Annie   m. 1877

612   Doyle, James. *Annie Howells and Achille Frechette.* Toronto: Univ. of Toronto Press, 1979. 131 pp.

Doyle covers both the lives and the careers of this couple in an overview; however, their famous siblings are not discussed in much detail. The book contains excellent photographs.

Hoxie, Vinnie R.   See **Ream, Vinnie**

Hull, Josephine   1884–1957

613   Carson, William G. B. *Dear Josephine: The Theatrical Career of Josephine Hull*. Norman: Univ. of Oklahoma Press, 1963. 313 pp.
Carson bases his book on the numerous private papers Hull left after her death. He focuses mainly on her career (1902 to 1957), but also details her relationship to her husband and their life together during that era.

Humphrey, Doris   1895–1958

614   Cohen, Selma J., ed. *Doris Humphrey: An Artist First*. Middletown, Conn.: Wesleyan Univ. Press, 1972. 305 pp.
Cohen presents an edited version of Humphrey's autobiography (*New Dance, 1961*), which covers her life to 1928. Then Cohen adds material to detail the rest of Humphrey's life. The book also includes a useful introduction, chronology, and bibliography.

615   Siegel, Marcia B. *Days on Earth: The Dance of Doris Humphrey*. New Haven: Yale Univ. Press, 1988. 333 pp.
Siegel admires Humphrey in this critical biography; yet, in focusing on the dancer's personality, she does not avoid its unpleasant aspects. Humphrey's dance style and career are not analyzed in enough detail in this book.

Hunter, Alberta   ca. 1895–1984

616   Taylor, Frank C., and Gerald Cook. *Alberta Hunter: A Celebration in Blues*. New York: McGraw-Hill, 1987. 311 pp.
In this authorized biography, the writers describe all of Hunter's life and career, including her retirement from entertaining and her subsequent career revival. They capture her personality especially vividly.

Hurston, Zora Neale   1901–1960

617   Hemenway, Robert E. *Zora Neale Hurston: A Literary Biography*. Urbana: Univ. of Illinois Press, 1977. 371 pp.
This is an informative biography that relies on archival materials to accurately determine the facts of Hurston's life. Hemenway also discusses her literary

career, which he interweaves well with his record of her life. He also demonstrates clearly how her life and her art interacted.

618   Howard, Lillie P. *Zora Neale Hurston*. Boston: Twayne Publishers, 1981. 192 pp.
See entry 26.

Hutchinson, Anne   1591–1643

619   Augur, Helen. *An American Jezebel: The Life of Anne Hutchinson*. New York: Bretano's, 1930. 320 pp.
Augur's focus is on Hutchinson's life in colonial America and her role as a preacher. The author also concentrates (with sympathy to her subject) on the trial. Some fictionalized scenes mar the historical integrity of this book.

620   Battis, Emery. *Saints and Sectaries: Anne Hutchinson and the Antinomian Controversy in the Massachusetts Bay Colony*. Chapel Hill: Univ. of North Carolina Press, 1963. 379 pp.
Battis is sympathetic to Hutchinson in this book, which details the years of her controversial preaching in Boston (1634 to 1638). He explains her heresy very precisely.

621   Bolton, Reginald P. *A Woman Misunderstood: Anne, Wife of William Hutchinson*. New York: Schoen Printing, 1931. 137 pp.
This is a popular account of the Hutchinson controversy in Boston; it is not useful to a serious student because it lacks an adequate scholarly apparatus.

622   Curtis, Edith. *Anne Hutchinson: A Biography*. Cambridge, Mass.: Washburn and Thomas, 1930. 122 pp.
Curtis does not use any fictionalization to recount Hutchinson's life; rather, her approach is completely factual. She is sympathetic to her subject, but her book, which also lacks an index, is too brief to provide an adequate life of the preacher.

623   Rugg, Winifred K. *Unafraid: A Life of Anne Hutchinson*. Boston: Houghton Mifflin, 1930. 263 pp.
This is a comprehensive book on Hutchinson's life, both in England and in America. Rugg mostly remains objective as she reports all the known facts of her subject's life, including the Boston trial. She details well all the influences on the young woman's development.

624   Williams, Selma R. *Divine Rebel: The Life of Anne Marbury Hutchinson.* New York: Holt, Rinehart and Winston, 1981. 246 pp.

Williams reviews her subject's life and controversial career from a decidedly feminist perspective. The book is carefully detailed and documented, both on Hutchinson's domestic life and her public career, including the trial. An extensive bibliography is also provided.

Hutton, Barbara   1912–1979

625   Heymann, C. David. *Poor Little Rich Girl: The Life and Legend of Barbara Hutton.* New York: Simon and Schuster, 1986. 451 pp.

This is a frank and detailed book dealing not only with Hutton's life, but also with the lives of her society friends. A bibliography is included.

626   Jennings, Dean. *Barbara Hutton: A Candid Biography.* New York: Frederick Fell Publishers, 1968. 301 pp.

Jennings's rather grim volume covers Hutton's life from her childhood to the year 1968. He considers her life to be sordid and wasted.

I

Irwin, Agnes   1841–1914

627   Repplier, Agnes. *Agnes Irwin: A Biography*. New York: Doubleday Publishing, 1934. 125 pp.

Repplier greatly admires her subject and provides a laudatory portrait of her in this book. Her narrative is especially good at showing Irwin's career before she began teaching at Radcliffe College.

J

Jackson, Helen Hunt   1830–1885

628 Banning, Evelyn I. *Helen Hunt Jackson*. New York: Vanguard Press, 1973. 248 pp.

Banning's account of Jackson's life is mainly derived from the Odell biography of 1939 (see below). This book is poorly documented and therefore is not useful to the serious student.

629 Odell, Ruth. *Helen Hunt Jackson (H.H.)*. New York: Appleton-Century, 1939. 326 pp.

This is a thoroughly researched and documented book. Odell opens with a discussion of Jackson's ancestry and covers all of her life fully. She is careful to sort out the facts of Jackson's life from the stories about her.

Jackson, Mahalia   1911–1972

630 Goreau, Laurraine. *Just Mahalia, Baby*. Waco, Tex.: Word Books, 1975. 611 pp.

Goreau has much praise for her subject. She also provides an interesting evaluation of Jackson's role in jazz, as well as discusses jazz as a black contribution to U.S. culture.

Jackson, Rachel D.   1767–1828

631 Caldwell, Mary F. *General Jackson's Lady: A Story of the Life and Times of Rachel Donelson Jackson*. Nashville: The Ladies' Hermitage Association, 1936. 555 pp.

This is a highly partisan biography of Mrs. Jackson that defends her reputation. Caldwell researched her subject completely and documents her book well.

Jackson, Rebecca Cox   1795–1871

632 Williams, Richard E. *Called and Chosen: The Story of Mother Rebecca Jackson and the Philadelphia Shakers*. Metuchen, N.J.: Scarecrow Press, 1981. 179 pp.

Williams quotes at length from Mother Jackson's journals in order to tell her life story. He also narrates, in the interspaces, the history of her ministry and religious community.

Jackson, Shirley   1919–1965

633 Friedman, Lenemaja. *Shirley Jackson*. Boston: Twayne Publishers, 1975. 245 pp.
See entry 26.

634 Oppenheimer, Judy. *Private Demons: The Life of Shirley Jackson*. New York: G. P. Putnam's Sons, 1988. 304 pp.
Oppenheimer has sympathy for Jackson's difficult and ultimately tragic life. She uses excellent sources of information here, such as the four Jackson children and Shirley's mother. The result is a book full of intimate and insightful details.

Jacobi, Mary Putnam   1842–1906

635 Putnam, Ruth, ed. *The Life and Letters of Mary Putnam Jacobi*. New York: G. P. Putnam's Sons, 1925. 354 pp.
Jacobi's life, her career, and her writings are all discussed thoroughly in this book; it includes a foreword by George Haven Putnam.

636 Truax, Rhoda. *The Doctors Jacobi*. Boston: Little, Brown, 1952. 270 pp.
Truax focuses on the marriage of the two physicians as well as on their individual careers. She is particularly apt at describing Mary's years of medical training and the social causes she espoused.

James, Alice   1848–1892

637 Strouse, Jean. *Alice James: A Biography*. Boston: Houghton Mifflin, 1980. 367 pp.
Strouse has written a well-balanced book, based on solid scholarship, about James's life. She is compassionate to her subject, but remains fairly objective; Strouse does not overstate her subject's accomplishments.

638 Yeazell, Ruth B. *The Death and Letters of Alice James*. Berkeley: Univ. of California Press, 1980. 214 pp.
Yeazell begins this book with a lengthy introduction that focuses on James's lifelong concern with death and dying. She does not exaggerate her subject's role

in American literary history, but merely reprints the best of her letters for the reader's own analysis.

Jamison, Judith   1934–

639   Maynard, Olga. *Judith Jamison: Aspects of a Dancer*. New York: Doubleday Publishing, 1982. 294 pp.

Maynard's book concentrates on both Jamison's dancing career and her personal life. The author has high praise for Jamison and discusses at length her work with Alvin Ailey.

Jemison, Mary   1743–1833

640   Seaver, James E. *A Narrative of the Life of Mary Jemison*. Canandaigua, N.Y.: J. D. Bemis, 1824. 189 pp.

The author claims that Jemison revealed her life story to him in an interview conducted on November 29, 1823. His book focuses on her seventy-eight years as an Indian captive, beginning in 1755. Many details of her story are provided, including the massacre of her white family and her two Indian marriages.

Jewett, Sarah Orne   1849–1909

641   Cary, Richard. *Sarah Orne Jewett*. New York: Twayne Publishers, 1962. 175 pp.

See entry 26.

642   Donovan, Josephine. *Sarah Orne Jewett*. New York: Frederick Ungar Publishing, 1980. 165 pp.

See entry 189.

643   Frost, John E. *Sarah Orne Jewett*. Kittery Point, Me.: The Gundalow Club, 1960. 174 pp.

This is a well-documented, detailed account of Jewett's public and private lives. Frost supplies some facts not found in the biography by Matthiessen (see below).

644   Matthiessen, Francis O. *Sarah Orne Jewett*. Boston: Houghton Mifflin, 1929. 160 pp.

Matthiessen writes an appreciative book on Jewett's life and works. He covers the essential details of her life while praising her writing talent. He also explains clearly how her life and art interacted.

Johnson, Claudia "Lady Bird"   1912–

645 Carpenter, Liz. *Ruffles and Flourishes*. New York: Doubleday Publishing, 1970. 264 pp.

Carpenter was Mrs. Johnson's press secretary in the White House; her book, written in an affectionate tone, describes their years together from a personal perspective.

646 Hall, Gordon L. *Lady Bird and Her Daughters*. Philadelphia: Macrae Smith, 1967. 256 pp.

Hall emphasizes the first lady's admirable personal traits. He also paints vivid portraits of the two Johnson daughters and their lives in the White House.

647 Montgomery, Ruth. *Mrs. LBJ*. New York: Henry Holt, 1964. 224 pp.

Montgomery is a friend to Mrs. Johnson, whom she quotes frequently in this book. The account is finely detailed on the family's life in the White House and on Mrs. Johnson's recollections of the JFK assassination.

648 Smith, Marie. *The President's Lady: An Intimate Biography of Mrs. Lyndon B. Johnson*. New York: Random House, 1964. 243 pp.

This is an informal look at the first lady that is based largely on anecdotes and quotations from her. (Some of her favorite recipes are reprinted here.) Harry Truman wrote a foreword to this book.

Johnson, Josephine W.   1910–

649 Wilk, Mary B. "The Inland Woman: A Study of the Life and Major Works of Josephine W. Johnson." Dissertation. Univ. of Massachusetts, 1978. 286 pp.

Wilk, who interviewed Johnson for this study, describes both her personal life and her writings (especially as they reflect her inner life). She analyzes Johnson's personality effectively.

Johnson, Luci   1947–

650 Hall, Gordon L. *Lady Bird and Her Daughters*. Philadelphia: Macrae Smith, 1967. 256 pp.

See under Johnson, Claudia "Lady Bird."

Johnson, Lynda 1943–

651 Hall, Gordon L. *Lady Bird and Her Daughters*. Philadelphia: Macrae Smith, 1967. 256 pp.
See under Johnson, Claudia "Lady Bird."

Johnston, Henrietta fl. 1708–1710—d. 1728 or 1729

652 Middleton, Margaret S. *Henrietta Johnston*. Columbia: Univ. of South Carolina Press, 1966. 88 pp.
Since little data is available on Johnston's life, Middleton draws a more detailed picture of the colonial Charleston in which her subject worked; her book is based on that community's records. The text reprints some of the artist's miniatures (but only in black and white).

Johnston, Mary 1870–1936

653 Cella, C. Ronald. *Mary Johnston*. Boston: Twayne Publishers, 1981. 164 pp.
See entry 26.

Jones, Jennifer 1919–

654 Linet, Beverly. *Star-Crossed: The Story of Robert Walker and Jennifer Jones*. New York: G. P. Putnam's Sons, 1986. 317 pp.
Linet's book on the romance of these two actors focuses on the 1940s when they were at the heights of their careers. She also explains in detail how their marriage ended.

Joplin, Janis 1943–1970

655 Carey, Gary. *Lenny, Janis, and Jimi*. New York: Pocket Books, 1975. 299 pp.
Carey, in this mostly objective book, devotes the greatest amount of space to Lenny Bruce. The author analyzes these three personalities clearly as he discusses the successes and failures of each one's career and early death.

656 Caserta, Peggy, and Dan Knapp. *Going Down with Janis*. Secaucus, N.J.: Lyle Stuart, 1973. 267 pp.

Caserta, who claims to have been Joplin's lover, writes a controversial book on their time together in San Francisco. The author is bitter toward Joplin at times, and is always very frank on sexual matters.

657   Dalton, David. *Janis.* New York: Simon and Schuster, 1972. 212 pp.

This book reprints Dalton's articles on Joplin written for *Rolling Stone*. He interviewed her at various points in her career, and uses those materials to describe her entire life, beginning with her childhood. His book reads as if it were one long interview with Joplin.

658   ———. *Piece of My Heart: The Life, Times and Legend of Janis Joplin.* New York: St. Martin's Press, 1986. 286 pp.

Dalton writes with affection for Joplin and her years in the music business. He begins with her early appearances and covers her career to its height.

659   Friedman, Myra. *Buried Alive: The Biography of Janis Joplin.* New York: William Morrow, 1973. 333 pp.

Friedman's biography of Joplin is intelligent and fairly well written. She describes vividly Joplin's character and the personal problems that caused her early death. The large volume of research that Friedman conducted, some among Joplin's family and friends, is evident throughout this book.

Jordan, Crystal Lee   1940–

660   Leifermann, Henry P. *Crystal Lee: A Woman of Inheritance.* New York: Macmillan Publishing, 1975. 200 pp.

This book details one major episode in Jordan's life: her efforts to establish a textile workers' union in her area of the south. Unfortunately, the book provides only a shallow view of the events in which Jordan participated.

Judson, Ann H.   1789–1826

661   Hall, Gordon L. *Golden Boats from Burma: The Life of Ann Hasseltine Judson, the First American Woman in Burma.* Philadelphia: Macrae Smith, 1961. 255 pp.

Hall's book, which contains much information on Judson's husband as well, relies on the Knowles biography (see below) for factual data.

662   Hubbard, Ethel D. *Ann of Ava.* New York: Missionary Education Movement of the United States and Canada, 1913. 245 pp.

This is a popular biography more suited for a general reader than for a serious student.

663   Knowles, James D. *Memoir of Ann H. Judson, Missionary to Burmah.* Boston: Lincoln and Edmonds, 1829. 324 pp.

Knowles relies heavily on Judson's surviving letters to tell her life story. The tone of his book is eulogistic.

664   Willson, Arabella M. *The Lives of Mrs. Ann H. Judson and Mrs. Sarah B. Judson, with a Biographical Sketch of Mrs. Emily C. Judson, Missionaries to Burmah.* New York: Derby and Miller, 1851. 356 pp.

Willson describes Ann's and Sarah's lives rather fully; a brief section of the text outlines Emily's life. The author's factual data is derived from the Knowles biography (see above).

665   Wyeth, W. N. *Ann H. Judson: A Memorial.* Cincinnati: W. N. Wyeth, 1888. 230 pp.

This is a popularized version of the missionary's life and works; it is not useful to a serious student.

Judson, Emily C.   1817–1854

666   Kendrick, Asahel C. *The Life and Letters of Mrs. Emily C. Judson.* New York: Sheldon, 1860. 426 pp.

Kendrick was a friend to the Judson family; as a result, this biography is sympathetic and uncritical. At times, its factual data is inaccurate.

667   Willson, Arabella M. *The Lives of Mrs. Ann H. Judson and Mrs. Sarah B. Judson, with a Biographical Sketch of Mrs. Emily C. Judson, Missionaries to Burmah.* New York: Derby and Miller, 1851. 356 pp.

See under Judson, Ann H.

Judson, Sarah B.   1803–1845

668   Judson, Emily C. *Memoir of Sarah B. Judson, a Member of the American Mission to Burmah.* New York: L. Colby, 1852. 250 pp.

Emily Judson's biography of Sarah is based on the papers Sarah and her husband kept at their mission. A first edition of this book appeared in 1848; however, the second edition contains a large appendix of informative notes.

669   Willson, Arabella M. *The Lives of Mrs. Ann H. Judson and Mrs. Sarah B. Judson, with a Biographical Sketch of Mrs. Emily C. Judson, Missionaries to Burmah.* New York: Derby and Miller, 1851. 356 pp.

See under Judson, Ann H.

Jumel, Eliza Bowen   1769–1865

670   Duncan, William C. *The Amazing Madame Jumel.* New York: Frederick A. Stokes, 1935. 321 pp.

Duncan researched many original sources in writing this thorough biography. He claims that the Burr-Hamilton duel was fought over Jumel, but he does not fully substantiate this conjecture.

671   Falkner, Leonard. *Painted Lady, Eliza Jumel: Her Life and Times.* New York: E. P. Dutton, 1962. 252 pp.

Falkner draws only a superficial portrait of his subject. He includes fictionalized scenes in this book, and he discusses all of Jumel's era, not just her own life.

672   Shelton, William H. *The Jumel Mansion.* Boston: Houghton Mifflin, 1916. 257 pp.

Shelton's early biography of Jumel remains a good source of the facts. For the most part, he used court documents and extant family letters as his sources; he sorted through these carefully to ensure accuracy.

K

Keller, Helen Adams   1880–1968

673   Brooks, Van Wyck. *Helen Keller: Sketch for a Portrait*. New York: E. P. Dutton, 1956. 166 pp.
While relating some of the major events in Keller's life, Brooks emphasizes the effects she had on her friends and all who met her. Brooks was a friend to Keller for twenty years and devotedly read everything she wrote, so that his knowledge of her is firsthand and complete.

674   Harrity, Richard, and Ralph G. Martin. *The Three Lives of Helen Keller*. New York: Doubleday Publishing, 1962. 189 pp.
The authors give a fairly thorough accounting of Keller's life, with a brief but substantive text and several decades worth of photographs. The illustrations are drawn from public life as well as her personal album of her early years. The book relays a vivid sense of Keller's very active life.

675   Lash, Joseph P. *Helen and Teacher: The Story of Helen Keller and Anne Sullivan Macy*. New York: Delacorte Press, 1980. 811 pp.
This is an extremely large and well-researched biography that quotes at length from both women's speeches and writings. Lash believes that the lives of Keller and Sullivan were so intertwined and interdependent on each other that a dual biography is necessary. The book contains a large section of notes, a bibliography, and a chronology chart.

676   Waite, Helen E. *Valiant Companions: Helen Keller and Anne Sullivan Macy*. Philadelphia: Macrae Smith, 1959. 223 pp.
This is a well-researched book written in an easy-to-read, narrative style, especially suitable for the general reader. The author studied the files at the Perkins Institute and discovered some previously unreported letters by and to Keller, the contents of which she includes here.

Kelley, Florence   1859–1932

677   Blumberg, Dorothy R. *Florence Kelley: The Making of a Social Pioneer*. Fairfield, N.J.: Augustus M. Kelley, 1967. 194 pp.

Blumberg's biography of Kelley is best on the years prior to 1899; she uses newly found letters (ca. 1967) written by her subject to give details of the years 1884 to 1894. Most of the book's attention is given to Kelley's career and ideas rather than to her private life.

678 Goldmark, Josephine. *Impatient Crusader: Florence Kelley's Life Story.* Urbana: Univ. of Illinois Press, 1953. 217 pp.

This is an early biography by a friend who is too admiring of Kelley to be objective. Blumberg's (see above) is a better biography, especially for the events of the 1880s and 1890s.

Kelly, Grace   1929–1982

679 Englund, Steven. *Grace of Monaco: An Interpretive Biography.* New York: Doubleday Publishing, 1984. 392 pp.

This is a fairly serious study that evaluates Kelly's various roles as a wife, mother, and member of Monaco's royalty. Englund also provides some insightful analyses of Kelly's acting career; Kelly cooperated in the preparation of this book until the time of her death.

680 Gaither, Gant. *Princess of Monaco.* New York: Henry Holt, 1957. 176 pp.

Gaither was a family friend to the Kellys. His romanticized version of Kelly's life focuses on her courtship by and marriage to Rainier of Monaco. The space devoted to her childhood and early acting career is brief.

681 Hart-Davis, Phyllida. *Grace: The Story of a Princess.* New York: St. Martin's Press, 1982. 141 pp.

Hart-Davis does not provide a balanced view of Kelly, for she writes only on the glamorous aspects of her life. All the periods of Kelly's life are discussed: her childhood, acting career, and royal marriage.

682 Lewis, Arthur H. *Those Philadelphia Kellys—with a Touch of Grace.* New York: William Morrow, 1977. 288 pp.

Lewis merely retells numerous unusual family stories and amusing anecdotes about the Kelly family, including many about Grace.

683 Robyns, Gwen. *Princess Grace.* New York: David McKay, 1976. 280 pp.

Although this book has been well researched, the space it devotes to Kelly's acting career is insufficient. Robyns provides some interesting details on her subject's daily life in the 1970s, including some new anecdotes.

684   Spada, James. *Grace: The Secret Lives of a Princess*. New York: Double-day Publishing, 1987. 360 pp.

Spada emphasizes Kelly's struggle throughout her life to win her father's respect and approval. The author is also candid about Kelly's sexual history and her poor relationships with her children; however, his attempts to psychoanalyze Kelly are awkward.

Kennedy, Ethel S.   1928–

685   David, Lester. *Ethel: The Story of Mrs. Robert F. Kennedy*. Cleveland: World Publishers, 1971. 274 pp.

David, who is sympathetic to Mrs. Kennedy, covers all of her life up to 1968 in this book. However, his text is padded with much information on the personality and career of RFK.

Kennedy, Jacqueline B.   1929–

686   Birmingham, Stephen. *Jacqueline Bouvier Kennedy Onassis*. New York: Grosset and Dunlap, 1978. 242 pp.

Birmingham is especially sympathetic to the traumas his subject faced in her childhood; nevertheless, his attempts to psychoanalyze her are weak. He also seems to dislike the Kennedy family, and his bias shows in this book.

687   Frischauer, Willi. *Jackie*. London: Michael Joseph, 1976. 255 pp.

Unfortunately, Frischauer bases his book on newspaper stories and anecdotes; the result is that he records in too much detail some of Jacqueline's hobbies: shopping and interior decorating. The biographer describes her most vividly before her first marriage; after that point her character is less clearly defined.

688   Gallagher, Mary B., and Frances S. Leighton, ed. *My Life with Jacqueline Kennedy*. New York: David McKay, 1969. 396 pp.

Gallagher was Mrs. Kennedy's personal secretary for all of her married life, until the summer of 1964; she bases her book on the diaries she kept during those years. Gallagher focuses more on herself than on her subject, and she shows some bitterness toward her former employer.

689   Hall, Gordon L., and Ann Pinchot. *Jacqueline Kennedy: A Biography*. New York: Frederick Fell, 1964. 275 pp.

This book, written shortly after JFK's assassination, is extremely sympathetic to his widow. The authors relate all the facts of her life, but they emphasize the White House years and her reaction to her husband's death.

690   Harding, Robert T., and A. L. Holmes. *Jacqueline Kennedy: A Woman for the World*. New York: Vanguard Press, 1966. 128 pp.

This undocumented book offers a superficial account of Mrs. Kennedy that briefly reviews her childhood, then focuses on her adult life. The two authors greatly admire her.

691   Heller, Deane, and David Heller. *Jacqueline Kennedy*. Derby, Conn.: Monarch Books, 1963. 222 pp.

Although this is merely a popular account of Mrs. Kennedy intended for the general reader, it is well written and compares her briefly to other first ladies (an interesting feature). All the periods of her life are covered, but the most emphasis is given to the White House years and JFK's assassination.

692   Heymann, C. David. *A Woman Named Jackie: An Intimate Biography of Jacqueline Kennedy Onassis*. Secaucus, N.J.: Lyle Stuart, 1989. 715 pp.

This book is based on the author's five years of research in the Secret Service, CIA, FBI, and White House files, and 825 interviews (none with Kennedy family members). Heymann focuses much attention on JFK as he writes of the couple's marriage, dwelling on the more sordid aspects of their life together. Heymann's thesis is that Mrs. Kennedy was actually a very strong-willed first lady—the opposite depiction of her soft-spoken, demure public image in the 1960s.

693   Kelley, Kitty. *Jackie Oh!* Secaucus, N.J.: Lyle Stuart, 1978. 352 pp.

Kelley's book emphasizes Jacqueline's marriage to Aristotle Onassis. The book is filled with unsubstantiated gossip, mostly derived from newspaper stories; imaginary conversations are also included here.

694   Thayer, Mary V. *Jacqueline Bouvier Kennedy*. New York: Doubleday Publishing, 1961. 127 pp.

This brief biography relies heavily on anecdotes to tell of Mrs. Kennedy's life. Thayer's approach is overly sentimental and therefore is not objective.

695   ———. *Jacqueline Kennedy: The White House Years*. Boston: Little, Brown, 1971. 362 pp.

This book was written as a sequel to Thayer's first volume on Mrs. Kennedy (see above). The book opens in 1960 and details the Kennedys' lives in the White House, focusing especially on the first lady's extensive remodeling project.

Kennedy, Joan B.   1936–

696   Chellis, Marcia. *Living with the Kennedys: The Joan Kennedy Story*. New York: Simon and Schuster, 1985. 240 pp.

Chellis worked as an administrative aide to Joan Kennedy from 1979 to 1982, so she emphasizes those years in her book. She describes her subject's unique personality traits and focuses on her problem with alcohol.

697 David, Lester. *Joan, the Reluctant Kennedy: A Biographical Profile*. New York: Funk and Wagnalls, 1974. 264 pp.

David describes his subject's life from her childhood through the year 1973. Unfortunately, the author relies too much on gossipy information and makes a lame attempt at psychoanalyzing Mrs. Kennedy.

Kennedy, Kathleen   1920–1948

698 McTaggart, Lynne. *Kathleen Kennedy: Her Life and Times*. New York: Dial Press, 1983. 248 pp.

McTaggart researched her subject thoroughly, including conducting interviews with Kennedy family members. Her theme is that Kathleen's brief life was both glamorous and tragic; that life is shown vividly against the background of the world affairs that affected it.

Kennedy, Rose F.   1890–

699 Cameron, Gail. *Rose: A Biography of Rose Fitzgerald Kennedy*. New York: G. P. Putnam's Sons, 1971. 247 pp.

Cameron's book, which presents an objective profile of its subject, is somewhat repetitious, yet clearly written. A dominant theme is Mrs. Kennedy's devout religious faith.

700 Gibson, Barbara, and Caroline Latham. *Life with Rose Kennedy*. New York: Warner Books, 1986. 194 pp.

Gibson served as Mrs. Kennedy's personal secretary in the 1970s; as a result, her book includes much on her employer's bouts with illness in that decade. This biography is also full of intimate details of the matriarch's daily life and her eccentric habits.

Kilgallen, Dorothy   1913–1965

701 Israel, Lee. *Kilgallen*. New York: Delacorte Press, 1979. 485 pp.

Israel has written the only full-length biography of Kilgallen. It details both her personal life and her professional career. The author theorizes that Kilgallen was murdered because she discovered new facts about the JFK assassination.

King, Coretta Scott   1927–

702   Vivian, Octavia. *Coretta*. Philadelphia: Fortress Press, 1970. 111 pp.
Coretta King is discussed in her own right in this book, not in relationship to her famous husband. Vivian admires Mrs. King and writes warmly about her.

King, Eleanor   1906–

703   Plett, Nicole, ed. *Eleanor King: Seventy Years in American Dance*. Albuquerque: Univ. of New Mexico Press, 1988. 80 pp.
This brief portrait of the choreographer is especially well illustrated; photographs of all her major performances, from the beginning of her career, are included.

King, Grace E.   1851–1932

704   Bush, Robert. *Grace King: A Southern Destiny*. Baton Rouge: Louisiana State Univ. Press, 1983. 317 pp.
This is a well-written biography that carefully details both the public and private lives of its subject. King's writing talent is also analyzed effectively by Bush, and her era in New Orleans's literary history is described evocatively.

705   Kirby, David. *Grace King*. Boston: Twayne Publishers, 1980. ca. 150 pp. See entry 26.

706   Slayton, Gail C. "Grace Elizabeth King: Her Life and Works." Dissertation. Univ. of Pennsylvania, 1974. 340 pp.
Slayton's study opens with a brief biography of King that primarily shows how she developed into a writer; this section of the dissertation relies on King's unpublished letters for data. The remainder of this study is a critical evaluation of King's various writings.

Kirchwey, Freda   1911–1976

707   Alpern, Sara. *Freda Kirchwey, A Woman of the Nation*. Cambridge: Harvard Univ. Press, 1987. 319 pp.
Alpern's biography is largely based on Kirchwey's private papers. It describes the subject's personality vividly but makes no evaluation of her career.

Kuhlman, Kathryn   1910–1976

708   Buckingham, Jamie. *Daughter of Destiny: Kathryn Kuhlman, Her Story*. Plainfield, N.J.: Logos International, 1976. 309 pp.

Buckingham focuses on his subject's years in Pittsburgh, a city he describes especially well. Emphasis is given to Kuhlman's public career as an evangelist and healer, rather than to her private life.

709   Hosier, Helen K. *Kathryn Kuhlman: The Life She Led, the Legacy She Left*. Old Tappan, N.J.: Fleming H. Revell, 1976. 160 pp.

Hosier has written a tribute to Kuhlman, not an objective biography. Some periods of her life are scarcely covered at all, while much space is devoted to defending Kuhlman from her critics.

L

La Flesche, Susette   See **Bright Eyes**

La Follette, Belle Case   1859–1931

710 Freeman, Lucy, Sherry La Follette, and George A. Zabriskie. *Belle: The Biography of Belle Case La Follette*. New York: Beaufort Books, 1986. 253 pp.

All of Belle's life is discussed in this book, but the focus is on her various career roles. This account is especially good at describing the political ideals she held and how they fit into the issues of her era.

Lake, Veronica   1919–1973

711 Lenburg, Jeff. *Peekaboo: The Story of Veronica Lake*. New York: St. Martin's Press, 1983. 253 pp.

This is not an adequate biography; the author's discussion of Lake's psychology and her film career is especially weak. Lake's mother, who seems to resent her daughter, cooperated with Lenburg in preparing this book.

Landers, Ann   1918–

712 Howard, Margo. *Eppie: The Story of Ann Landers*. New York: G. P. Putnam's Sons, 1982. 253 pp.

Since this book is written by Landers's daughter it gives insights into her family relationships. Howard discusses her mother's life in affectionate and polite terms.

713 Pottker, Jan, and Bob Speziale. *Dear Ann, Dear Abby: The Unauthorized Biography of Ann Landers and Abigail Van Buren*. New York: Dodd, Mead, 1987. 304 pp.

The authors did much research on their subjects, including numerous interviews with people who know the sisters. The result is a very detailed book that covers all aspects of their two lives, including their rivalry.

Lange, Dorothea N.   1895–1965

714   Elliott, George. *Dorothea Lange*. New York: Doubleday Publishing, 1966. 111 pp.

Elliott's well-written, introductory essay to this monograph discusses both Lange's life and her photography. A detailed chronology of her life as well as an extensive bibliography closes the book.

715   Meltzer, Milton. *Dorothea Lange: A Photographer's Life*. New York: Farrar, Straus and Giroux, 1978. 399 pp.

Meltzer's well-researched and detailed account quotes Lange herself frequently. He balances his coverage between her private life and career; Meltzer also psychoanalyzes his subject.

716   Ohrn, Karin B. *Dorothea Lange and the Documentary Tradition*. Baton Rouge: Louisiana State Univ. Press, 1980. 277 pp.

Ohrn discusses both Lange's life and her career. She does a particularly good job at describing the photographer's work between 1939 and 1965.

Larcom, Lucy   1824–1893

717   Addison, Daniel D. *Lucy Larcom: Life, Letters, and Diary*. Boston: Houghton Mifflin, 1894. 295 pp.

Addison was a friend to Larcom; he also consulted with her sister to produce this comprehensive biography. This book offers her life story primarily by quoting from her own diaries, letters, and notes for an autobiography; it is especially thorough from 1824 to 1859 and 1861 to 1889.

Lathrop, Julia   1858–1932

718   Addams, Jane. *My Friend, Julia Lathrop*. New York: Macmillan Publishing, 1935. 228 pp.

This book focuses on Lathrop's early career years when she worked with Addams; however, it covers all of her life in some detail. A final chapter discusses the years 1922 to 1932.

Lathrop, Rose Hawthorne   1851–1926

719   Burton, Katherine K. *Sorrow Built a Bridge: A Daughter of Hawthorne*. New York: Longmans, Green, 1937. 288 pp.

Burton's popular and sentimental book is aimed at a Catholic readership. Although she has done much research on Lathrop's life, she quotes dialogues without documenting her sources.

720   Hawthorne, Julian. *Hawthorne and His Wife*. Boston: Houghton Mifflin, 1884. 2 vols. 505 pp./464 pp.

This book, written by Lathrop's brother, depicts her childhood. There is sparse mention of her adult life in this account.

721   Maynard, Theodore. *A Fire Was Lighted*. Milwaukee: Bruce Publishing, 1948. 443 pp.

Maynard bases his biography on Lathrop's diary and other Hawthorne family papers. His coverage of her life falls into three divisions: her early years, her adult years starting at age twenty, and her career as Mother Alphonsa. His account is thorough but somewhat adulatory of its subject.

722   Walsh, James J. *Mother Alphonsa, Rose Hawthorne Lathrop*. New York: Macmillan Publishing, 1930. 275 pp.

Walsh, who worked with Lathrop, records many interesting facts about her methods. He discusses her background and growth to some extent, then focuses mainly on her career as Mother Alphonsa.

Lauder, Estée   1908–

723   Israel, Lee. *Estée Lauder: Beyond the Magic (An Unauthorized Biography)*. New York: Macmillan Publishing, 1985. 186 pp.

Israel wishes to show the reader the facts behind Lauder's public image. The book is mainly objective and includes comments on its subject's less attractive personality traits.

Lawrence, Margaret   1914–

724   Lightfoot, Sara L. *Balm in Gilead: Journey of a Healer*. Reading, Mass.: Addison-Wesley, 1988. 320 pp.

Lightfoot, Lawrence's admiring daughter, discusses all the stages of her mother's life and career in this candid book. She explains how her mother balanced her family life with the demands of a career.

Lazarus, Emma   1849–1887

725   Jacob, Heinrich E. *The World of Emma Lazarus*. New York: Schocken Books, 1949. 222 pp.

This is an honest, yet uncritical biography. It is well organized and includes a useful bibliography of Lazarus's scholarly writings.

726   Merriam, Eve. *Emma Lazarus: Woman with a Torch*. New York: Citadel Press, 1956. 160 pp.
Since one theme of this book is Lazarus as a Jewish poet, Merriam discusses the poet's family background in detail. She also quotes generously from the poems.

727   Vogel, Dan. *Emma Lazarus*. Boston: Twayne Publishers, 1980. 183 pp.
See entry 26.

Lee, Gypsy Rose   1914–1970

728   Preminger, Erik L. *Gypsy and Me: At Home and On the Road with Gypsy Rose Lee*. Boston: Little, Brown, 1984. 277 pp.
Preminger, Lee's son, wrote this admiring biography as a sequel to her autobiography. He discusses her daily life and travels from age forty-two until her death.

LeGuin, Ursula K.   1929–

729   Bucknall, Barbara J. *Ursula K. LeGuin*. New York: Frederick Ungar Publishing, 1981. 175 pp.
See entry 189.

730   Spivack, Charlotte. *Ursula K. LeGuin*. Boston: Twayne Publishers, 1984. 182 pp.
See entry 26.

Lennox, Charlotte R.   ca. 1729–1804

731   Maynadier, Gustavus H. *The First American Novelist?* Cambridge: Harvard Univ. Press, 1940. 79 pp.
In this brief yet informative book, Maynadier first describes the main events of Lennox's life, then he discusses her writing.

732   Small, Miriam R. *Charlotte Ramsay Lennox: An Eighteenth Century Lady of Letters*. Hamden, Conn.: Archon Books, 1969. 268 pp.
This complete biography of Lennox clearly depicts her personal relationships with several important literary figures of her day.

Lesley, Susan   1823–1904

733 Ames, Mary L., ed. *The Life and Letters of Peter and Susan Lesley*. New York: G. P. Putnam's Sons, 1909. 2 vols.

Susan Lesley is discussed here mainly in relationship to her husband. Their letters, which are reprinted in much of this text, cover the years 1838 to 1893.

Leslie, Miriam F.   1836–1914

734 Stern, Madeleine B. *Purple Passage: The Life of Mrs. Frank Leslie*. Norman: Univ. of Oklahoma Press, 1953. 281 pp.

This is the only complete biography available on Leslie. Its best features are an extensive secondary bibliography and checklists of the Leslie publications and Mrs. Leslie's own writings.

Levertov, Denise   1923–

735 Wagner, Linda W. *Denise Levertov*. New York: Twayne Publishers, 1967. 150 pp.

See entry 26.

Lewis, Ida   1842–1911

736 Brewerton, George D. *Ida Lewis, the Heroine of Lime Rock*. Newport, R.I.: A. J. Ward, 1869. 66 pp.

Lewis herself claimed that this brief account of her activities was accurate. However, an article in *Putnam's Magazine* (1910), based on an interview with Lewis, contains different facts about her.

Liliuokalani   1838–1917

737 Allen, Helena G. *The Betrayal of Liliuokalani: Last Queen of Hawaii, 1838–1917*. Glendale, Calif.: Arthur H. Clark, 1982. 432 pp.

This biography, which is totally biased in favor of its subject, was not researched adequately.

Lincoln, Mary Todd   1818–1882

738 Baker, Jean H. *Mary Todd Lincoln: A Biography*. New York: W. W. Norton, 1987. 500 pp.

This is a complete, definitive biography of Mrs. Lincoln that explains her life in her own terms. Baker is especially perceptive about her subject's victimization during her final years.

739   Evans, William A. *Mrs. Abraham Lincoln: A Study of Her Personality and Her Influence on Lincoln.* New York: Alfred A. Knopf, 1932. 377 pp.

Evans, a physician, makes a psychological study of Mrs. Lincoln. Because he makes large generalizations in so doing, his analysis is weak.

740   Helm, Katherine. *The True Story of Mary, Wife of Lincoln.* New York: Harper and Brothers, 1929. 309 pp.

Helm, a niece to her subject, pays tribute to Mrs. Lincoln in this book, which is based on Helm's family papers. The biography covers in equal proportion Mrs. Lincoln's life before and during her years as first lady.

741   Morrow, Honoré M. W. *Mary Todd Lincoln: An Appreciation of the Wife of Abraham Lincoln.* New York: William Morrow, 1928. 248 pp.

An overly sympathetic, admiring approach mars this book; its style is closer to that of a novel than a factual biography. It also lacks documentation of its sources and has no index.

742   Randall, Ruth P. *The Courtship of Mrs. Lincoln.* Boston: Little, Brown, 1957. 219 pp.

Randall interweaves her own narrative with letters exchanged between the couple. She concentrates on the years 1839 to 1842.

743   ———. *Mary Lincoln: Biography of a Marriage.* Boston: Little, Brown, 1953. 555 pp.

Randall is more sympathetic to Mrs. Lincoln than were her other biographers in the first half of this century. Her book is thorough and accurate, with well-documented new sources (ca. 1953).

744   Ross, Ishbel. *The President's Wife: Mary Todd Lincoln.* New York: G. P. Putnam's Sons, 1973. 384 pp.

Ross's popular and objective biography details all the periods of Mrs. Lincoln's life. Because this book has no footnotes it is not very useful to a serious student.

745   Sandburg, Carl. *Mary Lincoln, Wife and Widow.* New York: Harcourt, Brace, 1932. 357 pp.

Sandburg is not very sympathetic to Mrs. Lincoln's personal hardships. He focuses on the years of her marriage and widowhood, only briefly describing her early life. The second section of the book reprints relevant letters and documents.

746 Schreiner, Samuel A., Jr. *The Trials of Mrs. Lincoln.* New York: D. I. Fine, 1987. 333 pp.

Schreiner takes Mrs. Lincoln's defense in her insanity trial. He also describes her later years, including her stay in an asylum. One weak point of this book is its employment of imagined conversations.

747 Simmons, Dawn L. *A Rose for Mrs. Lincoln: A Biography of Mary Todd Lincoln.* Boston: Little, Brown, 1970. 197 pp.

Simmons's book, the result of much research, presents a balanced picture of all aspects of her subject's life. She is sympathetic to Mrs. Lincoln.

748 Townsend, William H. *Lincoln and His Wife's Home Town.* New York: Bobbs-Merrill, 1929. 384 pp.

Townsend provides a finely detailed picture of Mrs. Lincoln's early years in Lexington, Kentucky.

749 Turner, Justin G., and Linda L. Turner. *Mary Todd Lincoln: Her Life and Letters.* New York: Alfred A. Knopf, 1972. 750 pp.

The Turners use about six hundred of Mrs. Lincoln's letters to demonstrate the decline of her mental state over the years. The authors' many comments, which link these letters, explore Mrs. Lincoln's personality in depth.

750 Van der Heuvel, Gerry. *Crowns of Thorns and Glory: Mary Todd Lincoln and Varina Howell Davis, the Two First Ladies of the Civil War.* New York: E. P. Dutton, 1988. 352 pp.

See under Davis, Varina H.

Lincoln, Nancy Hanks   1784–1818

751 Briggs, Harold E., and Ernestine B. Briggs. *Nancy Hanks Lincoln: A Frontier Portrait.* New York: Bookman Associates, 1953. 135 pp.

This book appears to be about one-half fictionalization. Since few facts are known about their subject's life, the authors resort to discussing the daily life of a frontier woman of her era.

Lindbergh, Anne Morrow   1906–

752   Vaughan, David K. *Anne Morrow Lindbergh*. Boston: Twayne Publishers, 1986. ca. 150 pp.
See entry 26.

Livermore, Harriet   1788–1868

753   Livermore, Samuel T. *Harriet Livermore, the "Pilgrim Stranger."* Hartford: Press of Case, Lockwood and Brainard, 1884. 223 pp.
The Reverend Livermore includes his own commentary in this book, which also reprints letters of tribute from his subject's friends and includes her autobiographical writings and poetry.

Lohman, Ann S.   1812–1878

754   Browder, Clifford. *The Wickedest Woman in New York: Madame Restell, the Abortionist*. Hamden, Conn.: Archon Books, 1988. 217 pp.
Browder's book is based mainly on newspaper stories from Lohman's era; by necessity, then, he devotes much of his text to discussing her legal trials. Since Lohman left few personal records, it is difficult to create a detailed picture of her private life.

Lombard, Carole   1909–1942

755   Harris, Warren G. *Gable and Lombard*. New York: Simon and Schuster, 1974. 189 pp.
This book's emphasis is on the romance and marriage of this celebrated couple. It is an account based on gossip and anecdotes. The author makes a poor attempt at psychoanalyzing Lombard.

756   Maltin, Leonard. *Carole Lombard*. New York: Pyramid Publishers, 1976. 159 pp.
See entry 286.

757   Morella, Joe, and Edward Z. Epstein. *Gable and Lombard and Powell and Harlow*. New York: Dell Publishing, 1975. 204 pp.
See under Harlow, Jean.

758   Swindell, Larry. *Screwball: The Life of Carole Lombard*. New York: William Morrow, 1975. 301 pp.

Swindell offers a finely balanced portrait of the star. While he describes both her life and career, the latter receives more emphasis.

London, Charmian K.   1870–1955

759 Stasz, Clarice. *American Dreamers: Charmian and Jack London*. New York: St. Martin's Press, 1988. 362 pp.

This book opens with the love affair of this couple in 1903, then covers their subsequent relationship of eleven years. The biographer sees their marriage as one of equal partners and describes how Charmian influenced Jack's work.

Longworth, Alice Roosevelt   1884–1980

760 Brough, James. *Princess Alice: A Biography of Alice Roosevelt Longworth*. Boston: Little, Brown, 1975. 335 pp.

This is a popular biography of Longworth, based largely on newspaper articles. Brough covers all the aspects of her youth and adult life, focusing on her subject's political views and many friendships with eminent people.

761 Felsenthal, Carol. *Alice Roosevelt Longworth*. New York: G. P. Putnam's Sons, 1988. 320 pp.

This is a good biography; it opens with its subject's childhood and explains the many influences that shaped her brash personality. Felsenthal also describes the Roosevelt family feuds and some of Longworth's political activities.

762 Teichmann, Howard. *Alice: The Life and Times of Alice Roosevelt Longworth*. Englewood Cliffs, N.J.: Prentice-Hall. 1979. 286 pp.

Teichmann describes clearly his subject's intellectual makeup. He interviewed many of her friends for this book and his use of their dialogues is excellent.

Loos, Anita   1888–1981

763 Carey, Gary. *Anita Loos*. New York: Alfred A. Knopf, 1988. 416 pp.

Carey probes behind Loos's public image to reveal a basically puritanical and mild-mannered woman. His book includes many fine details about her, but also devotes much space to the famous people whom she knew.

Low, Juliette Gordon   1860–1927

764 Choate, Anne H., and Helen Ferris, eds. *Juliette Low and the Girl Scouts: The Story of an American Woman*. New York: Doubleday, Doran, 1928. 271 pp.

This unique biography comprises several chapters written by various people who knew Low well; each chapter focuses on one major episode in her life, presented in chronological order. The authors describe her life, works, and character in a laudatory manner.

765 List, Ely. *Juliette Low and the Girl Scouts: The Story of an American Woman, 1860–1927.* New York: Girl Scouts of the USA, 1960. 112 pp.

This brief, mainly laudatory account of Low's life, which was published to commemorate the centennial of her birth, focuses on her activities with the Girl Scouts.

766 Schultz, Gladys D., and Daisy G. Lawrence. *Lady from Savannah: The Life of Juliette Low.* Philadelphia: J. B. Lippincott, 1958. 383 pp.

Lawrence, Low's niece and the first Girl Scout, writes an insightful biography. The book's sources are Low's writings, as well as those of her mother and grandmother. Her life is discussed fairly frankly here, including her unhappy marriage.

Lowell, Amy   1874–1925

767 Benvenuto, Richard. *Amy Lowell.* Boston: Twayne Publishers, 1985. 163 pp.

See entry 26.

768 Damon, Samuel T. *Amy Lowell: A Chronicle, with Extracts from Her Correspondence.* Boston: Houghton Mifflin, 1935. 773 pp.

Damon's biography of Lowell places her in perspective and provides an honest account of her life and poetry. Since he was a friend to his subject, Damon offers many intimate details in this book. His quotations from her letters are judicious.

769 Gould, Jean. *Amy: The World of Amy Lowell and the Imagist Movement.* New York: Dodd, Mead, 1975. 372 pp.

This is a general, introductory biography that focuses on Lowell in the 1920s and on her intimate friendship with Ada Russell. It gives very little information about the imagist movement, despite its title.

770 Gregory, Horace. *Amy Lowell: A Portrait of the Poet in Her Time.* Nashville: Thomas Nelson, 1958. 213 pp.

Gregory's portrait of Lowell focuses on her character and her personal life. He reveals both her admirable and negative traits, while telling many literary anecdotes about her.

771   Wood, Clement. *Amy Lowell*. New York: H. Vinal, 1926. 185 pp.
Condescending to Lowell, both as a poet and as a woman, Wood is completely biased against her. He even describes all the bad influences she had on her acquaintances.

Lowell, Josephine S.   1843–1905

772   Stewart, William R. *The Philanthropic Work of Josephine Shaw Lowell*. New York: Macmillan Publishing, 1911. 584 pp.
This is a complete sourcebook on Lowell. It includes a sketch of her life, extracts from her reports, and a complete chronological list of her writings.

Loy, Mina   1882–1966

773   Kouidis, Virginia M. *Mina Loy, American Modernist Poet*. Baton Rouge: Louisiana State Univ. Press, 1980. 148 pp.
This first biography on Loy covers both her private life and career. Kouidis's approach to Loy is that of a feminist, but she does not overstate the poet's achievements.

Luce, Clare Boothe   1903–1987

774   Hatch, Alden. *Ambassador Extraordinary: Clare Boothe Luce*. New York: Henry Holt, 1956. 254 pp.
This informal, laudatory biography was written while Luce was the U.S. ambassador to Italy. It highlights all the major events of her life, beginning with her childhood, up to that time.

775   Shadegg, Stephen. *Clare Boothe Luce: A Biography*. New York: Simon and Schuster, 1971. 313 pp.
Shadegg bases this biography on his interviews with Luce and on her private papers. His account is totally factual; he makes no evaluations of her career nor provides insights into her personality or politics.

776   Sheed, Wilfred. *Clare Boothe Luce*. New York: E. P. Dutton, 1982. 183 pp.
Since Sheed was a close friend to Luce, his book on her is subjective. He discusses all the stages of her personal life and political career, but offers no analyses to the reader.

Luhan, Mabel Dodge   1879–1962

777   Frazer, Winifred L. *Mabel Dodge Luhan*. Boston: Twayne Publishers, 1984. 126 pp.
See entry 26.

778   Hahn, Emily. *Mabel: A Biography of Mabel Dodge Luhan*. Boston: Houghton Mifflin, 1977. 228 pp.
This biography is based on Luhan's writings and private papers. Hahn is sympathetic to her, but not exceedingly so. She focuses her attention on Luhan herself rather than on the famous people her subject befriended.

779   Rudnick, Lois P. *Mabel Dodge Luhan: New Woman, New Worlds*. Albuquerque: Univ. of New Mexico Press, 1984. 384 pp.
Rudnick uses Luhan's memoirs as her main source for this scholarly book; it provides an unembellished discussion of Luhan herself and her relationships with famous people.

Lyon, Mary   1797–1849

780   Banning, Evelyn I. *Mary Lyon of Putnam's Hill: A Biography*. New York: Vanguard Press, 1965. 189 pp.
This account of Lyon and her career in education was written for the general reader. The sources of the text are not well documented, but there is a short bibliography.

781   Fiske, Fidelia. *Recollections of Mary Lyon with Selections from Her Instructions to the Pupils of Mt. Holyoke Female Seminary*. Boston: American Tract Society, 1866. 333 pp.
This book is valuable for the contemporary reminiscences of Lyon by her friends and colleagues. It also contains extracts from her academic lectures and religious services.

782   Gilchrist, Beth B. *The Life of Mary Lyon*. Boston: Houghton Mifflin, 1910. 462 pp.
Gilchrist's is a sympathetic account and fine evaluation of Lyon's life. She explains her subject's intellect, as well as her educational and administrative methods.

783   Green, Elizabeth A. *Mary Lyon and Mount Holyoke: Opening the Gates*. Hanover, N.H.: Univ. Press of New England, 1979. 406 pp.

Green's book is based on archival records and is the most complete biography available on Lyon. It focuses on her founding of the college and quotes from her diaries and letters at length.

784   Hitchcock, Edward, ed. *The Power of Christian Benevolence Illustrated in the Life and Labors of Mary Lyon.* Northampton, Mass.: Hopkins, Bridgman, 1851. 486 pp.

A close friend to Lyon, Hitchcock provides an admiring account of her life and work. He bases his book on some of her letters that have since been lost.

M

McAuliffe, (Sharon) Christa   1948–1986

785   Hohler, Robert T. *"I Touch the Future—" : The Story of Christa McAuliffe*. New York: Random House, 1987. 262 pp.

The author, a reporter from McAuliffe's hometown newspaper, followed her preparations for space travel. He writes a lively, intimate portrait of the astronaut as he knew her.

McCarthy, Mary T.   1912–1989

786   Gelderman, Carol. *Mary McCarthy: A Life*. New York: St. Martin's Press, 1988. 448 pp.

This is a thorough and minutely detailed biography that covers all of McCarthy's life and career; it weaves the two together exceptionally well. Gelderman describes her subject's marriages clearly, particularly her union with Edmund Wilson, but she never speculates on McCarthy's psychology.

787   Grumbach, Doris. *The Company She Kept*. New York: Coward-McCann, 1967. 218 pp.

Grumbach interviewed McCarthy in preparing this biography, yet she discovered little new information about her subject. Instead of focusing on McCarthy's literary career and personal character, the biographer pays much attention to her four marriages and to her domestic life in general. Grumbach does demonstrate that much in McCarthy's books is autobiographical.

788   Hardy, Willene S. *Mary McCarthy*. New York: Frederick Ungar Publishing, 1981. 214 pp.

See entry 189.

789   McKenzie, Barbara. *Mary McCarthy*. New York: Twayne Publishers, 1967. 191 pp.

See entry 26.

McClintock, Barbara   1902–

790   Keller, Evelyn F. *Barbara McClintock: A Feeling for the Organism*. San Francisco: W. H. Freeman, 1983. 235 pp.

This well-written, insightful biography is based primarily on interviews with McClintock and her colleagues.

McCullers, Carson S.   1919–1967

791   Carr, Virginia S. *The Lonely Hunter: A Biography of Carson McCullers*. New York: Doubleday Publishing, 1975. 600 pp.

After many years of careful and detailed research, Carr has produced the definitive biography of McCullers. Though the approach is scholarly, the focus is on the life rather than the works. Excellent notes, a chronology, and a genealogy are included.

792   Cook, Richard M. *Carson McCullers*. New York: Frederick Ungar Publishing, 1975. 200 pp.

See entry 189.

793   Evans, Oliver. *The Ballad of Carson McCullers: A Biography*. New York: Coward-McCann, 1966. 220 pp.

Although this is a finely detailed and full biography, Evans makes some minor factual errors in his awkward commentary on McCullers's writings, along with his discussion of her life. He could have devoted more space to describing her personal traits.

794   McDowell, Margaret. *Carson McCullers*. Boston: Twayne Publishers, 1980. 158 pp.

See entry 26.

795   Sullivan, Margaret S. "Carson McCullers: The Conversion of Experience, 1917–1947." Dissertation. Duke Univ., 1966. 326 pp.

This is a very competent biography that relates the events of McCullers's life to the development of her literary talent.

MacDonald, Jeanette   1907–1965

796   Parish, James R. *The Jeanette MacDonald Story*. New York: Mason/ Charter, 1976. 181 pp.

Although Parish traces MacDonald's career in some detail, not enough attention is paid to her early years as an entertainer. However, Parish has researched this book well and his facts are accurate.

MacDowell, Katherine   See **Bonner, Sherwood**

McDowell, Mary E.   1854–1936

797 Wilson, Howard E. *Mary McDowell, Neighbor*. Chicago: Univ. of Chicago Press, 1929. 235 pp.

This biographer, while focusing on McDowell's social work in Chicago, pays tribute to her instead of providing any critical evaluation of her career.

McGinley, Phyllis   1905–1978

798 Wagner, Linda W. *Phyllis McGinley*. New York: Twayne Publishers, 1971. 128 pp.

See entry 26.

MacKay, Marie L.   1843–1928

799 Berlin, Ellin M. *Silver Platter*. New York: Doubleday Publishing, 1957. 454 pp.

Berlin, a granddaughter to her subject, covers all the stages of MacKay's life, focusing on her two marriages. Unfortunately, fictionalized elements mar this biography's seriousness.

McKinley, Ida Saxton   1847–1907

800 Leech, Margaret. *In the Days of McKinley*. New York: Harper and Brothers, 1959. 686 pp.

Leech discusses Mrs. McKinley's personality and medical history frankly and in detail. The author also focuses on her subject's relationship with her husband, whom the book also discusses at length.

McMain, Eleanor L.   1866–1934

801 Dubroca, Isabelle. *Good Neighbor Eleanor McMain of Kingsley House*. New Orleans: Pelican Publishing, 1955. 164 pp.

Dubroca, McMain's close friend, has written a laudatory biography that is prejudiced in its subject's favor.

McMein, Neysa   1888–1949

802   Gallagher, Brian. *Anything Goes: The Jazz Age Adventures of Neysa McMein and Her Extravagant Circle of Friends*. New York: Time Books, 1987. 241 pp.

This informative and insightful book is the result of much careful research.

Macy, Anne Sullivan   1866–1936

803   Braddy, Nella. *Anne Sullivan Macy: The Story behind Helen Keller*. New York: Doubleday Publishing, 1933. 365 pp.

Braddy, a friend to both of these women, provides an insightful and comprehensive biography of Macy that begins in her childhood. The biographer also focuses in close detail on Macy's teaching of and friendship for Keller.

804   Hickok, Lorena A. *The Touch of Magic: The Story of Helen Keller's Great Teacher, Anne Sullivan Macy*. New York: Dodd, Mead, 1961. 184 pp.

This brief book summarizes the major events of Macy's life and emphasizes her best character traits throughout its text.

805   Keller, Helen A. *Teacher: Anne Sullivan Macy, a Tribute by the Foster-child of Her Mind*. New York: Doubleday Publishing, 1955. 247 pp.

Keller tries to remain objective in this book but cannot; she has adulation for her teacher, who spent a lifetime of devotion to her pupil. Keller also explains in some detail how she learned language from Macy.

806   Lash, Joseph P. *Helen and Teacher: The Story of Helen Keller and Anne Sullivan Macy*. New York: Delacorte Press, 1980. 811 pp.

See under Keller, Helen A.

807   Waite, Helen E. *Valiant Companions: Helen Keller and Anne Sullivan Macy*. Philadelphia: Macrae Smith, 1959. 223 pp.

See under Keller, Helen A.

Macy, Henrietta Gardner   1854–1927

808   Bacheler, Clementine, and Jessie O. White. *Nun of the Ca'Frollo: The Life and Letters of Henrietta Gardner Macy*. New York: W. F. Payson, 1931. 321 pp.

The authors, who both were friends to Macy, use her letters to tell most of her story, interspersed with their own comments and summaries of her life.

Madison, Dolly Payne   1768–1849

809   Anthony, Katharine S. *Dolly Madison: Her Life and Times.* New York: Doubleday Publishing, 1949. 426 pp.

This is a good biography on the first lady and her era for a general reader. However, at times Mrs. Madison becomes lost on a stage crowded with the famous men of her day.

810   Arnett, Ethel S. *Mrs. James Madison: The Incomparable Dolley.* Greensboro, N.C.: Piedmont Press, 1972. 520 pp.

This fully documented biography, based mainly on primary sources, covers all of Mrs. Madison's life.

811   Beebe, Elswyth T. *Dolly Madison: Her Life and Times.* New York: Crowell-Collier Press, 1970. 184 pp.

This biographer re-creates some scenes and dialogue that feature Mrs. Madison, thereby fictionalizing parts of his book. He also shows only her positive character traits, depicting her as a devoted wife and unsurpassed first lady.

812   Clark, Allen C. *The Life and Letters of Dolly Madison.* Washington, D.C.: Press of W. F. Roberts, 1914. 517 pp.

Clark depends heavily on Mrs. Madison's eloquent letters to tell her life story.

813   Dean, Elizabeth L. *Dolly Madison, the Nation's Hostess.* Boston: D. Lothrop, 1928. 250 pp.

Dean covers all eighty years of the first lady's life in a fair amount of detail. The reader receives a clear view of life in her era and of the country's early leaders.

814   Goodwin, Maud W. *Dolly Payne Madison.* New York: Charles Scribner's Sons, 1896. 287 pp.

Although Goodwin focuses only on Mrs. Madison's admirable qualities and includes much about her subject's domestic life, this is still a perceptive book on her. It is based mainly on Dolly's letters and some essential documents, and eschews much political discussion.

815   Moore, Virginia. *The Madisons.* New York: McGraw-Hill, 1978. 568 pp.

Moore is totally biased in favor of the Madisons in this book, which details their private and public lives. She is especially interested in how they worked together as partners and learned from each other.

Mailliard, Anna W.   See **Ward, Anna**

Mankin, Helen Douglas   1896–1956

816 Spritzer, Lorraine N. *The Belle of Ashby Street: Helen Douglas Mankin and Georgia Politics.* Athens: Univ. of Georgia Press, 1982. 188 pp.

In this biography, which focuses on Mankin's political career rather than on her personal life, the author's extensive research is obvious. While Spritzer describes Mankin's personality vividly, a more elaborate overview of Southern politics in Mankin's era would help the reader's understanding.

Mann, Mary Peabody   1806–1887

817 Tharp, Louise H. *The Peabody Sisters of Salem.* Boston: Little, Brown, 1950. 372 pp.

See under Hawthorne, Sophia P.

818 ———. *Until Victory: Horace Mann and Mary Peabody.* Boston: Little, Brown, 1953. 367 pp.

Although Mary Peabody's letters help tell this story, Tharp discusses Horace Mann at greater length. Tharp's thorough and careful research results in some new insights into their marriage and their work together.

Mansfield, Jayne   1932–1967

819 Mann, May. *Jayne Mansfield.* New York: Drake Publishers, 1973. 300 pp.

Although the author purports to be a very close friend to Mansfield, she nonetheless chronicles in this book the most awful, inhumane aspects of Mansfield's life.

820 Strait, Raymond. *The Tragic Secret Life of Jayne Mansfield.* Chicago: Henry Regnery, 1974. 207 pp.

Although Strait worked as Mansfield's press secretary for ten years, his is not a well-written biography of her. He emphasizes her life's sordidness while discussing her entire sexual history.

Marks, Jeannette A.   1875–1964

821 Wells, Anna M. *Miss Marks and Miss Woolley.* Boston: Houghton Mifflin, 1978. 268 pp.

Wells describes the relationship of these two college teachers without sensationalizing their love for each other. She quotes from the letters written between them and concludes her book with a bibliography of Miss Marks's writings.

Marlowe, Julia   1866–1950

822   Barry, John D. *Julia Marlowe*. Boston: R. G. Badger, 1899. 87 pp.

This is a short sketch of Marlowe's life and acting career, produced when she was at the height of her popularity. The book is ornately illustrated.

823   Russell, Charles E. *Julia Marlowe: Her Life and Art*. New York: D. Appleton, 1926. 582 pp.

Russell's focus is on Marlowe's forty-year career rather than on her personal life. He lavishes admiration and praise on his subject as he traces the development of her acting. His book also includes a history of Marlowe's best roles.

824   Sothern, Edward H. *Julia Marlowe's Story*. Ed. Fairfax Downey. New York: Rinehart, 1953. 237 pp.

Marlowe actually dictated this book to her husband and fellow actor, Edward Sothern. As a result, he writes in the first person, as if Marlowe were speaking. The editor has added one chapter of his own to the text.

Martin, Anne H.   1875–1951

825   Howard, Anne B. *The Long Campaign: A Biography of Anne Martin*. Reno: Univ. of Nevada Press, 1985. 220 pp.

Howard's feminist study is a well-balanced biography of her subject, employing Martin's many extant papers for its information.

Martin, Lillien J.   1851–1943

826   deFord, Miriam A. *A Psychologist Unretired: The Life Pattern of Lillien J. Martin*. Stanford: Stanford Univ. Press, 1948. 127 pp.

This is a very good, comprehensive biography that includes a useful bibliography.

Martinez, Maria M.   1887–1980

827   Marriott, Alice. *Maria: The Potter of San Ildefonso*. Norman: Univ. of Oklahoma Press, 1948. 294 pp.

This is a popularized biography containing drawn illustrations rather than photographs of Martinez's work (which lessens the book's value). It does, however, contain a useful bibliography and chronology.

828   Peterson, Susan. *The Living Tradition of Maria Martinez*. New York: Harper and Row, 1977. 300 pp.

Peterson praises both Martinez and her art in this basically descriptive book. Though Patterson does not evaluate her subject, the book contains many fine illustrations of Martinez's art and a very good bibliography.

Mason, Lucy Randolph   1882–1959

829 Salmond, John A. *Miss Lucy of the CIO: The Life and Times of Lucy Randolph Mason, 1882–1959*. Athens: Univ. of Georgia Press, 1988. 240 pp.
In this well-researched book, Salmond details Mason's personality traits and intellectual ideas that aided her in her career. However, the author gives less attention to her private life.

Maxwell, Martha   1923–

830 Benson, Maxine. *Martha Maxwell, Rocky Mountain Naturalist*. Lincoln: Univ. of Nebraska Press, 1986. 335 pp.
Benson's biography is carefully researched and filled with informative details. She quotes frequently from Maxwell's letters and provides good notes to the entire text.

Mead, Margaret   1901–1978

831 Bateson, Mary C. *With a Daughter's Eye: A Memoir of Margaret Mead and Gregory Bateson*. New York: William Morrow, 1984. 242 pp.
Bateson is fairly candid and thorough on her mother's personality, her parents' marriage, and the details of Mead's relationship to Ruth Benedict. However, this book does not discuss Mead's work in any depth or breadth.

832 Cassidy, Robert. *Margaret Mead: A Voice for the Century*. New York: Universe Books, 1982. 176 pp.
Mead cooperated in the preparation of this book. Cassidy follows a chronological approach to Mead's life and work, demonstrating how the latter affected the former. He shows some of the less attractive sides of her personality and explains her views on social and political issues.

833 Howard, Jane. *Margaret Mead: A Life*. New York: Simon and Schuster, 1984. 527 pp.
Howard interviewed approximately three hundred people to gather information on Mead, and the result is an overly detailed account of her character and career. While the book describes best the years after 1945, it is not a critical or intellectual biography of Mead.

834 Rice, Edward. *Margaret Mead: A Portrait.* New York: Harper and Row, 1979. 204 pp.

Rice, a personal friend to Mead, discusses her career achievements while he writes about all the stages of her life. Many new aspects of her marriage and her family life are introduced in this book.

Mecom, Jane Franklin   1712–1794

835 Van Doren, Carl C. *Jane Mecom.* New York: Viking Press, 1950. 255 pp.

This is a well-written, scholarly book by the major biographer of Benjamin Franklin, Mecom's brother. The text, which is based on the many surviving letters between brother and sister, also presents a fine depiction of life in eighteenth-century Boston.

Mendl, Elsie D.   See DeWolfe, Elsie

Menken, Adah Isaacs   1835–1868

836 Falk, Bernard. *The Naked Lady; or, Storm Over Adah: A Biography of Adah Isaacs Menken.* London: Hutchinson, 1934. 306 pp.

This biography, which covers all of Menken's life and career, is much more detailed and accurate than are earlier books on her.

837 Gerson, Noel B. *The Queen of the Plaza: A Biography of Adah Isaacs Menken.* New York: Funk and Wagnalls, 1964. 307 pp.

Gerson's sources for this biography are Menken's own diary and poetry. He uses them to discuss the more sordid aspects of her life; he also questions her acting ability.

838 Lesser, Allen. *Enchanting Rebel: The Secret of Adah Isaacs Menken.* New York: Beech-hurst Press, 1947. 284 pp.

In this well-researched book, Lesser does a good job of clearing away the legends about Menken to get at the facts. He covers her career in detail, as well as discusses her four marriages and numerous friendships with the famous.

839 Mankowitz, Wolf. *Mazeppa: The Lives, Loves and Legends of Adah Isaacs Menken.* Briarcliff Manor, N.Y.: Stein and Day, 1982. 300 pp.

Mankowitz describes all the legends extant about Menken. Throughout the text his approach to the actress and her adventures in the United States and Europe is rather humorous.

840   Northcott, Richard. *Adah Isaacs Menken: An Illustrated Biography*. London: Press Printers, 1921. 56 pp.
This brief, illustrated sketch of Menken mistakes some of the facts of her life.

Mercer, Mabel   1900–1984

841   Haskins, James. *Mabel Mercer: A Life*. New York: Atheneum Publishers, 1987. 217 pp.
Haskins, an admirer of Mercer, provides a mostly anecdotal portrait of her. Based on interviews with her friends and colleagues, the book describes her personal life clearly.

Metalious, Grace   1924–1964

842   Toth, Emily. *Inside Peyton Place: The Life of Grace Metalious*. New York: Doubleday Publishing, 1981. 395 pp.
Toth covers all of her subject's life and brief fame as an author. She views Metalious as a feminist, a position that cannot be substantiated from the evidence presented in this biography.

Meyer, Lucy Rider   1849–1922

843   Horton, Isabelle. *High Adventure: The Life of Lucy Rider Meyer*. New York: The Methodist Book Concern, 1928. 359 pp.
Horton, who had access to many primary sources, writes an affectionate account of Meyer. Unfortunately, the book has no index, bibliography, or footnotes to aid the serious student.

Miles, Emma Bell   1879–1919

844   Edwards, Grace T. "Emma Bell Miles: Appalachian Author, Artist, and Interpreter of Folk Culture." Dissertation. Univ. of Virginia, 1981. 325 pp.
Edwards critically assesses both Miles's life and career, concentrating on the years 1904–1919. The student also highlights Miles's childhood and her last years of illness.

Millay, Edna St. Vincent   1892–1950

845   Atkins, Elizabeth. *Edna St. Vincent Millay and Her Times*. Chicago: Univ. of Chicago Press, 1936. 266 pp.

This account of Millay's life and art was written when the poet was still young; it is best at depicting her at the height of her career. Unfortunately, Atkins's tone is overly adulatory, and she overvalues Millay's poetry.

846 Brittin, Norman A. *Edna St. Vincent Millay.* New York: Twayne Publishers, 1967. 192 pp.

See entry 26.

847 Cheney, Anne. *Millay in Greenwich Village.* University: Univ. of Alabama Press, 1975. 160 pp.

Cheney focuses on the years 1918 through 1925 and attempts to psychoanalyze Millay based on her relationships with men during that period. The biographer provides many details of Millay's life for those years and discusses the influences on her.

848 Gould, Jean. *The Poet and Her Book: A Biography of Edna St. Vincent Millay.* New York: Dodd, Mead, 1969. 308 pp.

This is a fairly well written and highly detailed biography of the poet. Gould relies on facts rather than on incidental anecdotal material to describe Millay's life.

849 Gurko, Miriam. *Restless Spirit: The Life of Edna St. Vincent Millay.* New York: Thomas Y. Crowell, 1962. 271 pp.

Gurko provides a good introduction to the poet's life for the general reader. She retells the major episodes of that life as references to them appear in her poetry.

850 Sheean, Vincent. *Indigo Bunting: A Memoir of Edna St. Vincent Millay.* New York: Harper and Brothers, 1951. 131 pp.

Sheean's book, a memorial to his friend Millay, describes her pursuits in her later years, particularly bird-watching. He details her personality and her private life in the 1940s very effectively.

Miller, Alice D.   1874–1942

851 Miller, Henry W. *All Our Lives: Alice Duer Miller.* New York: Coward-McCann, 1945. 299 pp.

Although Miller's husband wrote this account of her life, it is not a very detailed book. He is biased in his narrative, which provides an informal portrait of Miller rather than a full biography of her.

Miller, Bertha Mahoney   1882–1969

852 Ross, Eulalie S. *The Spirited Life: Bertha Mahoney Miller and Children's Books*. Boston: The Horn Book, 1973. 274 pp.

Ross's book concentrates on Miller's work in behalf of children's literature and on her bookstore exclusively for children. The author includes a selected bibliography prepared by Virginia Haviland.

Miller, Marilyn   1898–1936

853 Harris, Warren G. *The Other Marilyn: A Biography of Marilyn Miller*. New York: Arbor House, 1985. 248 pp.

This candid biography covers all of Miller's personal life and career; its introduction explains the similarities between her life and that of Marilyn Monroe.

Mills, Susan Lincoln   1825–1912

854 James, Elias O. *The Story of Cyrus and Susan Mills*. Stanford: Stanford Univ. Press, 1953. 275 pp.

James, a friend to this couple for forty years, provides a warm picture of their life and work at Mills College, while he emphasizes the basic themes that ran through their lives.

Minnelli, Liza   1946–

855 Parish, James R., and Jack Ano. *Liza! An Unauthorized Biography*. New York: Pocket Books, 1975. 173 pp.

Unfortunately, this book relies heavily on gossip to describe Liza's childhood and the style of her adult life. Parish also discusses Judy Garland at some length here, as well as the mother-daughter relationship between the two women.

856 Petrucelli, Alan W. *Liza! Liza! An Unauthorized Biography*. New York: Karz-Cohl Publishing, 1983. 174 pp.

Petrucelli, who greatly admires Minnelli, produces a biography that includes many trivial details. He also depicts imaginary scenes and conversations, rendering the book closer to fiction than to biography.

857 Spada, James, and Karen Swenson. *Judy and Liza*. New York: Doubleday Publishing, 1983. 216 pp.

See under Garland, Judy.

Mitchell, Lucy Sprague   1878–1967

858   Antler, Joyce. *Lucy Sprague Mitchell: The Making of a Modern Woman.* New Haven: Yale Univ. Press, 1987. 436 pp.

Antler's approach to Mitchell is that of a feminist; as a result, her book describes how Mitchell's life was a balance between career and family. Among Antler's sources for this book were Mitchell's four children, who provided a unique perspective on her home life.

Mitchell, Margaret   1900–1949

859   Edwards, Anne. *The Road to Tara: The Life of Margaret Mitchell.* New York: Ticknor and Fields, 1983. 369 pp.

Edwards spends too much space in this biography describing the history of Mitchell's novel, *Gone with the Wind.* She highlights portions of Mitchell's daily life and quotes from a few of her important letters.

860   Farr, Finis. *Margaret Mitchell of Atlanta: The Author of "Gone with the Wind."* New York: William Morrow, 1965. 244 pp.

Based on an unpublished memoir written by Mitchell's brother, in addition to her personal papers, Farr's book describes all the stages of Mitchell's life and her time as a celebrity.

Mitchell, Maria   1818–1889

861   Kendall, Phebe M. *Maria Mitchell: Life, Letters and Journals.* Boston: Lee and Shephard, 1896. 293 pp.

Kendall, Mitchell's sister, is best at providing details about her subject's childhood. Since Kendall zealously protects her famous sister's private life, this biography includes few intimate details and nothing that would be detrimental to Mitchell's reputation.

862   Wright, Helen. *Sweeper in the Sky.* New York: Macmillan Publishing, 1949. 253 pp.

Wright, who used Mitchell's private papers to prepare this book on her life and career, presents a sympathetic and admiring portrait of her subject. Wright also employs some fictionalization in this book, especially when describing Mitchell's childhood.

Mitchell, Martha Beall   1918–1976

863   McLendon, Winzola. *Martha: The Life of Martha Mitchell.* New York: Random House, 1979. 400 pp.

The biographer, who was a friend to Mitchell, offers no evaluation of her life in this book. Instead, she merely details the stages of her subject's life, concentrating on Mitchell's last five years, when she was seriously ill.

Monroe, Harriet   1860–1936

864   Cahill, Daniel J. *Harriet Monroe*. New York: Twayne Publishers, 1974. 148 pp.
See entry 26.

865   Williams, Ellen. *Harriet Monroe and the Poetry Renaissance: The First Ten Years of "Poetry," 1912–1922*. Urbana: Univ. of Illinois Press, 1977. 312 pp.
Williams perceptively assesses Monroe's contributions to *Poetry* and that magazine's impact on American arts in general. By consulting the extant letter files of *Poetry,* Williams produces a complete account of this ten-year period.

Monroe, Marilyn   1926–1962

866   Guiles, Fred L. *Legend: The Life and Death of Marilyn Monroe*. Briarcliff Manor, N.Y.: Stein and Day, 1984. 501 pp.
Guiles focuses his attention on re-creating Monroe's psychology and on demonstrating how her childhood traumas affected her adult life. However, the author is not always precise in defining his subject's personality.

867   ———. *Norma Jean: The Life of Marilyn Monroe*. New York: McGraw-Hill, 1969. 341 pp.
Guiles, who attempts to remain objective, writes in opposition to the many myths about Monroe. He both employs details accurately and evaluates Monroe's life competently.

868   Hoyt, Edwin P. *Marilyn: The Tragic Venus*. New York: Duell, Sloan and Pearce, 1965. 279 pp.
After interviewing many people who knew Monroe, Hoyt writes a basic, sympathetic account of her life.

869   Kahn, Roger. *Joe and Marilyn: A Memory of Love*. New York: William Morrow, 1986. 269 pp.
Kahn, a sportswriter, discusses DiMaggio at greater length than he does Monroe. He compassionately details the couple's lives before, during, and after their marriage. Kahn's frank account endeavors to clear away myths about the pair.

870   Lembourn, Hans J. *Diary of a Lover of Marilyn Monroe*. Trans. Hallberg Hallmundsson. New York: Arbor House, 1979. 214 pp.

Lembourn, who claims to have been Monroe's lover for one period of forty days, recalls that episode in this book. His recollected conversations sound fictitious, and his writing style is either awkward or poorly translated.

871   McCann, Graham. *Marilyn Monroe: The Body in the Library*. New Brunswick, N.J.: Rutgers Univ. Press, 1988. 241 pp.

McCann attempts to recover the true Marilyn from behind her public image, refuting earlier biographers' descriptions of her personality. This writer pays little attention to the actress's career, preferring to discuss her private life.

872   Mailer, Norman. *Marilyn: A Biography*. New York: Grosset and Dunlap, 1973. 270 pp.

Mailer bases the facts in his book on those in Guiles's *Norma Jean* (see above), to which he adds much speculation. While Mailer discusses all the stages of Monroe's life, he does so "in the subjunctive tense."

873   Martin, William T. *Will Acting Spoil Marilyn Monroe?* New York: Doubleday Publishing, 1956. 128 pp.

This is not a full biography, merely an extended sketch of the actress. Martin bases his text on interviews with Monroe and her colleagues.

874   Mellen, Joan. *Marilyn Monroe*. New York: Pyramid Publishers, 1973. 157 pp.

See entry 286.

875   Murray, Eunice, and Rose Shade. *Marilyn: The Last Months*. New York: Pyramid Publishers, 1975. 157 pp.

Murray, Monroe's housemaid for the last year of her life, narrates her account of that period. She theorizes that Monroe was an accidental suicide.

876   Pepitone, Lena, and William Stadiem. *Marilyn Monroe, Confidential: An Intimate Personal Account*. New York: Simon and Schuster, 1979. 251 pp.

Since Pepitone was Monroe's personal maid from 1957 to 1962, she is able to provide some intimate details about the actress and to offer a clear picture of her personality.

877   Rollyson, Carl E. *Marilyn Monroe: A Life of the Actress*. Ann Arbor: UMI Research Press, 1986. 255 pp.

Rollyson, while providing a basic review of Monroe's private life, concentrates more on her acting career. He takes her seriously as an actress and shows how she developed her craft over the years.

878   Rosten, Norman. *Marilyn Monroe: An Untold Story*. New York: New American Library, 1973. 125 pp.

Rosten, a longtime friend to Monroe, writes a fairly objective and very informative book on her life. He understands her well and describes her personal life and psychological problems clearly, especially for the year 1962.

879   Shevey, Sandra. *The Marilyn Scandal: Her True Life Revealed by Those Who Knew Her*. New York: William Morrow, 1988. 360 pp.

While Shevey reiterates much data about Monroe that is already known, her views on the actress are unusual. In particular, she psychoanalyzes Monroe very differently than anyone has done before.

880   Slatzer, Robert F. *The Life and Curious Death of Marilyn Monroe*. New York: Pinnacle House, 1974. 348 pp.

Slatzer has two main focuses in his book: his own brief marriage to Monroe and his speculation about her death. This book also reprints important documents concerning the actress's death.

881   Steinem, Gloria. *Marilyn*. New York: Holt, Rinehart and Winston, 1986. 182 pp.

In this well-researched book Steinem theorizes that Monroe was not murdered. Steinem also becomes involved in some speculation about the actress's psychology. She comments accurately and shrewdly on Monroe's personal problems.

882   Summers, Anthony. *Goddess: The Secret Lives of Marilyn Monroe*. New York: Macmillan Publishing, 1985. 415 pp.

Summers, in this heavily documented book, concentrates on the nature and causes of Monroe's decline and death. Conversely, he says little about her childhood or early life.

883   Zolotow, Maurice. *Marilyn Monroe*. New York: Harcourt, Brace and World, 1960. 340 pp.

This is a serious book that covers all of Monroe's life and attempts to separate the true woman from the manufactured public image. The biographer did much research on his subject and is fairly successful at explaining her psychology.

Moody, Harriet C. T.   1857–1932

884 Dunbar, Olivia H. *A House in Chicago*. Chicago: Univ. of Chicago Press, 1947. 288 pp.

About half of this book comprises letters that famous people wrote to Moody. Then Dunbar focuses on Moody's role in Chicago's literary history. She also details the lives of some of Moody's closest friends.

Moon, Lottie D.   1840–1912

885 Allen, Catherine B. *The New Lottie Moon Story*. Nashville: Broadman Press, 1980. 320 pp.

Allen's is the first lengthy, modern book on Moon's life and missionary work. Therefore, it supersedes the inadequate biography by Lawrence (see below).

886 Lawrence, Una R. *Lottie Moon*. Nashville: Sunday School Board of the Southern Baptist Convention, 1927. 317 pp.

This is not an adequately comprehensive book on Moon's life and career.

Moore, Anne Carroll   1871–1961

887 Sayers, Frances O. *Anne Carroll Moore: A Biography*. New York: Atheneum Publishers, 1972. 303 pp.

Sayers writes an adulatory account of Moore's life and work, but one that is also honest and understanding. The biographer's factual data is all well documented, and she is apt at describing the character of this complex woman.

Moore, Grace   1901–1947

888 Farrar, Rowena R. *Grace Moore and Her Many Worlds*. Cranbury, N.J.: Cornwall Books, 1982. 312 pp.

Farrar covers the singer's entire life, from childhood to death, and writes candidly but not sensationally on Moore's private life. This book includes a very thorough discography.

Moore, Marianne C.   1887–1972

889 Engel, Bernard F. *Marianne Moore*. New York: Twayne Publishers, 1964. 176 pp.

See entry 26.

890   Phillips, Elizabeth. *Marianne Moore*. New York: Frederick Ungar Publishing, 1982. 247 pp.

See entry 189.

Moorehead, Agnes   1906–1974

891   Sherk, Warren. *Agnes Moorehead: A Very Private Person*. Philadelphia: Dorrance, 1976. 137 pp.

In this, the only book-length biography available on Moorehead, Sherk writes from a fundamentalist outlook.

Morgan, Anna   1851–1936

892   Sozen, Joyce L. C. "Anna Morgan: Reader, Teacher, and Director." Dissertation. Univ. of Illinois, 1961. 208 pp.

Sozen opens with a brief review of Morgan's early life and the influences on her. The majority of the study describes Morgan's career, particularly from 1878 to 1925 in Chicago.

Morgan, Julia   1872–1957

893   Boutelle, Sara H. *Julia Morgan Architect*. New York: Abbeville Press, 1988. 271 pp.

Boutelle's emphasis is on Morgan's career and her ideas on architecture rather than on her personal life. The biographer is sympathetic to her subject, yet gives an honest account of her lengthy career, including the details of many of her projects. Color photographs in the text show Morgan's best buildings.

Morgan, Vicki   1953?–1983

894   Basichis, Gordon. *Beautiful Bad Girl: The Vicki Morgan Story*. Santa Barbara, Calif.: Santa Barbara Press, 1985. 303 pp.

The author describes Morgan's life with a fair amount of detail. He concentrates primarily on her last years as a mistress to wealthy men and on her death in 1983.

Mortimer, Mary   1816–1877

895   Norton, Minerva B. *A True Teacher: Mary Mortimer*. New York: Fleming H. Revell, 1894. 341 pp.

Norton obtained information for this biography from some of Mortimer's former students at Milwaukee College. The book also reprints some of Mortimer's personal letters.

Morton, Sarah W. 1759–1846

896 Pendleton, Emily, and Milton Ellis. *Philenia: The Life and Works of Sarah Wentworth Morton, 1759–1846.* Orono: Univ. of Maine Press, 1931. 122 pp.

This is the fullest and most authoritative account of Morton's life and career that is available.

Moses, Grandma 1860–1961

897 Kallir, Otto, ed. *Grandma Moses: American Primitive.* New York: Doubleday Publishing, 1946. n.p.

Louis Bromfield provides a well-written introduction to this book. The biographical data on the artist was provided by her daughter-in-law, Dorothy H. Moses.

Moskowitz, Belle 1877–1933

898 Perry, Elisabeth I. *Belle Moskowitz: Feminine Politics and the Exercise of Power in the Age of Alfred E. Smith.* New York: Oxford Univ. Press, 1987. 304 pp.

Perry, a granddaughter to Moskowitz, pays tribute to her and her accomplishments in this scholarly book. Her focus is on Moskowitz's career as a political organizer, specifically for Al Smith.

Mott, Lucretia Coffin 1793–1880

899 Bacon, Margaret H. *Valiant Friend: The Life of Lucretia Mott.* New York: Walker, 1980. 265 pp.

This biographer depends heavily on primary sources for this complete life of Mott. Bacon shows Mott's family life, as well as her public career; the two intermesh well as she describes them in her narrative.

900 Cromwell, Otelia. *Lucretia Mott.* Cambridge: Harvard Univ. Press, 1958. 241 pp.

Cromwell details Mott's public crusades and her friendships with her colleagues, often by quoting Mott herself. Although this book includes many informative notes, it does not show enough detail about the era in question.

901   Hallowell, Anna D. *James and Lucretia Mott*. Boston: Houghton Mifflin, 1884. 566 pp.

This biography, written by Mott's granddaughter, is useful since she can provide an intimate portrait of the Motts, and because it reprints many extracts from Lucretia's letters.

902   Hare, Lloyd C. M. *The Greatest American Woman, Lucretia Mott*. New York: American Historical Society, 1937. 307 pp.

This book is a competent, factual account of Mott's life. Although Hare provides a clear depiction of Mott against her historical setting, he does not evaluate her career or provide any insights into her character.

Moulton, Louise C.   1835–1908

903   Whiting, Lilian. *Louise Chandler Moulton: Poet and Friend*. Boston: Little, Brown, 1910. 294 pp.

Whiting pays tribute to her friend in this sympathetic, well-organized account of her life. She shows Moulton in relationship to many famous literary people of her era, in the United States and abroad.

Mowatt, Anna Cora   1819–1870

904   Barnes, Eric W. *The Lady of Fashion: The Life and the Theatre of Anna Cora Mowatt*. New York: Charles Scribner's Sons, 1954. 402 pp.

This book describes fully all of Mowatt's personal life and career, and depicts the society of that period. Barnes also provides a complete bibliography in his text.

905   Blesi, Marius. "The Life and Letters of Anna Cora Mowatt." Dissertation. Univ. of Virginia, 1938. 166 pp.

Blesi first describes Mowatt's life and then discusses her career in detail in this study.

Mudge, Isadore G.   1875–1957

906   Waddell, John N. "The Career of Isadore G. Mudge: A Chapter in the History of Reference Librarianship." Dissertation. Columbia Univ., 1973. 354 pp.

In this study based on her private papers, Waddell discusses the interaction of various familial and educational influences on Mudge's life and career.

Munford, Mary Cooke   1865–1938

907 Bowie, Walter R. *Sunrise in the South*. Richmond, Va.: William Byrd Press, 1942. 158 pp.

Bowie, a nephew to Munford, provides the only complete account of her life and works in this insightful book.

Murfree, Mary N.   1850–1922

908 Cary, Richard. *Mary N. Murfree*. New York: Twayne Publishers, 1967. 192 pp.

See entry 26.

909 Parks, Edd W. *Charles Egbert Craddock (Mary Noailles Murfree)*. Chapel Hill: Univ. of North Carolina Press, 1941. 258 pp.

This critical biography is the only complete study of Murfree's life that is available. It is carefully documented and includes an extensive bibliography.

Murphy, Sara W.   1883–1975

910 Donnelly, Honoria M., and Richard N. Billings. *Sara and Gerald: Villa America and After*. New York: Times Books, 1984. 254 pp.

Donnelly, the Murphys' daughter, recalls her parents' lives clearly by use of intimate family stories. She focuses both on their lively years in ex-patriate society and on their lonely later life back in the United States.

911 Tomkins, Calvin. *Living Well Is the Best Revenge*. New York: Viking Press, 1971. 148 pp.

Tomkins's memoir of the Murphys was first published as a series in the *New Yorker*. He recalls Sara and her era chiefly by employing anecdotes and remembrances by her friends.

Murray, Judith Sargent   1751–1820

912 Field, Vena B. *Constantia: A Study of the Life and Works of Judith Sargent Murray, 1751–1820*. Orono: Univ. of Maine Press, 1931. 118 pp.

This meticulous, scholarly book is the definitive biography of Murray.

Myerson, Bess   1924–

913 Dworkin, Susan. *Miss America, 1945: Bess Myerson's Own Story*. New York: Harper and Row, 1987. 229 pp.

In this sympathetic book, Dworkin discusses the Miss America pageant of 1945 in some detail and follows Myerson through the events of the year of her reign. The author also provides some details about her subject's life after 1945.

N

Nāhienaena   1815?–1836

914 Sinclair, Marjorie. *Nāhi 'ena 'ena: Sacred Daughter of Hawaii.* Honolulu: Univ. Press of Hawaii, 1976. 177 pp.

Since no extensive record of this woman's life is available, Sinclair must make some surmises. Nevertheless, the book is well written and displays a clear understanding of Hawaiian life in the 1820s and 1830s.

Nation, Carry   1846–1911

915 Asbury, Herbert. *Carry Nation.* New York: Alfred A. Knopf, 1929. 314 pp.

Asbury's biography is detailed and objective; he derives his factual data from Nation's autobiography. He uses psychology well to interpret her personal traits.

916 Beals, Carleton. *Cyclone Carry: The Story of Carry Nation.* Radnor, Penn.: Chilton Books, 1962. 364 pp.

Beals includes some fictionalization of Nation's life and crusades in this book. He bases his facts and interpretations largely on her autobiography (which is not always accurate).

917 Taylor, Robert L. *Vessel of Wrath: The Life and Times of Carry Nation.* New York: New American Library, 1966. 373 pp.

Taylor's account of Nation focuses on the humorous aspects of her causes as well as her eccentric personality. He relies on the Beals and Asbury biographies of her (see above) for his facts.

Nelson, Rebecca J.   1845–?

918 Nelson, Joseph R. *Lady Unafraid.* Caldwell, Idaho: Caxton Printers, 1951. 278 pp.

In this book Nelson proudly discusses his mother's accomplishments as a missionary at age seventeen. He recounts the events of 1862 when she taught members of the Ojibway tribe and was formally adopted by them.

Nesbit, Evelyn   1885–1967

919 Mooney, Michael M. *Evelyn Nesbit and Stanford White: Love and Death in the Gilded Age*. New York: William Morrow, 1976. 320 pp.

Much of the first half of this book deals exclusively with Stanford White. Then, Nesbit's career as a chorus girl is detailed, and her marriage to Harry Thaw is examined. The book contains an unreliable index.

Nevelson, Louise B.   1900–1988

920 Glimcher, Arnold B. *Louise Nevelson*. New York: Praeger Publishers, 1972. 172 pp.

Nevelson's entire life and career are covered in this biography, but it is especially good on the hardships of her early career and her early life in general. This book includes bibliographical references and many photographs of Nevelson's art.

Newcomb, Kate Pelham   1885–1956

921 Comandini, Adele. *Doctor Kate, Angel on Snowshoes: The Story of Kate Pelham Newcomb*. New York: Rinehart, 1956. 339 pp.

This is a clearly written, basic biography of Newcomb. The author details her years in medical school, then concentrates on her courtship, marriage, and subsequent career in Wisconsin.

Nicholson, Eliza Jane   See **Rivers, Pearl**

Nieriker, May Alcott   1840–1879

922 Ticknor, Caroline. *May Alcott: A Memoir*. Boston: Little, Brown, 1928. 307 pp.

May Alcott is described in this book mainly by reference to her letters and journals and those of her family. Ticknor describes her subject's personality well.

Nin, Anais   1903–1977

923 Knapp, Bettina. *Anais Nin*. New York: Frederick Ungar Publishing, 1978. 168 pp.

See entry 189.

924   Scholar, Nancy. *Anais Nin*. Boston: Twayne Publishers, 1984. 175 pp. See entry 26.

Nixon, Patricia Ryan   1912–

925   David, Lester. *The Lonely Lady of San Clemente: The Story of Pat Nixon*. New York: Thomas Y. Crowell, 1978. 235 pp.

David's chronology in this book is awkward and may confuse the reader. He includes many details about Mrs. Nixon's past and present life, based on interviews with her friends. Unfortunately, he sometimes includes too many gossipy items in his account.

926   Eisenhower, Julie N. *Pat Nixon: The Untold Story*. New York: Simon and Schuster, 1986. 480 pp.

Mrs. Eisenhower's awkwardly organized book deals more with her father and his politics than it does with her mother. She admires her mother but does not give the reader any insights into her character.

Nordica, Lillian   1859–1914

927   Glackens, Ira. *Yankee Diva: Lillian Nordica and the Golden Age of Opera*. New York: Coleridge Press, 1963. 366 pp.

This is a thorough and detailed biography that remains objective. Glackens focuses more on Nordica's private life than on her artistic talent or career.

Normand, Mabel   1894–1930

928   Fussell, Betty H. *Mabel*. New York: Ticknor and Fields, 1982. 239 pp.

Fussell's book reads more like a novel than a biography. She writes an entertaining narrative on her subject, which she interrupts to quote from the letters and interviews involved in her research. Furthermore, Fussell does not substantiate all her claims.

Norsworthy, Naomi   1877–1916

929   Higgins, Frances C. *The Life of Naomi Norsworthy*. Boston: Houghton Mifflin, 1918. 243 pp.

A former student, Higgins pays tribute to her teacher in this book. The author begins with her subject's childhood and traces the major influences on Norsworthy. Higgins also provides details about her subject's successful career and admirable personal character.

Nutting, Mary A.   1858–1948

930   Marshall, Helen E. *Mary Adelaide Nutting: Pioneer of Modern Nursing.* Baltimore: Johns Hopkins Univ. Press, 1972. 396 pp.

No other full-length biography of Nutting is available, and this one is adequate. It contains a useful bibliography of her publications on nursing.

O

Oakley, Annie 1860–1926

931 Cooper, Courtney R. *Annie Oakley—Woman at Arms*. New York: Duffield, 1927. 270 pp.

Cooper pads her book with some unnecessary details and digressions. She bases her text on the autobiographical notes and scrapbooks that remain from Oakley's life, but greater care with these materials would have produced a more valuable biography.

932 Havighurst, Walter. *Annie Oakley of the Wild West*. New York: Macmillan Publishing, 1954. 246 pp.

Havighurst's well-documented study of Oakley is especially skillful at re-creating her circus performances. His habit of using invented dialogue is a poor aspect of this book.

933 Sayers, Isabelle S. *Annie Oakley and Buffalo Bill's Wild West*. New York: Dover Publishers, 1981. 89 pp.

Sayers focuses more on Oakley's performances than on her personal life. By consulting newspaper stories from the era, the author details Oakley's circus act and includes her early years before joining the Bill Cody Company. Unfortunately, this book has no index or bibliography.

Oates, Joyce Carol 1938–

934 Creighton, Joanne V. *Joyce Carol Oates*. Boston: Twayne Publishers, 1979. 173 pp.

See entry 26.

935 Friedman, Ellen G. *Joyce Carol Oates*. New York: Frederick Ungar Publishing, 1980. 238 pp.

See entry 189.

O'Connor, Flannery 1925–1964

936 Getz, Lorine M. *Flannery O'Connor: Her Life, Library, and Book Reviews*. New York: Edwin Mellen Press, 1980. 223 pp.

This is an informative sourcebook that lists the holdings in O'Connor's library and reprints reviews of her writing. Getz discusses the author's early years in better detail than her mature and declining years.

937   McFarland, Dorothy T. *Flannery O'Connor*. New York: Frederick Ungar Publishing, 1976. 132 pp.
See entry 189.

938   Walters, Dorothy A. *Flannery O'Connor*. New York: Twayne Publishers, 1973. 172 pp.
See entry 26.

O'Keeffe, Georgia   1887–1986

939   Castro, Jan G. *The Art and Life of Georgia O'Keeffe*. New York: Crown Publishers, 1985. 192 pp.
Castro provides the basic biographical facts on O'Keeffe while praising her art. Included in the more than one hundred illustrations are photographs of some of the objects that most inspired the artist.

940   Goodrich, Lloyd, and Doris Bry. *Georgia O'Keeffe*. New York: Praeger Publishers, 1970. 195 pp.
The authors provide a general biographical introduction to O'Keeffe. They also discuss at some length the development of her artistic style.

941   Lisle, Laurie. *Portrait of an Artist: A Biography of Georgia O'Keeffe*. New York: Washington Square Press, 1987. 496 pp.
This book concentrates almost completely on O'Keeffe's life rather than on her art. No in-depth analysis of her character is presented, but the facts are all given clearly, up through her death.

942   Pollitzer, Anita. *A Woman on Paper: Georgia O'Keeffe*. New York: Simon and Schuster, 1988. 290 pp.
Pollitzer was a friend to O'Keeffe primarily in the artist's early life (pre-1917). The author is especially vivid and informative in describing those years. Pollitzer's correspondence with the artist is drawn upon heavily throughout the book.

Onassis, Jacqueline K.   See **Kennedy, Jacqueline B.**

O'Neill, Carlotta Monterey   1888–1970

943 Gelb, Arthur, and Barbara Gelb. *O'Neill*. New York: Harper and Row, 1974. 990 pp.

The Gelbs's book details much of Carlotta's life with her husband and her own problems with mental illness. The authors are sympathetic to her, especially in their twenty-page epilogue, which describes her life as a widow.

O'Neill, Rose Cecil   1874–1944

944 McCanse, Ralph A. *Titans and Kewpies: The Life and Art of Rose O'Neill*. New York: Vantage Press, 1968. 220 pp.

This is the fullest biography that is available on O'Neill. It is well illustrated, including photographs of her at various stages of her career.

Ossoli, Marchesa   See **Fuller, Margaret**

Oughton, Diana   1942–1970

945 Powers, Thomas. *Diana: The Making of a Terrorist*. Boston: Houghton Mifflin, 1971. 225 pp.

Oughton's family cooperated with Powers in the preparation of this book. While he covers all of her life, he does emphasize her political activities. Powers has difficulty breaking through his subject's enigmatic personality to understand her motivations.

Ozick, Cynthia   1928–

946 Lowin, Joseph. *Cynthia Ozick*. Boston: Twayne Publishers, 1986. ca. 150 pp.

See entry 26.

P

Page, Ruth   1900–

947 Martin, John. *Ruth Page: An Intimate Biography*. New York: Marcel Dekker, 1977. 342 pp.

Martin, a professional dance critic, writes a vividly detailed book on Page's life and career, based on anecdotes. The book's foreword was written by Margot Fonteyn.

Paige, Mabeth Hurd   1870–1961

948 Aldrich, Clara C. *Lady in Law: A Biography of Mabeth Hurd Paige*. Chicago: Ralph F. Seymour, 1950. 347 pp.

This biographer treats Paige sympathetically but not sentimentally. The book details all of the subject's life, focusing particularly on the twenty-two years she worked in the Minnesota state legislature.

Palmer, Alice F.   1855–1902

949 Palmer, George H. *The Life of Alice Freeman Palmer*. Boston: Houghton Mifflin, 1908. 354 pp.

Literary critics of his era praised this biography by Palmer's husband for its warmth and humanity, as well as for its excellent writing. He strikes a fine balance between his wife's private life and professional career, especially for the years she was president of Wellesley College.

Palmer, Bertha   1849–1918

950 Ross, Ishbel. *Silhouette in Diamonds: The Life of Mrs. Potter Palmer*. New York: Harper and Brothers, 1960. 276 pp.

This is a popular biography that is suitable for a general reader. Ross read Palmer's personal papers to write this book, which covers the years 1871 to 1918. A bibliography is included.

Parker, Bonnie   1911–1934

951   Parker, Emma K. *The True Story of Bonnie and Clyde*. New York: New American Library, 1968. 175 pp.

This book is narrated by Bonnie's mother, Emma K. Parker, and Clyde's sister, Nella B. Cowan, so it provides some intimate details about the couple. An interesting introduction, written by Nelson Algren, is included.

952   Treherne, John E. *The Strange History of Bonnie and Clyde*. Briarcliff Manor, N.Y.: Stein and Day, 1985. 263 pp.

Treherne covers his subjects' lives from their childhoods through their deaths. He is especially concerned with analyzing their posthumous fame. He considers Bonnie to be an exhibitionist who was devoted to Clyde.

Parker, Dorothy R.   1893–1967

953   Frewin, Leslie R. *The Late Mrs. Dorothy Parker*. New York: Macmillan Publishing, 1986. 345 pp.

Frewin's biography shows both the positive and the negative aspects of Parker's character and how they affected her life. Anecdotes about the Algonquin Round Table abound. Some of the material for this book was derived from John Keats's biography of Parker (see below).

954   Keats, John. *You Might As Well Live: The Life and Times of Dorothy Parker*. New York: Simon and Schuster, 1970. 319 pp.

Keats finely details all of Parker's life, including the low points. The book lacks a bibliography of Parker's writings.

955   Kinney, Arthur F. *Dorothy Parker*. Boston: Twayne Publishers, 1979. 204 pp.

See entry 26.

956   Meade, Marion. *Dorothy Parker: What Fresh Hell Is This?* New York: Random House, 1988. 459 pp.

Meade fully describes all the periods of Parker's life, beginning with a discussion of her ancestors. Many of Parker's witty anecdotes are repeated in the book, but the more sordid aspects of her life are also treated. Meade neither describes nor analyzes Parker's writing.

957   Pearl, Jane H. "Dorothy Parker, Herself: A Psychobiography of the Literary Artist." Dissertation. Northwestern Univ., 1982. 152 pp.

Pearl's study employs the analytic methods of Heinz Kohut, who developed a psychology of the self. She evaluates the influences of Parker's early life and demonstrates how they harmed her as an adult.

Parsons, Elsie Clews   1875–1971

958   Hare, Peter H. *A Woman's Quest for Science: Portrait of Anthropologist Elsie Clews Parsons*. Buffalo: Prometheus Books, 1985. 192 pp.

This is an accurate, factual approach to Parsons's life, but the book does not attempt to evaluate her character or her career. Parsons was Hare's grandaunt, so he had access to her personal papers, from which he often quotes in this book.

Parsons, Louella   1893–1972

959   Eells, George. *Hedda and Louella*. New York: G. P. Putnam's Sons, 1972. 360 pp.

See under Hopper, Hedda.

Parsons, Lucy E.   1859–1942

960   Ashbaugh, Carolyn. *Lucy Parsons: American Revolutionary*. Chicago: Charles H. Kerr Publishing, 1976. 288 pp.

This biography focuses on Parsons's public career more than on her private life. The author does not provide much analysis of the events in the life nor does she give any insights into Parsons's motivations.

Patrick, Mary Mills   1850–1940

961   Jenkins, Hester D. *An Educational Ambassador to the Near East: The Story of Mary Mills Patrick and an American College in the Orient*. New York: Fleming H. Revell, 1925. 314 pp.

Jenkins treats Patrick like a heroine in this book. She pays tribute to her subject's career as a missionary, educator, and college founder in Turkey.

Patterson, Eleanor "Cissy"   1884–1948

962   Healy, Paul F. *Cissy: The Biography of Eleanor M. "Cissy" Patterson*. New York: Doubleday Publishing, 1966. 421 pp.

This popular biography was written with the aid of Patterson's daughter. It is especially good at describing Patterson's journalistic work, and it is also candid about her politics.

963 Hoge, Alice A. *Cissy Patterson.* New York: Random House, 1966. 237 pp.

A grandniece to Patterson wrote this popular biography. As a result, it contributes many useful personal and family details on its subject, but it does a good deal of name-dropping at the same time.

964 Martin, Ralph G. *Cissy.* New York: Simon and Schuster, 1979. 512 pp.

Martin's book is weak on both Patterson's life and her career. He dwells on the scandals in which she was involved, and writes in a romantic tone.

Paul, Alice   1885–1977

965 Irwin, Inez H. *The Story of Alice Paul and the National Woman's Party.* Fairfax, Va.: Denlingers Publishers, 1964. 501 pp.

Irwin's detailed study focuses on Paul's role in the struggle for women's rights. Very little space is given to her private life, despite the length of this book.

966 Lunardini, Christine A. *From Equal Suffrage to Equal Rights: Alice Paul and the National Woman's Party, 1910–1928.* New York: New York Univ. Press, 1986. 230 pp.

Lunardini is primarily concerned with Paul's role as a leading feminist. The author argues that Paul deserves a more prominent place in the history of the women's suffrage movement.

Peabody, Elizabeth P.   1804–1894

967 Baylor, Ruth M. *Elizabeth Palmer Peabody, Kindergarten Pioneer.* Philadelphia: Univ. of Pennsylvania Press, 1965. 228 pp.

Baylor emphasizes Peabody's educational theories and practices. She also provides some basic biographical information, as well as a good bibliography.

968 Tharp, Louise H. *The Peabody Sisters of Salem.* Boston: Little, Brown, 1950. 372 pp.

See under Hawthorne, Sophia P.

Peale, Sarah M.   1800–1885

969 King, Joan. *Sarah M. Peale: America's First Woman Artist*. Boston: Branden Press, 1987. 296 pp.

King's book employs fictionalized elements to complete the story of Peale's life. Many accurate domestic and family details are included, but King makes no analysis of Peale's character.

Peck, Annie Smith   1850–1935

970 Olds, Elizabeth F. *Women of the Four Winds: The Adventures of Four of America's First Women Explorers*. Boston: Houghton Mifflin, 1985. 263 pp.

See under Akeley, Delia.

Pennell, Abby Reed   d. 1909

971 Coffin, Robert P. T. *Captain Abby and Captain John: An Around-the-World Biography*. New York: Macmillan Publishing, 1939. 375 pp.

Coffin bases his information on the Pennell family papers, especially the diaries from which he quotes. In telling their unique story, the author exaggerates the accomplishments of this couple.

Pennybacker, Anna J.   1861–1938

972 Knox, Helen. *Mrs. Percy V. Pennybacker*. New York: Fleming H. Revell, 1916. 192 pp.

Knox writes an appreciative tribute to Mrs. Pennybacker in this survey of her life and public works. The book was written on the occasion of the subject's retirement as President of the General Federation of Women's Clubs.

Perkins, Frances   1882–1965

973 Martin, George. *Madame Secretary, Frances Perkins*. Boston: Houghton Mifflin, 1976. 589 pp.

This sympathetic biography deals only with Perkins's public life. Martin bases his book on her own records of her years in social work and government.

974 Mohr, Lillian H. *Frances Perkins: "That Woman in FDR's Cabinet!"* Croton-on-Hudson, N.Y.: North River Press, 1979. 328 pp.

Though Mohr describes Perkins's public life in more detail than the private life, she offers some useful insights into her subject's character and career.

975 Severn, Bill. *Frances Perkins, a Member of the Cabinet.* New York: Hawthorn Books, 1976. 256 pp.

Only a small section of this biography deals with Perkins's early years and personal life. The focus throughout is on her political activities, particularly during the New Deal.

Perkins, Lucy Fitch   1865–1937

976 Perkins, Eleanor E. *Eve among the Puritans.* Boston: Houghton Mifflin, 1956. 328 pp.

This biography, written by Perkins's daughter, captures the subject's personality especially well. The biographer focuses on her mother's childhood and young years, with very little said about her writing career.

Peter, Sarah W.   1800–1877

977 King, Margaret R. *Memoirs of the Life of Mrs. Sarah Peter.* Cincinnati: R. Clarke, 1889. 2 vols.

This admiring account of Peter's life is written by her daughter-in-law. She quotes at length from Peter's European letters.

978 McAllister, Anna S. *In Winter We Flourish: The Life and Letters of Sarah Worthington King Peter, 1800–1877.* New York: Longmans, Green, 1939. 398 pp.

McAllister, after thorough research, covers fully all the eras of Peter's personal life and public career, beginning with a description of her genealogy. Although this book has no bibliography, it provides notes on the sources of each chapter.

Peterkin, Julia   1880–1961

979 Landress, Thomas H. *Julia Peterkin.* Boston: Twayne Publishers, 1976. 160 pp.

See entry 26.

Phelps, Almira Hart   1793–1884

980 Bolzau, Emma L. *Almira Hart Lincoln Phelps: Her Life and Work.* West Collinswood, N.J.: Emma L. Bolzau Publisher, 1936. 534 pp.

A definitive biography of Phelps that is based on much careful research, this book quotes at length from Phelps herself and contains an extensive bibliography.

Phelps, Elizabeth S.   1815–1852

981   Bennett, Mary A. *Elizabeth Stuart Phelps*. Philadelphia: Univ. of Pennsylvania Press, 1939. 172 pp.
This early biography of Phelps discusses the details of her life and makes a critical analysis of her writing. It includes a good bibliography.

982   Kessler, Carol F. " 'The Woman's Hour': The Life and Novels of Elizabeth Stuart Phelps (1844–1911)." Dissertation. Univ. of Pennsylvania, 1977. 507 pp.
Kessler's study is very thorough on Phelps's personal life; she describes how her subject's experiences influenced her writing. Phelps's ancestry and childhood are discussed at length, as are her relationships to her parents and their effects on her intellectual growth.

Phillipps, Adelaide   1833–1882

983   Waterston, Anna C. L. Q. *Adelaide Phillipps: A Record*. Boston: A. Williams, 1883. 170 pp.
This biography was written solely to pay tribute to Phillipps, yet it records all the major facts of the life as interpreted by her friend Waterston.

Phillips, Ann Terry   1813–1886

984   Bartlett, Irving H. *Wendell and Ann Phillips: The Community of Reform, 1840–1880*. New York: W. W. Norton, 1981. 249 pp.
Bartlett's book comprises two long essays: one is on Wendell Phillips exclusively, and the second is on his marriage. The biographer's major source of information was the recently discovered (ca. 1981) Phillips letters, from which he quotes at length.

Phillips, Lena M.   1881–1955

985   Sergio, Lisa. *A Measure Filled: The Story of Lena Madesin Phillips*. Washington, D.C.: R. B. Luce, 1972. 246 pp.
This detailed book covers all of its subject's career without being biased in her favor. Its main sources were her letters, essays, and speeches.

Pickford, Mary   1894–1979

986 Carey, Gary. *Doug and Mary: A Biography of Douglas Fairbanks and Mary Pickford*. New York: E. P. Dutton, 1977. 248 pp.

Carey emphasizes the years 1916 to 1933, the period of this couple's courtship and marriage. He gives no new information about them and makes some small factual errors.

987 Herndon, Booton. *Mary Pickford and Douglas Fairbanks: The Most Popular Couple the World Has Ever Known*. New York: W. W. Norton, 1977. 324 pp.

Although this book is well researched and fully documented, its attempts to psychoanalyze its subjects are faulty. Herndon is best at describing Pickford's private life and her late career.

988 Windeler, Robert. *Sweetheart: The Story of Mary Pickford*. New York: Praeger Publishers, 1974. 226 pp.

Windeler wishes to tell the true story of the actress and to dismiss the legends about her. In order to achieve this, he discusses both her triumphs and her hardships. He depicts her as an actress, a businesswoman, and a wife.

Pinckney, Eliza(beth) L.   1722?–1793

989 Ravenel, Harriott H. *Eliza Pinckney*. New York: Charles Scribner's Sons, 1896. 331 pp.

Ravenel, a great-great-granddaughter to Pinckney, bases this book primarily on her ancestor's letters. Politics are eschewed in favor of domestic details and a close look at South Carolina society in the 1740s. Only Pinckney's favorable attributes are mentioned.

Pinkham, Lydia E.   1819–1883

990 Burton, Jean. *Lydia Pinkham Is Her Name*. New York: Farrar, Straus, 1949. 279 pp.

Burton's book is about both Pinkham and the business she founded. Her approach is too simplistic and undocumented to be of use to a serious student; the book also lacks an index.

991 Stage, Sarah. *Female Complaints*. New York: W. W. Norton, 1981. 304 pp.

Stage's scholarly book deals not only with Pinkham, but also with the business aspects of early American medicine. She describes with understanding the role of American women in the decades just before and after 1900.

992 Washburn, Robert C. *The Life and Times of Lydia Pinkham.* New York: G. P. Putnam's Sons, 1931. 221 pp.

This undocumented biography pads its discussion of Pinkham's life with discursive details on her environs. More details of her life might have been included here if some of Washburn's work had not been censored by Pinkham's granddaughter.

Pittman, Portia M.   1883–1978

993 Hill, Roy L. *Booker T.'s Child: The Life and Times of Portia Marshal Washington Pittman.* Newark, N.J.: McDaniel Press, 1974. 90 pp.

Hill's biography is scholarly and well written. It includes many photographs from the Washington family's private album.

994 Stewart, Ruth A. *Portia: The Life of Portia Washington Pittman, the Daughter of Booker T. Washington.* New York: Doubleday Publishing, 1977. 154 pp.

Stewart, who knew Booker T. Washington's family personally, relies on anecdotes to depict Portia. She begins her account with her subject's birth and highlights well the elements of her education and musical career.

Plath, Sylvia   1932–1963

995 Aird, Eileen. *Sylvia Plath: Her Life and Work.* New York: Harper and Row, 1973. 114 pp.

Aird's first chapter presents a brief biography of Plath. She then proceeds to examine the biographical aspects of her writings, focusing on *The Bell Jar* in particular.

996 Barnard, Caroline K. *Sylvia Plath.* Boston: Twayne Publishers, 1978. 132 pp.

See entry 26.

997 Butscher, Edward. *Sylvia Plath: Method and Madness.* New York: Seabury Press, 1976. 338 pp.

Butscher writes a highly detailed, accurate biography of Plath. He is sympathetic to her and focuses on her psychological relationship to her father. Butcher also employs A. Alvarez's writings to explain Plath's suicide.

998 Holbrook, David. *Sylvia Plath: Poetry and Existence*. New York: Humanities Press, 1976. 308 pp.

Holbrook produces a psychological study of Plath as an individual and Plath as an artist. He basically views her as schizophrenic and evaluates her career in that light.

999 Patterson, Rena M. "Sylvia Plath: A Study of Her Life and Art." Dissertation. State University of New York at Buffalo, 1978. 165 pp.

Patterson describes Plath's personal life and writings in chronological order. She explains how the poems reflect Plath's emotional states at various points in her life.

1000 Steiner, Nancy H. *A Closer Look at Ariel: A Memory of Sylvia Plath*. New York: Harper's Magazine Press, 1972. 83 pp.

This sympathetic book written by Plath's college roommate examines her college years. Steiner offers some new nuances to the poet's personality.

1001 Uroff, Margaret D. *Sylvia Plath and Ted Hughes*. Urbana: Univ. Of Illinois Press, 1979. 245 pp.

Uroff details both the personal and professional relationships between this husband and wife. She writes factually to dispel the many myths that have grown to surround their marriage.

1002 Wagner-Martin, Linda. *Sylvia Plath: A Biography*. New York: Simon and Schuster, 1987. 282 pp.

This is a fairly well detailed biography despite the fact that Wagner-Martin was hindered: many important documents about the poet's life are still restricted from public view. The biographer aims at giving a balanced view of Plath, neither as victim nor as heroine solely.

Pocahontas   1595–1617

1003 Barbour, Philip L. *Pocahontas and Her World*. Boston: Houghton Mifflin, 1970. 320 pp.

In this carefully researched book, Barbour describes all that is known of Pocahontas's life and dismisses some of the legends about her. The book also includes an extensive bibliography.

1004   Mossiker, Frances. *Pocahontas: The Life and the Legend*. New York: Alfred A. Knopf, 1976. 383 pp.

This is a popular biography written for a general reader. Although the author quotes at length from primary sources, her book also includes some unsubstantiated speculations.

1005   Robertson, Whyndham. *Pocahontas Alias Matooka*. Richmond, Va.: J. W. Randolph and English, 1887. 84 pp.

Robertson's biography of Pocahontas comprises just a limited section of this book; the rest of the text discusses forty or more Virginians who played a role in her story.

1006   Woodward, Grace S. *Pocahontas*. Norman: Univ. of Oklahoma Press, 1969. 227 pp.

Woodward, a historian, writes an accurate account of Pocahontas based on much research. She describes her subject as an individual, not as a mythic character; the book's best sections are on her last years.

Poe, Eliza(beth) A.   1787?–1811

1007   Smith, Geddeth. *The Brief Career of Eliza Poe*. Madison, N.J.: Fairleigh Dickinson Univ. Press, 1988. 174 pp.

Smith writes the only full-length biography on the brief life and career of Edgar A. Poe's mother. He bases his book on primary sources and includes a section of informative notes.

Polk, Sarah C.   1803–1891

1008   Nelson, Anson, and Fanny Nelson. *Memorials of Sarah Childress Polk, Wife of the Eleventh President of the U.S.* New York: A. D. F. Randolph, 1892. 284 pp.

The Nelsons focus on their subject's married life and her response to her husband's political career. They also describe the changes she brought to the White House. The book closes with a discussion of her forty years' widowhood.

Porter, Katherine Anne   1890–1980

1009   Givner, Joan. *Katherine Anne Porter: A Life*. New York: Simon and Schuster, 1982. 572 pp.

Givner, who was commissioned by Porter to write this biography, had access to all the author's personal papers. As a result, this factual book describes each stage of Porter's life fully. However, Givner does not evaluate her subject's character.

1010 Hardy, John E. *Katherine Anne Porter*. New York: Frederick Ungar Publishing, 1973. 160 pp.

See entry 189.

1011 Hendrick, George. *Katherine Anne Porter*. New York: Twayne Publishers, 1965. 176 pp.

See entry 26.

Post, Emily 1873–1960

1012 Post, Edwin. *Truly Emily Post*. New York: Funk and Wagnalls, 1961. 249 pp.

Post, Emily's son, wrote this somewhat fictionalized biography shortly after her death. He offers a wealth of details on all the periods of her private life. He describes very clearly the impact her writing had on her society.

Post, Marjorie M. 1887–1973

1013 Wright, William. *Heiress: The Rich Life of Marjorie Merriweather Post*. Washington, D.C.: New Republic Books, 1978. 265 pp.

This study follows an awkward chronology. Its approach is also confused, being sometimes detached toward and alternately critical of its subject.

Powell, Maud 1868–1920

1014 Shaffer, Karen A., and Neva G. Greenwood. *Maud Powell: Pioneer American Violinist*. Ames: Iowa State Univ. Press, 1988. 530 pp.

This biography is written too much in praise of Powell to be useful to a serious student. Although all the facts of the musician's life are recorded accurately here, none of her inner complexities are explained.

Prentiss, Elizabeth P. 1818–1878

1015 Prentiss, George L. *The Life and Letters of Elizabeth Prentiss*. New York: A. D. F. Randolph, 1882. 573 pp.

This complete biography of Prentiss was written by her husband. It includes selections from her personal journals, written from age twenty until her death.

Preston, Margaret J.   1820–1897

1016   Allan, Elizabeth P. *The Life and Letters of Margaret Junkin Preston.* Boston: Houghton Mifflin, 1903. 378 pp.

This biography, written by Preston's stepdaughter, is the only one available on her. An appendix contains a lengthy appreciation of Preston and her work, written by James A. Harrison.

Price, Nina Mae   1882–1974

1017   Wheeler, Shirley P. *Dr. Nina and the Panther.* New York: Dodd, Mead, 1976. 278 pp.

Wheeler, Price's daughter, wrote this book about the doctor's life and career; she has nothing but high praise for her subject.

R

Ragghianti, Marie   1943?–

1018   Maas, Peter. *Marie: A True Story.* New York: Random House, 1983. 420 pp.

Marie's entire life story is told in the first quarter of this book. Then, the author focuses on her trial and its results; unfortunately, he relies heavily on re-created dialogues in this section.

Rainey, Gertrude "Ma"   1886–1939

1019   Lieb, Sandra R. *Mother of the Blues: A Study of Ma Rainey.* Amherst: Univ. of Massachusetts Press, 1981. 226 pp.

Chapter one presents a concise biography of Rainey. The remainder of this scholarly book focuses on her singing career and the meanings of the lyrics she sang.

Rand, Ayn   1905–1982

1020   Baker, James T. *Ayn Rand.* Boston: Twayne Publishers, 1987. ca. 150 pp.

See entry 26.

1021   Branden, Barbara. *The Passion of Ayn Rand.* New York: Doubleday Publishing, 1987. 442 pp.

This is a full-length biography that gives many details of Rand's life. Branden, a close friend to Rand and a follower of her philosophy, may be too involved with her subject to be objective.

1022   Branden, Nathaniel, and Barbara Branden. *Who Is Ayn Rand? An Analysis of the Novels of Ayn Rand, with a Biographical Essay.* New York: Random House, 1962. 239 pp.

The Brandens, close friends and followers of Rand, include in this book one lengthy biographical essay. The tone throughout the text is warm and admiring.

Rankin, Jeannette   1880–1973

1023   Giles, Kevin S. *Flight of the Dove: The Story of Jeannette Rankin.* Beaverton, Ore.: Touchstone Press, 1980. 256 pp.

This biography is flawed by Giles's awkward writing style and grammatical errors.

1024   Harris, Ted C. "Jeannette Rankin: Suffragist, First Woman Elected to Congress, and Pacifist." Dissertation. Univ. of Georgia, 1972. 398 pp.

Harris describes in clear detail all of Rankin's public career, from her work for women's rights in 1900 to her advocacy of feminism in the 1970s. He also discusses her congressional career.

1025   Josephson, Hannah. *Jeannette Rankin: First Lady in Congress: A Biography.* New York: Bobbs-Merrill, 1974. 227 pp.

This is a sympathetic biography of Rankin's career written by a friend of over twenty years; Rankin cooperated with her in its production. The book covers Rankin's six decades in public life, but provides few personal details about her.

1026   Schaffer, Ronald. "Jeannette Rankin, Progressive-Isolationist." Dissertation. Princeton Univ., 1959. 277 pp.

Schaffer details all of Rankin's adult life, beginning in 1908. He also describes her political career and evaluates the contributions she made through it.

Rawlings, Marjorie Kinnan   1896–1953

1027   Bellman, Samuel I. *Marjorie Kinnan Rawlings.* New York: Twayne Publishers, 1974. 168 pp.

See entry 26.

1028   Bigelow, Gorden E. *Frontier Eden: The Literary Career of Marjorie Kinnan Rawlings.* Gainesville: Univ. of Florida Press, 1967. 162 pp.

Bigelow concentrates more on Rawlings' career than on her personal life. However, he describes her character well as he focuses heavily on the biographical aspects of her writing.

1029   Silverthorne, Elizabeth. *Marjorie Kinnan Rawlings: Sojourner at Cross Creek.* Woodstock, N.Y.: Overlook Press, 1988. 374 pp.

This sympathetic biography highlights Rawlings's daily life at her Florida home; nevertheless, it also gives a full account of her entire life. Silverthorne includes in her text a discussion of the causes that Rawlings advocated.

Reagan, Nancy Davis   1921–

1030   Adler, Bill. *Ronnie and Nancy: A Very Special Love Story*. New York: Crown Publishers, 1985. 216 pp.

This account of the couple is not a frank depiction of their marriage; instead, Adler employs a romantic tone throughout his text. The book also presents the highlights of Mrs. Reagan's early life.

1031   Hannaford, Peter. *The Reagans: A Personal Portrait*. New York: Coward, McCann and Geoghegan, 1983. 317 pp.

Hannaford's text gives little space to Mrs. Reagan. Very few personal details are provided about her or her husband, for whom Hannaford was once a speechwriter.

1032   Leighton, Frances S. *The Search for the Real Nancy Reagan*. New York: Macmillan Publishing, 1987. 288 pp.

This book's weaknesses are its overly sympathetic approach to the subject and its emphasis on her husband and his political career. Leighton does not make her sources clear to the reader.

Ream, Vinnie   1847–1914

1033   Hoxie, Richard L. *Vinnie Ream*. Washington, D.C.: Press of the Gibson Brothers, 1908. 64 pp.

Hoxie, Ream's husband, wrote this brief account of her life and career, which focuses on the years 1865 to 1878. He includes some newspaper stories relating to her career and to her death.

Repplier, Agnes   1855–1950

1034   Repplier, Emma. *Agnes Repplier: A Memoir, by Her Niece*. Philadelphia: Dorrance, 1957. 171 pp.

This account of Repplier focuses on her personal life rather than on her career. The biographer draws on her own memories and those of her family to depict Repplier's early life and personal traits. Her many travels are also described in detail here.

1035   Stokes, George S. *Agnes Repplier, Lady of Letters*. Philadelphia: Univ. of Pennsylvania Press, 1949. 274 pp.

Stokes's overview covers, on the surface, all the events in Repplier's long life. He interviewed her for this book and clearly admires her; the result is that he shows few negative aspects of her character in this biography.

Restell, Madame   See **Lohman, Ann S.**

Richmond, Mary   1861–1928

1036   Pumphrey, Muriel W. "Mary Richmond and the Rise of Professional Social Work in Baltimore: The Foundation of a Creative Career." Dissertation. Columbia Univ., 1956. 512 pp.

This study treats Richmond's entire life and career in rich detail. It begins by showing her family's influence on her early years and follows her in minute detail throughout her life. Even her personality and leisure pursuits are described in this work.

Rinehart, Mary Roberts   1876–1958

1037   Cohn, Jan. *Improbable Fiction: The Life of Mary Roberts Rinehart.* Pittsburgh: Univ. of Pittsburgh Press, 1980. 293 pp.

Cohn's book focuses equally on Rinehart's private life and on her writing career. Taking a modern perspective on her subject, Cohn demonstrates how Rinehart balanced her family life and her career.

Rivers, Pearl   1849–1896

1038   Harrison, James H. *Pearl Rivers, Publisher of the Picayune.* New Orleans: Tulane Univ. Press, 1932. 63 pp.

This brief book describes all of Rivers's life and work. It also clearly explains New Orleans's newspaper history.

Rives, Amélie   1863–1945

1039   Taylor, Welford D. *Amélie Rives (Princess Troubetzkoy).* New York: Twayne Publishers, 1973. 162 pp.

See entry 26.

Roberts, Elizabeth Madox   1881–1941

1040   Campbell, Harry M., and Ruel E. Foster. *Elizabeth Madox Roberts: American Novelist.* Norman: Univ. of Oklahoma Press, 1956. 283 pp.

This is a complete account of Roberts's life and literary career, which opens with her biography. Her letters and her fiction are quoted from frequently in the text. Unfortunately, this book lacks an index and a bibliography.

1041 McDowell, Frederick P. W. *Elizabeth Madox Roberts.* New York: Twayne Publishers, 1963. 176 pp.
See entry 26.

1042 Spears, Woodridge. "Elizabeth Madox Roberts: A Biography and Critical Study." Dissertation. Univ. of Kentucky, 1953. 278 pp.
Spears covers all of Roberts's life, beginning with her birth. The main theme of this study is Roberts's growth as an artist and the many influences on her, including those of her parents and ancestors.

Robertson, Alice Mary   1854–1931

1043 Spaulding, Joe P. "The Life of Alice Mary Robertson." Dissertation. Univ. of Oklahoma, 1959. 227 pp.
Spaulding bases this study mainly on Robertson's private papers. He describes all her life, beginning with her ancestry; her achievements are also noted throughout the text.

Robertson, Anna Mary   See Moses, Grandma

Robins, Margaret D.   1868–1945

1044 Dreier, Mary E. *Margaret Dreier Robins: Her Life, Letters and Work.* Covelo, Calif.: Island Press, 1950. 278 pp.
This biography was written by Robins's sister, who is not objective. The most useful sources in this book are its quotations from Robins's letters.

1045 Payne, Elizabeth A. *Reform, Labor, and Feminism: Margaret Dreier Robins and the Women's Trade Union League.* Champaign: Univ. of Illinois Press, 1988. 200 pp.
Payne's book is scholarly and thorough. In it she focuses on Robins's work for the WTUL, and how it functioned under her leadership.

Robinson, Harriet H.   1825–1911

1046 Bushman, Claudia L. *"A Good Poor Man's Wife": Being a Chronicle of Harriet Hanson Robinson and Her Family in Nineteenth Century New England.* Hanover, N.H.: Univ. Press of New England, 1981. 276 pp.

In this well-documented book, Bushman presents the facts of Robinson's life without evaluating them. Many fine details of her domestic and family life are provided, but they are balanced with an account of her suffrage work.

Rockefeller, Abby A.   1874–1948

1047 Chase, Mary E. *Abby Aldrich Rockefeller*. New York: Macmillan Publishing, 1950. 159 pp.

This memoir provides a warm but not overly admiring portrait of its subject. It is too sketchy to be considered a complete biography.

Rogers, Ginger   1911–

1048 McGilligan, Patrick. *Ginger Rogers*. New York: Pyramid Publishers, 1975. 159 pp.

See entry 286.

Rogers, Mary J.   1882–1955

1049 Lyons, Jeanne M. *Maryknoll's First Lady*. New York: Dodd, Mead, 1964. 327 pp.

Lyons, who knew her subject personally, writes an affectionate account of her life and work. This book also discusses the works of the Maryknoll Sisters in Europe in the 1930s and 1940s.

Roosevelt, Anna "Bamie"   See **Cowles, Anna R.**

Roosevelt, Anna Eleanor   1906–1975

1050 Boettiger, John R. *A Love in Shadow*. New York: W. W. Norton, 1978. 279 pp.

Boettiger's book tells the history of his parents' marriage. He also describes in some detail his mother's relationship with her own mother, Eleanor Roosevelt.

Roosevelt, Edith Kermit   1861–1948

1051 Morris, Sylvia J. *Edith Kermit Roosevelt: Portrait of a First Lady*. New York: Coward, McCann and Geoghegan, 1980. 581 pp.

This is an excellent biography that is well researched and has complete documentation. Morris is insightful on her subject, who was a very private person.

Roosevelt, Eleanor R.   1884–1962

1052   Black, Ruby A. *Eleanor Roosevelt*. New York: Duell, Sloan and Pearce, 1940. 331 pp.

Black briefly reviews her subject's early years and then concentrates on her life as first lady and family member. Black admires Mrs. Roosevelt and consequently says nothing negative about her.

1053   Douglas, Helen G. *The Eleanor Roosevelt We Remember*. New York: Hill and Wang, 1963. 173 pp.

Douglas, a friend to her subject for more than twenty years, recalls that friendship in this favorable sketch. She describes Mrs. Roosevelt's character vividly by use of anecdotes.

1054   Faber, Doris. *The Life of Lorena Hickok: E. R.'s Friend*. New York: William Morrow, 1980. 384 pp.

See under Hickok, Lorena.

1055   Hareven, Tamara K. *Eleanor Roosevelt: An American Conscience*. New York: Quadrangle Books, 1968. 326 pp.

This is an objective and scholarly book about the first lady's public life, but with little discussion of her private side. It also details her advocacy of various political and social causes.

1056   Hickok, Lorena A. *Eleanor Roosevelt: Reluctant First Lady*. New York: Dodd, Mead, 1980. 176 pp.

The first twelve chapters of this book are the best; they tell how Mrs. Roosevelt faced the major transitions in her married life as FDR rose to the Presidency. The remainder of the book is a sentimental recollection of the travels of the author with her intimate friend, Eleanor.

1057   Johnson, George. *Eleanor Roosevelt*. Derby, Conn.: Monarch Books, 1962. 142 pp.

This popular account of Mrs. Roosevelt's life was written for the general reader. The text is fairly well written, but it is not of much use to a serious student; it lacks an index.

1058   Kearney, James R. *Anna Eleanor Roosevelt: The Evolution of a Reformer*. Boston: Houghton Mifflin, 1968. 352 pp.

Kearney chronicles Mrs. Roosevelt's emergence as a national leader for social reforms, particularly in the years 1933 to 1941. Very little of her early life or later career is discussed by the author in this otherwise balanced portrait.

1059   Lash, Joseph P. *Eleanor and Franklin: The Story of Their Relationship, Based on Eleanor Roosevelt's Private Papers*. New York: W. W. Norton, 1971. 765 pp.

Lash's book, which ends with the year 1945, is full of new details about this couple; he includes a candid discussion of their marital problems. Lash also highlights Eleanor's accomplishments as first lady.

1060   ———. *Eleanor Roosevelt: A Friend's Memoir*. New York: Doubleday Publishing, 1964. 374 pp.

Lash, a friend to his subject since 1939, focuses on the years 1939 to 1942 in this book. His account is very detailed but is also subjective.

1061   ———. *Eleanor: The Years Alone*. New York: W. W. Norton, 1972. 368 pp.

This is Lash's companion volume to his *Eleanor and Franklin* (see above). His admiring book discusses Mrs. Roosevelt's public and private lives as a widow by frequently quoting from her.

1062   ———. *"Life Was Meant To Be Lived": A Centenary Portrait of Eleanor Roosevelt*. New York: W. W. Norton, 1984. 197 pp.

Lash provides an overview of his subject's life in this lavishly illustrated book. Too much of his text reviews the problems with her marriage.

1063   ———. *Love, Eleanor: Eleanor Roosevelt and Her Friends*. New York: Doubleday Publishing, 1982. 534 pp.

Lash offers ample commentary in this book, which reprints Eleanor's correspondence in part. He explains precisely his own relationship to her and discusses all of her life in some detail. The book is best at explaining her state role in the 1930s.

1064   Roosevelt, Elliott, and James Brough. *Mother R: Eleanor Roosevelt's Untold Story*. New York: G. P. Putnam's Sons, 1977. 288 pp.

The author, in his third volume about his parents, focuses on his mother's widowhood. He is less harsh to her here than he was in his first volume (see below).

1065 ————. *A Rendezvous with Destiny: The Roosevelts of the White House.* New York: G. P. Putnam's Sons, 1975. 460 pp.

The Roosevelts' son continues the story of his parents' marriage and careers, focusing on the presidential years. He discusses his father more than his mother in this text.

1066 ————. *An Untold Story: The Roosevelts of Hyde Park.* New York: G. P. Putnam's Sons, 1973. 319 pp.

Mrs. Roosevelt's son discusses his parents' marriage in the years 1916 to 1932 in this book. He writes in a very unflattering tone about his mother's domestic and maternal roles.

1067 Roosevelt, James, and Bill Libby. *My Parents: A Differing View.* Chicago: Playboy Press, 1976. 369 pp.

James Roosevelt's view of his parents is more balanced and less critical than is that of his brother Elliott (see above). Although this book is not well organized, it does present some intimate anecdotes about the couple.

1068 Scharf, Lois. *Eleanor Roosevelt: First Lady of American Liberalism.* Boston: Twayne Publishers, 1987. 232 pp.

Scharf provides a sympathetic account that is an introductory survey of Mrs. Roosevelt's life. However, no single aspect of the life is given in much detail.

1069 Steinberg, Alfred. *Mrs. R: The Life of Eleanor Roosevelt.* New York: G. P. Putnam's Sons, 1958. 384 pp.

Steinberg details all the periods of his subject's life, but deals best with her years in politics. He does not provide any substantial character analysis of her, but rather gives a simple portrait without much depth to it.

1070 Youngs, J. William. *Eleanor Roosevelt: A Personal and Public Life.* Boston: Little, Brown, 1984. 246 pp.

This biography achieves a fine balance between Mrs. Roosevelt's public and private roles. Although the author is sensitive to her, his discussions of her personal problems are frank.

Roosevelt, Sara Delano   1855–1941

1071 Kleeman, Rita S. *Gracious Lady: The Life of Sara Delano Roosevelt.* New York: Appleton-Century, 1935. 333 pp.

This book narrates all the eras of its subject's life. The author's main sources of information were Sara's own diary, as well as those of her parents.

Rorer, Sarah Tyson   1849–1937

1072 Weigley, Emma S. *Sarah Tyson Rorer: The Nation's Instructress in Dietetics and Cookery.* New York: American Philosophical Society, 1977. 196 pp.

This book traces both Rorer's private life and public career, focusing on her roles as lecturer and teacher. Weigley bases her work largely on Rorer's own writings, and as a result, delineates her personality clearly.

Rosenberg, Ethel   1915–1953

1073 Gardner, Virginia. *The Rosenberg Story.* New York: Masses and Mainstream, 1954. 126 pp.

This partisan biography presents the basic facts of Mrs. Rosenberg's life. Gardner denies that the couple were guilty of spying.

1074 Meeropol, Robert, and Michael Meeropol. *We Are Your Sons: The Legacy of Ethel and Julius Rosenberg, Written by Their Children.* Boston: Houghton Mifflin, 1975. 282 pp.

This book reprints some of Ethel's letters from prison to her two sons. Their depiction of the Rosenbergs' family life and their parents' personalities are done precisely.

1075 Philipson, Ilene. *Ethel Rosenberg: Beyond the Myths.* New York: Franklin Watts, 1988. 390 pp.

All of Mrs. Rosenberg's life is described in this book; the biographer also delineates her complex personality well. This book is based on several informative sources, including Ethel's letters from prison, her psychiatrist's notes, and recently released (ca. 1988) government files on the Rosenberg case.

Ross, Betsy G.   1752–1836

1076 Parry, Edwin S. *Betsy Ross, Quaker Rebel.* Philadelphia: John C. Winston, 1930. 252 pp.

Parry, a great-great-grandson to his subject, uses original sources to re-create her life story. He also covers the Revolutionary War to a great extent in his text.

Rourke, Constance M.   1885–1941

1077 Bellman, Samuel I. *Constance Rourke*. Boston: Twayne Publishers, 1981. 164 pp.
See entry 26.

1078 Rubin, Joan S. *Constance Rourke and American Culture*. Chapel Hill: Univ. of North Carolina Press, 1980. 244 pp.
This book exhibits meticulous scholarship. It covers both Rourke's personal life and her career, with an emphasis on her contribution to American culture.

Rowson, Susanna H.   ca. 1762–1824

1079 Brandt, Ellen B. *Susanna Haswell Rowson: America's First Best-Selling Novelist*. Chicago: Serba Press, 1975. ca. 430 pp.
Brandt's is a detailed, comprehensive account of Rowson's life and works. The book describes her personality vividly while it places her in perspective in U.S. literary history.

1080 Nason, Elias. *A Memoir of Mrs. Susanna Rowson*. Albany: Joel Munsell, 1870. 212 pp.
Rowson's life is outlined broadly in this book. Nason's account relies on a remembrance written by Rowson's friend Samuel L. Knapp in the early 1800s.

1081 Parker, Patricia L. *Susanna Rowson*. Boston: Twayne Publishers, 1986. 160 pp.
See entry 26.

Royall, Anne Newport   1769–1854

1082 Jackson, George S. *Uncommon Scold: The Story of Anne Royall*. Boston: Bruce Humphries, 1939. 161 pp.
Jackson offers a shallow picture of Royall's career. Although he is sympathetic to her, he does not seem to understand her completely.

1083 James, Bessie R. *Anne Royall's USA*. New Brunswick, N.J.: Rutgers Univ. Press, 1972. 447 pp.
James's factual account of Royall's life and career centers on the years 1831 to 1854; she especially details the writer's many travels. This book makes use of legal documents and public records from that era.

1084   Maxwell, Alice S., and Marion B. Dunlevy. *Virago! The Story of Anne Newport Royall (1769–1854)*. Jefferson, N.C.: McFarland, 1985. 305 pp.

This biography, which is written from a feminist viewpoint, focuses on Royall's constant struggles to gain a place in and then respect in a man's profession. The biographers describe in detail her famous trial of 1829. This book also contains an extensive bibliography of Royall's writings.

1085   Porter, Sarah H. *The Life and Times of Anne Royall*. Cedar Rapids, Iowa: The Torch Press Book Shop, 1909. 298 pp.

This biography describes its subject's life and career, while detailing the era in which she lived. The book also reprints Royall's "Sketches of History and Manners in the U.S. (1826)."

Rubinstein, Helena   1870–1965

1086   O'Higgins, Patrick. *Madame: An Intimate Biography of Helena Rubinstein*. New York: Viking Press, 1971. 296 pp.

O'Higgins, a former secretary to Rubinstein, writes a great deal in this book about his own life and his travels with her. He relies too much on gossip to tell her story.

Russell, Lillian   1861–1922

1087   Burke, John. *Duet in Diamonds: The Flamboyant Saga of Lillian Russell and Diamond Jim Brady in America's Gilded Age*. New York: G. P. Putnam's Sons, 1972. 286 pp.

Burke's book focuses on the respective careers of these two personalities as well as on their celebrated friendship. He has done much research on their era, and he defines its social milieu very well.

1088   Morell, Parker. *Lillian Russell: The Era of Plush*. New York: Random House, 1940. 319 pp.

Morell's account of Russell is actually more about her interesting era than about the woman herself. The best feature of this book is its collection of period photographs.

Rutherford, Mildred L.   1852–1928

1089   Clare, Virginia P. *Thunder and Stars: The Life of Mildred Rutherford*. Oglethorpe, Ga.: Oglethorpe Univ. Press, 1941. 245 pp.

Clare has written a sentimental account of Rutherford's life. This biography is too subjective to be useful to a serious student.

S

Sabin, Florence Rena   1871–1953

1090   Bluemel, Elinor. *Florence Sabin: Colorado Woman of the Century*. Boulder: Univ. of Colorado Press, 1959. 238 pp.

Bluemel merely writes an overview highlighting the main achievements of Sabin's life. While she admires her subject and shows her personality clearly, Bluemel is not always factually correct.

Sacajawea   ca. 1786–1812?

1091   Clark, Ella E., and Margot Edmonds. *Sacagawea of the Lewis and Clark Expedition*. Berkeley: Univ. of California Press, 1979. 171 pp.

This account of the Indian guide's life is sympathetic but not overly adulatory. Their book is divided into two sections: the events of the Lewis and Clark expedition involving their subject, and her life after the expedition. The authors place Sacajawea's death in 1884, which is far too late.

1092   Hebard, Grace R. *Sacajawea: A Guide and Interpreter of the Lewis and Clark Expedition*. Glendale, Calif.: Arthur H. Clark, 1933. 340 pp.

Although Hebard based her book on much research, it contains one major flaw: she confuses the Indian guide with another woman of the same name for the years after the expedition. She also devotes a good deal of space to describing the career of Sacajawea's son.

1093   Howard, Harold P. *Sacajawea*. Norman: Univ. of Oklahoma Press, 1971. 218 pp.

One of the better-prepared, more detailed studies of Sacajawea, this book contains useful maps and a good bibliography.

1094   Schultz, James W. *Bird Woman (Sacajawea)*. Boston: Houghton Mifflin, 1918. 235 pp.

Schultz interviewed (ca. 1870) two Indians who claimed to have known Sacajawea personally; he relates their narratives in this text, but their veracity is questionable. The book includes a useful appendix that reprints all the sections of Lewis and Clark's journals referring to their Indian guide.

St. Denis, Ruth   1877–1968

1095 Shawn, Ted. *Ruth St. Denis: Pioneer and Prophet, Being a History of Her Cycle of Oriental Dances*. San Francisco: John Henry Nash, 1920. 2 vols.

This is a lavishly illustrated book (volume two has virtually no text), in which Shawn praises his wife's work. Since only 350 copies of this book were produced, it may prove difficult to locate.

1096 Shelton, Suzanne. *Divine Dancer: A Biography of Ruth St. Denis*. New York: Doubleday Publishing, 1981. 338 pp.

This is a complete and objective biography on the dancer's private life and public career. It provides intimate details on her marriage to Ted Shawn and their work together.

1097 Terry, Walter. *Miss Ruth: The "More Living Life" of Ruth St. Denis*. New York: Dodd, Mead, 1970. 206 pp.

Terry, a friend to his subject, makes use of her personal records to write this authorized biography. His book includes all the essential facts of St. Denis's life and career.

Salmon, Lucy Maynard   1853–1927

1098 Brown, Louise F. *Apostle of Democracy: The Life of Lucy Maynard Salmon*. New York: Harper and Brothers, 1943. 315 pp.

Brown's book is actually a compilation of materials from Salmon's extensive private papers. The biographer writes interconnecting chapters between these materials to describe the main events of the life, starting at age six; she explains well the basic struggles of Salmon's life as a woman.

Sampson, Deborah   1760–1827

1099 Mann, Herman. *The Female Review: The Life of Deborah Sampson, the Female Soldier in the War of the Revolution*. Boston: J. K. Wiggin and W. P. Lunt, 1866. 267 pp.

This book saw several editions, beginning in 1797 with a romanticized tale that Sampson had related to Mann. This edition of 1866 is most useful for its notes and an introduction by John A. Vinton. The text focuses on Sampson's three years of service in the Revolutionary War.

Sandburg, Lillian S.   See **Steichen, Lillian**

Sandoz, Mari   1896–1966

1100   Stauffer, Helen W. *Mari Sandoz: Story Cather of the Plains*. Lincoln: Univ. of Nebraska Press, 1982. 322 pp.

Stauffer chiefly discusses Sandoz's life as it relates to her writing. When Stauffer does describe her subject, both her faults and virtues are touched upon.

Sanford, Maria L.   1836–1920

1101   Whitney, Helen A. *Maria Sanford*. Minneapolis: Univ. of Minnesota Press, 1922. 322 pp.

Whitney opens her book with Sanford's unfinished autobiography (of about forty pages). The biographer then describes the remainder of her subject's life, relying on primary sources for the facts.

Sanger, Margaret H.   1879–1966

1102   Dash, Joan. *A Life of One's Own*. New York: Harper and Row, 1973. 113 pp.

Dash details both the public activities and the private relationships of her subject. Her account is chronological, with some psychoanalysis of Sanger included.

1103   Douglas, Emily T. *Margaret Sanger: Pioneer of the Future*. New York: Holt, Rinehart and Winston, 1970. 274 pp.

Douglas provides numerous details on Sanger's private life, her public career, and her professional friendships. Douglas re-creates her subject's personality well and speaks of her in an admiring tone.

1104   Gray, Madeline. *Margaret Sanger: A Biography of the Champion of Birth Control*. New York: Richard Marek, 1979. 494 pp.

Gray's emphasis is on Sanger's personal life rather than on her public crusades. Although Gray did much research on her subject (including reviewing previously unpublished materials), some of her facts are inaccurate.

1105   Kennedy, David M. *Birth Control in America: The Career of Margaret Sanger*. New Haven: Yale Univ. Press, 1970. 320 pp.

This scholarly and well-researched study concentrates primarily on Sanger's crusade for birth control, while explaining her character clearly. The book contains an extensive bibliography.

1106   Lader, Lawrence. *The Margaret Sanger Story: The Fight for Birth Control*. New York: Doubleday Publishing, 1955. 352 pp.

This sympathetic portrait of Sanger and her work seems to praise her indiscriminately. Lader describes the social and political issues of Sanger's day very well.

Sarton, May   1912–

1107   Sibley, Agnes. *May Sarton*. New York: Twayne Publishers, 1972. 160 pp.
See entry 26.

Savitch, Jessica   1947–1983

1108   Blair, Gwenda. *Almost Golden: Jessica Savitch and the Selling of Television News*. New York: Simon and Schuster, 1988. 352 pp.

Blair opens with a detailed account of Savitch's early life, then carefully records her career rise and tragic downfall. The biographer, who regrettably did not have the cooperation of her subject's family, relies on some undocumented sources for facts.

1109   Nash, Alanna. *Golden Girl: The Story of Jessica Savitch*. New York: E. P. Dutton, 1988. 320 pp.

Nash depicts Savitch as being almost two persons: one on camera and the other off. The author psychoanalyzes her subject; to accomplish this, she relies on material from the autobiography.

Sawyer, Ruth   1880–1970

1110   Haviland, Virginia. *Ruth Sawyer*. New York: H. Z. Walck, 1965. 78 pp.

This monograph is based on Haviland's interviews with Sawyer. The biographer provides a fair amount of details about Sawyer's life, then focuses on her works.

Schiff, Dorothy   1903–1989

1111   Potter, Jeffrey. *Men, Money and Magic: The Story of Dorothy Schiff*. New York: Coward, McCann and Geoghegan, 1976. 352 pp.

Schiff cooperated with Potter and provided him with her personal papers (from which he quotes). He focuses on the more gossipy details of her public and private lives.

Schlafly, Phyllis S.   1924–

1112   Felsenthal, Carol. *The Sweetheart of the Silent Majority: The Biography of Phyllis Schlafly*. New York: Doubleday, 1981. 337 pp.

This book, in which Felsenthal attempts to clarify Schlafly's political views, is the result of numerous interviews with her subject's friends and adversaries. The book's text is equally balanced between a discussion of Schlafly's personal life and her public career.

Schuyler, Catherine V.   1734–1803

1113   Humphreys, Mary G. *Catherine Schuyler*. New York: Charles Scribner's Sons, 1897. 251 pp.

Humphreys is so sympathetic to her subject that she discusses only her favorable character traits. Schuyler's role as a wife and mother receives the most emphasis.

Scott, Evelyn   1893–1963

1114   Callard, D. A. *"Pretty Good for a Woman": The Enigmas of Evelyn Scott*. New York: W. W. Norton, 1985. 202 pp.

Rather than writing a complete biography of Scott, Callard merely outlines the events of her life in chronological order. Too much text is devoted to describing the plots of Scott's novels and quoting from reviews of them.

Scripps, Ellen Browning   1836–1932

1115   Britt, Albert. *Ellen Browning Scripps: Journalist and Idealist*. New York: Oxford Univ. Press, 1960. 134 pp.

This is the most complete biography available on Scripp's life and career. The book is filled with rich details on all aspects of her life.

Scudder, Ida Sophia   1870–1960

1116   Jeffery, Mary P. *Dr. Ida of India: The Life Story of Ida S. Scudder*. New York: Fleming H. Revell, 1938. 212 pp.

This book deals only partially with Dr. Scudder's life and work. Much of the text deals with descriptions of her female patients in India and their way of life.

1117   Wilson, Dorothy C. *Dr. Ida: The Story of Dr. Ida Scudder of Vellore*. New York: McGraw-Hill, 1959. 358 pp.

This biography, which relies on some fictionalization, is written in a sincere and admiring spirit.

Seaman, Elizabeth C.   See **Bly, Nellie**

Seberg, Jean   1938–1979

1118 Richards, David. *Played Out: The Jean Seberg Story*. New York: Random House, 1981. 386 pp.
Although Seberg's entire life is covered by Richards, his focus is on her mental illnesses. The book is filled with accurate details, but the author produces no insights into Seberg's character.

Sedgwick, Catharine M.   1789–1867

1119 Dewey, Mary, ed. *The Life and Letters of Catharine Sedgwick*. New York: Harper and Brothers, 1872. 446 pp.
This is an extensive and useful early biography of Sedgwick that reprints many of her letters, as edited by Dewey.

1120 Foster, Edward H. *Catharine Maria Sedgwick*. New York: Twayne Publishers, 1974. 167 pp.
See entry 26.

Sedgwick, Edie   1943–1971

1121 Stein, Jean. *Edie: An American Biography*. Ed. George Plimpton. New York: Alfred A. Knopf, 1982. 455 pp.
Stein presents in this book a collection of 250 interviews with Sedgwick's friends and relatives, so this is actually an oral biography. Some use of documents in the text helps round out the actress's life.

Seelye, Sarah Emma   1841–1898

1122 Dannett, Sylvia G. L. *She Rode with the Generals: The True and Incredible Story of Sarah Emma Seelye, Alias Franklin Thompson*. Nashville: Thomas Nelson, 1960. 326 pp.
Dannett provides a full biography of her subject, including her later years. She takes a Freudian approach to Seelye's story and also tries to demonstrate which of her claims were true and which were exaggerated.

Seid, Ruth   See **Sinclair, Jo**

Seton, Elizabeth A. Bayley 1774–1821

1123 Cushing, Richard Cardinal. *Blessed Mother Seton*. Boston: The Daughters of St. Paul, 1963. 97 pp.

Cardinal Cushing tells Mother Seton's life story in about fifty pages, emphasizing her religious nature and admirable character. The remainder of the book reprints devotional writings by Mother Seton.

1124 de Barberey, Helene B., and Joseph B. Code. *Elizabeth Seton*. New York: Macmillan Publishing, 1927. 594 pp.

This biography, whose source is a French book printed in 1868, provides the details of Mother Seton's life, as well as reprinting some of her letters and journals. Code writes an essay that updates the activities of the Sisters of Charity after the death of their founder.

1125 Dirvin, Joseph I. *Mrs. Seton, Foundress of the American Sisters of Charity*. New York: Farrar, Straus, 1962. 498 pp.

Dirvin is biased on Mother Seton's behalf in this thorough, penetrating study that focuses both on her life and her works.

1126 Feeney, Leonard. *Elizabeth Seton, an American Woman: Her Story*. New York: American Press, 1938. 272 pp.

Father Feeney has written an appreciative biography of Mother Seton from a Roman Catholic viewpoint. His writing style is both informal and informative.

1127 Laverty, Sr. Rose M. *Loom of Many Threads: The English and French Influences on the Character of Elizabeth Ann Bayley Seton*. New York: The Paulist Press, 1958. 258 pp.

This scholarly, well-researched book was written chiefly in admiration of Mother Seton, yet it also presents a detailed account of her life. The biographer is primarily interested in which character traits the saint inherited from her ancestors.

1128 Melville, Annabelle M. *Elizabeth Bayley Seton, 1774–1821*. New York: Charles Scribner's Sons, 1951. 411 pp.

Melville covers all of her subject's life in this scholarly book. Although she is admiring of Mother Seton, the tone of her narrative is not overly laudatory.

1129 White, Charles I. *Mother Seton, Mother of Many Daughters*. New York: E. Dunigan and Brother, 1853. 581 pp.

White's dignified and highly respectful narrative accurately records all the facts of Mother Seton's life.

Seward, Frances M.   1805–1865

1130   Conrad, Earl. *The Governor and His Lady: The Story of William Henry Seward and His Wife Frances*. New York: G. P. Putnam's Sons, 1959. 433 pp.
This unscholarly biography relies, in part, on such devices as imagined conversations. Although this book is based on Mrs. Seward's letters, her husband emerges more clearly than she does.

Sharp, Katharine L.   1865–1914

1131   Grotzinger, Laurel A. *The Power and the Dignity: Librarianship and Katharine Sharp*. Metuchen, N.J.: Scarecrow Press, 1966. 331 pp.
Grotzinger discusses all of Sharp's life in this biography, but emphasizes her years as a librarian. The biographer clearly demonstrates the contributions Sharp made to her profession.

Sheed, Maisie Ward   1889–1975

1132   Sheed, Wilfred. *Frank and Maisie: A Memoir with Parents*. New York: Simon and Schuster, 1986. 304 pp.
Sheed, the son of this couple, describes their marriage and their career together as Catholic publishers. He also highlights their friendships with famous people.

Shepard, Helen G.   See **Gould, Helen**

Sherman, Ellen Ewing   1824–1888

1133   McAllister, Anna S. *Ellen Ewing, Wife of General Sherman*. New York: Benzinger Brothers, 1936. 379 pp.
McAllister's book, which emphasizes Mrs. Sherman's Roman Catholic faith, is an intimate biography, based on the subject's own letters. Mrs. Sherman's son wrote a foreword to this book in which he praises its accuracy.

Shore, Dinah   1917–

1134   Cassiday, Bruce. *Dinah! A Biography*. New York: Franklin Watts, 1979. 212 pp.
Although Cassiday covers all of Shore's life, his main emphasis is on her career years. He neither provides any insights into her personality nor describes that personality effectively.

Sigourney, Lydia H.   1791–1865

1135   Haight, Gordon S. *Mrs. Sigourney, the Sweet Singer of Hartford*. New Haven: Yale Univ. Press, 1930. 201 pp.

Haight's well-documented biography is the result of careful research on his subject's private life and literary career. He is unsympathetic to her and her poetry, which he judges as mediocre.

Simpson, Wallis   See **Windsor, Wallis**

Sinclair, Jo   1913–

1136   Sandberg, Elisabeth. "Jo Sinclair: Toward a Critical Biography." Dissertation. Univ. of Massachusetts, 1985. 230 pp.

Sandberg's first chapter describes Sinclair's family background, early life, and public employment. The rest of the study describes Sinclair's literary development and her canon.

Skinner, Maud Durbin   d. 1936

1137   Skinner, Cornelia O. *Family Circle*. Boston: Houghton Mifflin, 1948. 310 pp.

Skinner recalls the lives of both her parents in this remembrance, which begins by discussing their American ancestors. This book is candid and relies to a good extent on her parents' well-written memoirs.

Slocum, Frances   1773–1847

1138   Meginness, John F. *The Biography of Frances Slocum*. Williamsport, Penn.: Heller Brothers' Printing House, 1891. 238 pp.

This is the fullest and most carefully detailed book on Slocum's life. It includes a bibliography.

1139   Phelps, Martha B. *Frances Slocum, the Lost Sister of Wyoming*. New York: Knickerbocker Press, 1905. 167 pp.

Phelps, Slocum's grandniece, wrote this account for the benefit of her own children and grandchildren. The book lists the authorities that Phelps researched in preparing her narrative.

1140   Todd, John. *The Lost Sister of Wyoming: An Authentic Narrative*. Northampton, Mass.: J. H. Butler, 1842. 160 pp.

This is the earliest book that tells the full story of Slocum's capture by the Delaware Indians in the Wyoming Valley of Pennsylvania.

Slye, Maud   1879–1954

1141 McCoy, J. J. *The Cancer Lady: Maud Slye and Her Heredity Studies.* Nashville: Thomas Nelson, 1977. 191 pp.

This biography, written for a general reader, lacks documentation. The biographer takes a feminist approach to examine Slye.

Smedley, Agnes   1894–1950

1142 MacKinnon, Janice R., and Stephen R. MacKinnon. *Agnes Smedley: The Life and Times of an American Radical.* Berkeley: Univ. of California Press, 1987. 425 pp.

This is a good bibliography that explains all of Smedley's life and political activities. The book is equally proportioned between her public and private lives; it quotes from her letters to provide a distinct picture of Smedley.

Smith, Abigail Adams   1765–1813

1143 Roof, Katharine M. *Colonel William Smith and Lady: The Romance of Washington's Aide and Young Abigail Adams.* Boston: Houghton Mifflin, 1929. 347 pp.

This book focuses on the courtship and marriage of Abigail Adams, daughter of John Adams, Sr. In her research, Roof consulted the Adams's family letters and journals, from which she quotes frequently.

Smith, Amanda Berry   1837–1915

1144 Cadbury, M. H. *The Life of Amanda Smith: The African Sybil, the Christian Saint.* Birmingham, England: Cornish Brothers, 1916. 84 pp.

This book is particularly good on Smith's later life, a period not covered in her autobiography (which had ended with the year 1892).

Smith, Bessie   1894–1937

1145 Albertson, Chris. *Bessie.* Briarcliff Manor, N.Y.: Stein and Day, 1972. 253 pp.

Albertson covers the years 1912 to 1937 in this biography, which focuses on Smith's personal life and problems more than on her singing career. He provides new information about her, given to him by her niece.

Smith, Elizabeth Oakes   1806–1893

1146 Wyman, Mary A. *Two American Pioneers: Seba Smith and Elizabeth Oakes Smith*. New York: Columbia Univ. Press, 1927. 249 pp.

Wyman clearly presents both the literary and political settings for the Smiths' era, so that the reader can fully appreciate Elizabeth's accomplishments. The book includes an extensive bibliography.

Smith, Emma Hall   1804–1879

1147 Newell, Linda K., and Valeen T. Avery. *Mormon Enigma: Emma Hall Smith, Prophet's Wife, Elect Lady, Polygamy's Foe, 1804–1879*. New York: Doubleday Publishing, 1984. 394 pp.

The authors remain objective in this biography of a controversial figure. They have created a thorough view of her life and her crusade, based on much research.

Smith, Jessie W.   1863–1935

1148 Schnessel, S. Michael. *Jessie Willcox Smith*. New York: Thomas Y. Crowell, 1977. 224 pp.

Schnessel writes a basic, factual account of the entire chronology of Smith's life. The book's best feature is its set of 163 illustrations by the artist, many of which are in color.

Smith, Lillian   1897–1966

1149 Blackwell, Louise, and Frances Clay. *Lillian Smith*. New York: Twayne Publishers, 1971. 152 pp.

See entry 26.

1150 Loveland, Anne C. *Lillian Smith, a Southerner Confronting the South: A Biography*. Baton Rouge: Louisiana State Univ. Press, 1986. 289 pp.

This is a fairly complete biography of Smith that also assesses her literary career and achievements. Although the book is a result of much careful research, it lacks a bibliography.

Smith, Margaret Chase   1897–

1151 Graham, Frank. *Margaret Chase Smith: Woman of Courage*. New York: Day, 1964. 188 pp.

Graham wrote this overview of Smith's life and career as a source of information for U.S. voters in an election year. The book is highly flattering to Smith, while retaining an informal narrative.

Smith, Sophia   1796–1870

1152 Hanscom, Elizabeth D., and Helen F. Greene. *Sophia Smith and the Beginnings of Smith College*. Northampton, Mass.: Smith College Press, 1925. 120 pp.

This book pays tribute to Smith and her efforts in founding Smith College for Women; it is based on a narrative by John Morton Greene about the institution's first days.

Southworth, E. D. E. N.   1819–1899

1153 Boyle, Regis L. *Mrs. E. D. E. N. Southworth, Novelist*. Washington, D.C.: The Catholic Univ. of America Press, 1939. 171 pp.

This is a full-length study of the life and works of Mrs. Southworth. It includes four appendices that deal specifically with cataloging her literary output.

Spencer, Anne   1882–1975

1154 Greene, J. Lee. *Time's Unfading Garden: Anne Spencer's Life and Poetry*. Baton Rouge: Louisiana State Univ. Press, 1977. 204 pp.

Greene provides a sensitive and comprehensive biography of all the stages of Spencer's life. He interviewed his subject late in her life and quotes her fairly often in this book.

Spencer, Elizabeth   1921–

1155 Prenshaw, Peggy W. *Elizabeth Spencer*. Boston: Twayne Publishers, 1985. 200 pp.

See entry 26.

Spofford, Harriet P.   1835–1921

1156 Halbeisen, Elizabeth K. *Harriet Prescott Spofford: A Romantic Survival*. Philadelphia: Univ. of Pennsylvania Press, 1935. 273 pp.

This is a complete critical biography of Spofford which has an unusually thorough index and bibliography. Halbeisen describes well Spofford's work and her place in New England literary circles from 1850 to 1920.

Sprague, Kate C.   See **Chase, Kate**

Stafford, Jean   1915–1979

1157   Roberts, David. *Jean Stafford: A Biography*. Boston: Little, Brown, 1988. 494 pp.

Roberts did much research on his subject, and as a result he understands her character. He makes effective use of quotations from her letters and from revealing sections in her fiction. However, he focuses so heavily on the sordid details of her life that he gives too little attention to her accomplishments.

1158   Walsh, Mary E. *Jean Stafford*. Boston: Twayne Publishers, 1985. 113 pp.

See entry 26.

Stanford, Jane Lathrop   1828–1905

1159   Berner, Bertha. *Mrs. Leland Stanford: An Intimate Account*. Stanford: Stanford Univ. Press, 1935. 231 pp.

Berner was a private secretary to Mrs. Stanford from 1884 to 1905, the years on which she focuses in this book. Her account is detailed and prejudiced in favor of Mrs. Stanford, yet it does not interpret her character or career.

Stanton, Elizabeth Cady   1815–1902

1160   Banner, Lois W. *Elizabeth Cady Stanton: A Radical for Woman's Rights*. Boston: Little, Brown, 1980. 189 pp.

Banner's sympathetic account of Stanton begins with her childhood and evaluates her character development; although it is the public career that Banner emphasizes in Stanton's adult years, Banner is apt at describing Stanton's approach to and thoughts on feminism.

1161   Griffith, Elisabeth. *In Her Own Right: The Life of Elizabeth Cady Stanton*. New York: Oxford Univ. Press, 1984. 268 pp.

Griffith covers all the major events of Stanton's life, including the controversies. She believes the major influences on Stanton's development as a feminist were her two parents and Lucretia Mott.

1162   Lutz, Alma. *Created Equal: A Biography of Elizabeth Cady Stanton, 1815–1902*. New York: John Day, 1940. 345 pp.

Lutz skims over Stanton's early life, then focuses mainly on her active career in suffrage, after the 1860s. This biographer is especially apt at describing the vital relationship between Stanton and Susan B. Anthony.

1163   Oakley, Mary Ann. *Elizabeth Cady Stanton*. Old Westbury, N.Y.: The Feminist Press, 1972. 148 pp.

Oakley describes Stanton's political career in its entirety, not just her work for women's rights. However, this book could have been more neatly organized and could have detailed Stanton's era more fully.

1164   Wise, Winifred E. *Rebel in Petticoats: Elizabeth Cady Stanton*. Philadelphia: Chilton Books, 1960. 204 pp.

Wise has written a vivid account of Stanton that highlights her role as a social reformer. This book contains two bibliographies: one of writings by Stanton, and the other of writings about her.

Stanwyck, Barbara   1907–

1165   DiOrio, Al. *Barbara Stanwyck: A Biography*. New York: Coward, McCann and Geoghegan, 1984. 249 pp.

Although DiOrio describes Stanwyck's childhood, there are not too many private details about her life in this book. He describes all of her career, but spends too much space paraphrasing the plots of her major films.

1166   Smith, Ella. *Starring Miss Barbara Stanwyck*. New York: Crown Publishers, 1973. 352 pp.

Smith focuses chiefly on Stanwyck's film career, with few comments on her personal life. She has mostly praise for the actress's work, which she follows from silent movies to major film roles to television acting.

1167   Vermilye, Jerry. *Barbara Stanwyck*. New York: Pyramid Publishers, 1975. 159 pp.

See entry 286.

1168   Wayne, Jane E. *Stanwyck*. New York: Arbor House, 1985. 220 pp.

Because Stanwyck did not grant this author an interview, no new intimate or perceptive details of her character are included in this book. Wayne discusses all the aspects of the actress's life and career, with an emphasis on her romance with Robert Taylor.

Starr, Pearl   1867–1925

1169   Hicks, Edwin P. *Belle Starr and Her Pearl*. Little Rock, Ark.: C. A. Harper, 1963. 183 pp.
See under Starr, Shirley "Belle."

Starr, Shirley "Belle"   1848–1889

1170   Breihan, Carl W., and Charles A. Rosamond. *Bandit Belle: The Story of the Notorious Belle Starr*. Seattle: Hangman Press, 1970. 144 pp.
This book report on Belle Starr is not too extensive. Instead, the authors include in their text the autobiography of Henry Starr (written in jail) and some reports of other notorious men of that era.

1171   Hicks, Edwin P. *Belle Starr and Her Pearl*. Little Rock, Ark.: C. A. Harper, 1963. 183 pp.
This is the only book-length account of Belle Starr that includes the story of her daughter Pearl. This is mostly an entertaining narrative, with a good foreword by Homer Croy.

1172   Rascoe, Burton. *Belle Starr*. New York: Random House, 1941. 340 pp.
Rascoe carefully writes his text on Starr by consulting old newspaper accounts of her exploits. He provides his reader with the tall tales extant about Starr and also makes a critical analysis of her life and career.

1173   Shirley, Glenn. *Belle Starr and Her Times: The Literature, the Facts, and the Legends*. Norman: Univ. of Oklahoma Press, 1982. 324 pp.
Shirley provides a very distinct picture of Starr and her era in the West. He not only accurately delineates her life's history, but he also describes and refutes the many false stories surrounding her.

Steichen, Lillian   1883–1977

1174   Sandburg, Helga. *A Great and Glorious Romance: The Story of Carl Sandburg and Lillian Steichen*. New York: Harcourt, Brace, Jovanovich, 1978. 380 pp.
Mrs. Sandburg's daughter is the author of this intimate account of her parents' marriage, and quotes from their love letters at length. Carl Sandburg receives more space in this book than does his wife.

Stein, Gertrude   1874–1946

1175 Brinnin, John M. *The Third Rose: Gertrude Stein and Her World*. Boston: Little, Brown, 1959. 427 pp.

Brinnin's is a full-length and balanced biography of Stein that describes both her private life and her public image. He perceptively finds the true woman behind the myths about her.

1176 Hobhouse, Janet. *Everybody Who Was Anybody: A Biography of Gertrude Stein*. New York: G. P. Putnam's Sons, 1975. 244 pp.

Hobhouse, an art critic, offers a detailed and well-documented account that focuses on Stein's place in the artistic and literary circles in Paris. The biographer, who remains objective, quotes from Stein's own writings to describe her life.

1177 Hoffman, Michael J. *Gertrude Stein*. Boston: Twayne Publishers, 1976. 160 pp.

See entry 26.

1178 Mellow, James R. *Charmed Circle: Gertrude Stein and Company*. New York: Praeger Publishers, 1974. 528 pp.

Mellow provides a densely detailed book on Stein and her artistic world. The biographer's approach is sympathetic, yet always accurate, as he focuses on Stein the writer, the sister, and the companion to other creative people.

1179 Rogers, W. G. *When This You See Remember Me: Gertrude Stein in Person*. New York: Rinehart, 1948. 247 pp.

This is a personal memoir of Stein written in an informal style. While the biographer offers a few interesting anecdotes, his discussion of Stein's work is not significant.

1180 Sprigge, Elizabeth. *Gertrude Stein: Her Life and Work*. New York: Harper and Brothers, 1956. 277 pp.

Sprigge, who is sympathetic to Stein, discusses her life and writing career without evaluating either. In speaking of Stein's books, Sprigge summarizes them rather than providing a critical review.

1181 Toklas, Alice B. *What Is Remembered*. New York: Holt, Rinehart and Winston, 1963. 186 pp.

Toklas's book repeats many of the same facts and anecdotes found in Stein's *The Autobiography of Alice B. Toklas* (see below). She does not draw a very intimate portrait of Stein; instead, she stays close to Stein's public image.

Stephens, Kate   1853–1938

1182 Habein, Margaret. "Kate Stephens: A Study of Her Life and Writings." Dissertation. Univ. of Kansas, 1952. 133 pp.

Habein's study reveals how Stephens's writings reflect her personal life and ideas. This dissertation covers all of Stephens's career and has a complete bibliography of her works.

Stettheimer, Florine   1871–1944

1183 Tyler, Parker. *Florine Stettheimer: A Life in Art.* New York: Farrar, Straus, 1963. 194 pp.

Tyler goes into a fair amount of detail on the artist's life in his text. The book also reprints some of her best paintings, but lacks a bibliography.

Stone, Lucinda H.   1814–1900

1184 Perry, Belle M. *Lucinda Hinsdale Stone: Her Life Story and Reminiscences.* Detroit: Blinn Publishing, 1902. 369 pp.

Perry pays tribute to her close friend in this book, which also describes all of her life. The text includes autobiographical sketches by Stone, her pupils' recollections of her, and an introduction by Ellen M. Henrotin.

Stone, Lucy   1818–1893

1185 Blackwell, Alice S. *Lucy Stone: Pioneer of Woman's Rights.* Boston: Little, Brown, 1930. 313 pp.

Blackwell, Stone's daughter, writes a careful explanation of her mother's work in the suffrage movement, including new details. Blackwell admires her mother but does not eulogize her in this book.

1186 Hays, Elinor R. *Morning Star: A Biography of Lucy Stone, 1818–1893.* New York: Harcourt, Brace and World, 1961. 339 pp.

Hays uses Stone's family papers to describe her life in this illuminating biography. This book is especially perceptive on Stone's relationship with her husband and her daughter Alice.

Stowe, Harriet Beecher   1811–1896

1187 Adams, John R. *Harriet Beecher Stowe.* New York: Twayne Publishers, 1964. 172 pp.

See entry 26.

1188   Fields, Annie. *The Life and Letters of Harriet Beecher Stowe*. Boston: Houghton Mifflin, 1898. 406 pp.

Fields is very sympathetic to her friend Stowe in this book. Its biographical facts are accurate and Fields's personal knowledge of her subject is impressive.

1189   Gerson, Noel B. *Harriet Beecher Stowe*. New York: Praeger Publishers, 1976. 218 pp.

This is an adequate, basic biography that presents the major facts of Stowe's life. However, too much irrelevant data crowds the book, so Stowe's personality never emerges clearly.

1190   Gilbertson, Catherine P. *Harriet Beecher Stowe*. New York: Appleton-Century, 1937. 330 pp.

This is a mostly objective and balanced book on Stowe's writing career and her role in her era. Unfortunately, its sources are not documented.

1191   Johnston, Johanna. *Runaway to Heaven: The Story of Harriet Beecher Stowe*. New York: Doubleday Publishing, 1963. 490 pp.

Johnston views Stowe as a complex woman whose life was full of conflicts, many of which she describes in this book. All of the stages of Stowe's life are covered; the text even includes a genealogy chart on the Stowe and Beecher families.

1192   McCray, Florine T. *The Life-Work of the Author of "Uncle Tom's Cabin."* New York: Funk and Wagnalls, 1889. 440 pp.

McCray wrote this unauthorized biography while Stowe was still alive. McCray praises her subject frequently in the text, which also summarizes the plots of Stowe's novels at length.

1193   Scott, John A. *Woman against Slavery: The Story of Harriet Beecher Stowe*. New York: Thomas Y. Crowell, 1978. 169 pp.

Scott's emphasis is on Stowe's antislavery sentiments; therefore, he explains thoroughly the social and political aspects of slavery in her era. Scott describes Stowe's other writings as well, such as those set in New England.

1194   Stowe, Charles E. *The Life of Harriet Beecher Stowe*. Boston: Houghton Mifflin, 1889. 313 pp.

This biography was written by Stowe's son in close collaboration with her. She is in essence analyzing her own life in this account, and naturally the record presented is prejudiced in her behalf. The book also includes many quotations from her correspondence.

1195 Wagenknecht, Edward. *Harriet Beecher Stowe: The Known and the Unknown*. New York: Oxford Univ. Press, 1965. 267 pp.

Wagenknecht provides a vivid, detailed picture of Stowe in her various life roles: as wife, as daughter, as mother, as writer. He sums up her personality effectively in his text, which deals more with Stowe's personal life than her writings.

1196 Wilson, Forrest. *Crusade in Crinoline: The Life of Harriet Beecher Stowe*. Philadelphia: J. B. Lippincott, 1941. 706 pp.

This is a very good biography that contains many new facts about Stowe and some newly found (ca. 1941) letters written by her. Wilson explores all her life, documents his sources well, and presents a balanced view of her character. The book's scholarly apparatus is excellent.

1197 Wise, Winifred E. *Harriet Beecher Stowe: Woman with a Cause*. New York: G. P. Putnam's Sons, 1965. 190 pp.

Wise's main focus is on Stowe as an abolitionist. She is shown chiefly in the context of her Calvinistic upbringing, while Wise details the effects the Civil War had on Stowe.

Straight, Dorothy W.   See **Whitney, Dorothy**

Stratton-Porter, Gene   1863–1924

1198 Meehan, Jeannette P. *Lady of the Limberlost: The Life and Letters of Gene Stratton-Porter*. New York: Doubleday Publishing, 1928. 369 pp.

This is a highly personal account of the author written by her daughter. Meehan relies heavily on her mother's correspondence to describe all the stages of her life, including her courtship and marriage.

1199 Richards, Bertrand F. *Gene Stratton-Porter*. Boston: Twayne Publishers, 1980. 165 pp.

See entry 26.

1200 Saxton, Eugene F. *Gene Stratton-Porter: A Little Story of the Life and Works and Ideals of "The Bird Woman."* New York: Doubleday and Page, 1915. 52 pp.

This brief biography was issued by Stratton-Porter's publishers to advertise her career; it claims to be based on "intimate records" about her.

Streisand, Barbra   1942–

1201   Considine, Shaun. *Barbra Streisand: The Woman, the Myth, the Music.* New York: Delacorte Press, 1985. 355 pp.

Considine has written a mostly serious biography of the singer that covers all of her life and career. He frankly discusses her faults, but not all the details of her intimate life.

1202   Spada, James. *Streisand: The Woman and the Legend.* New York: Doubleday Publishing, 1981. 249 pp.

Spada's book, which relies on anecdotes to tell its story, pays tribute to Streisand rather than describing her character in any detail. He chronicles all of her major performances, often quoting from favorable reviews.

1203   Zec, Donald, and Anthony Fowles. *Barbra: A Biography of Barbra Streisand.* New York: St. Martin's Press, 1982. 253 pp.

These authors show Streisand in more depth than do her other biographers (see above); Zec and Fowles penetrate beyond the public image of the singer to reveal her true character. They also offer extensive quotations from her friends and colleagues.

Strong, Anna L.   1885–1970

1204   Pringle, Robert W. "Anna Louise Strong: Propagandist of Communism." Dissertation. Univ. of Virginia, 1970. 220 pp.

Pringle details Strong's political work in the United States and elsewhere in this study. He covers all aspects of her journalism career, beginning when Strong is awarded her Ph.D.

1205   Strong, Tracy B., and Helene Keyssar. *Right in Her Soul: The Life of Anna Louise Strong.* New York: Random House, 1984. 399 pp.

Although this is an informative book, it does not adequately detail all of Strong's life. Her radical politics are discussed more fully than are her career in journalism and its impact.

Stuart, Ruth McEnery   1849–1917

1206   Fletcher, Mary F. "Ruth McEnery Stuart: A Biography and Critical Study." Dissertation. Louisiana State Univ., 1955. 135 pp.

This is a good biography providing the fullest account of Stuart's life that is available. It includes a listing of her papers held at Tulane University Library in New Orleans.

Suckow, Ruth   1892–1960

1207   Kissane, Leedice M. *Ruth Suckow*. New York: Twayne Publishers, 1969.
175 pp.
See entry 26.

Sullavan, Margaret   1896–1960

1208   Quirk, Lawrence J. *Margaret Sullavan: Child of Fate*. New York: St.
Martin's Press, 1986. 224 pp.
Quirk is sympathetic to Sullavan, but not overly so. His portrait of her is well
balanced, and he includes interesting details about her movie appearances.

Sullivan, Anne   See **Macy, Anne S.**

Surratt, Mary E.   1820–1865

1209   Campbell, Helen J. *The Case for Mrs. Surratt*. New York: G. P. Putnam's
Sons, 1943. 272 pp.
Campbell does not provide documentation of her sources in this biography. Her
book includes the basic facts of Surratt's early life that are seldom seen in print.

Susann, Jacqueline   1921–1974

1210   Mansfield, Irving, and Jean L. Block. *Life with Jackie*. New York: Ban-
tam Books, 1983. 276 pp.
Mansfield, Susann's widower, mainly pays tribute to her in this book, which
avoids any scandalous information. He does not provide any in-depth evaluation
of her character, since he focuses on detailing their domestic life together.

1211   Seaman, Barbara. *Lovely Me: The Life of Jacqueline Susann*. New York:
William Morrow, 1987. 416 pp.
Seaman, who is sympathetic to Susann, details her early life and the influences
on her personal development. This is an authorized biography that documents its
sources awkwardly.

Swain, Clara A.   1834–1910

1212   Wilson, Dorothy C. *Palace of Healing*. New York: McGraw-Hill, 1968.
245 pp.

This popular narrative is the most detailed one available on Swain; unfortunately, it is not documented. Wilson focuses on Swain's work rather than on her personal life.

Swallow, Ellen H.   1842–1911

1213   Clarke, Robert. *Ellen Swallow: The Woman Who Founded Ecology.* Chicago: Follett Publishing, 1973. 276 pp.

Although his is a factual biography, Clarke's writing style romanticizes Swallow too much. It is comprehensive on her life, beginning at her birth, but it also places excessive emphasis on the ecology movement of the 1970s.

Swanson, Gloria   1898–1983

1214   Madsen, Axel. *Gloria and Joe: The Star-Crossed Love Affair of Gloria Swanson and Joe Kennedy.* New York: Arbor House, 1988. 328 pp.

This account, which is sympathetic to Swanson, focuses as much on her early career as it does on her three-year love affair with Kennedy. Madsen's book is accurate on her biographical facts and does not sensationalize its subject.

Szold, Henrietta   1860–1945

1215   Dash, Joan. *Summoned to Jerusalem: The Life of Henrietta Szold.* New York: Harper and Row, 1979. 348 pp.

In this balanced view of Szold that is based, in part, on her own diaries, Dash offers many details of Szold's private life and demonstrates how they affected her career.

1216   Fineman, Irving. *Woman of Valor: The Life of Henrietta Szold, 1860–1945.* New York: Simon and Schuster, 1961. 448 pp.

Fineman, in this biography commissioned by Hadassah, covers all of Szold's life and her work for various causes, especially Zionism. However, he does not provide an especially well-balanced or personal portrait of this woman. He praises her highly, but does not offer enough details to explain her various projects properly.

1217   Lowenthal, Marvin. *Henrietta Szold: Life and Letters.* New York: Viking Press, 1942. 350 pp.

In order to tell Szold's life story (up to 1941), Lowenthal relies on her correspondence and that of her family. Her personality and her career are both described clearly in this book.

1218   Zeitlin, Rose. *Henrietta Szold: The Record of a Life*. New York: Dial Press, 1952. 263 pp.

Although this is another authorized biography, it is not overly biased in Szold's favor. Its chronology, which focuses on her career as a Zionist, is sometimes confusing.

T

Tabor, Elizabeth "Baby Doe"   1854–1935

1219   Gandy, Lewis C. *The Tabors: A Footnote of Western History*. New York: Press of the Pioneers, 1935. 291 pp.

This book focuses more on the husband than on the wife; it also details silver and gold mining in the early West. Gandy effectively sorts the facts from the legends about the Tabors.

1220   Hall, Gordon L. *The Two Lives of Baby Doe*. Philadelphia: Macrae Smith, 1962. 252 pp.

This is a popular biography that is not useful to a serious student; no new data on Tabor is included in this book. It also lacks an index and documentation.

1221   O'Connor, Richard. *The Legend of Baby Doe: The Life and Times of the Silver Queen of the West*. New York: G. P. Putnam's Sons, 1974. 273 pp.

This book focuses on Baby Doe's character and mores, particularly in relationship to the values of her era. An interesting discussion of her large collection of souvenirs concludes this biography.

Taft, Jessie   1882–1960

1222   Robinson, Virginia, ed. *Jessie Taft, Therapist and Social Work Educator: A Professional Biography*. Philadelphia: Univ. of Pennsylvania Press, 1962. 384 pp.

This is a rich sourcebook on Taft's life and career. Besides containing her biography, it reprints selections from her writings and provides a full bibliography of them.

Tallchief, Maria   1925–

1223   Maynard, Olga. *Bird of Fire: The Story of Maria Tallchief*. New York: Dodd, Mead, 1961. 201 pp.

Maynard deeply admires her subject and this fact renders her book less than objective. She carefully details the dancer's childhood and early career, calling on the family's letters for her facts; the later career is covered more briefly.

Talmadge, Constance 1900–1973

1224 Loos, Anita. *The Talmadge Girls: A Memoir*. New York: Viking Press, 1978. 204 pp.

Loos's book focuses on Constance and Norma, as well as on their mother. Loos relies on anecdotes to tell much of their story, but her awkward chronology can confuse the reader.

1225 Talmadge, Margaret L. *The Talmadge Sisters*. Philadelphia: J. B. Lippincott, 1924. 245 pp.

Margaret Talmadge was the mother of the three actresses, so her book includes personal details not found elsewhere. She describes their family life, their childhoods, and their three careers up to 1924.

Talmadge, Natalie 1899–1969

1226 Talmadge, Margaret L. *The Talmadge Sisters*. Philadelphia: J. B. Lippincott, 1924. 245 pp.

See under Talmadge, Constance.

Talmadge, Norma 1897–1957

1227 Loos, Anita. *The Talmadge Girls: A Memoir*. New York: Viking Press, 1978. 204 pp.

See under Talmadge, Constance.

1228 Talmadge, Margaret L. *The Talmadge Sisters*. Philadelphia: J. B. Lippincott, 1924. 245 pp.

See under Talmadge, Constance.

Tarbell, Ida M. 1857–1944

1229 Brady, Kathleen. *Ida Tarbell: Portrait of a Muckraker*. New York: G. P. Putnam's Sons, 1984. 286 pp.

Brady bases her book on Tarbell's private papers. She makes good use of detail and produces a study that is both factually accurate and sympathetic to Tarbell; she describes her subject's inner life with great clarity.

1230   Tomkins, Mary E. *Ida M. Tarbell*. New York: Twayne Publishers, 1974. 182 pp.
See entry 26.

Tartt, Ruby Pickens   1880–1974

1231   Brown, Virginia P., and Laurella Owens. *Toting the Lead Row: Ruby Pickens Tartt, Alabama Folklorist*. University: Univ. of Alabama Press, 1981. 180 pp.
The authors begin with a detailed description of Tartt's work as a folklorist for the WPA and her life in that era. Approximately two-thirds of the book reprints some of the data Tartt collected on that assignment.

Taylor, Elizabeth   1932–

1232   Allan, John B. *Elizabeth Taylor*. Derby, Conn.: Monarch Books, 1961. 139 pp.
Taylor's life story and acting career are described in a fair amount of detail. The book is addressed to the general reader; it has no index.

1233   David, Lester, and Jhan Robbins. *Richard and Elizabeth*. New York: Thomas Y. Crowell, 1977. 242 pp.
The authors of this dual biography (of Taylor and Burton) follow their subjects from childhood through their adult careers and marriages (to each other and to others). Most of the material sounds gossipy and may derive from newspaper stories.

1234   Kelley, Kitty. *Elizabeth Taylor: The Last Star*. New York: Simon and Schuster, 1981. 448 pp.
Kelley, who does not admire her subject, maintains a skeptical tone throughout this book. The text is based heavily on gossip and anecdotes; it does not examine Taylor's life in depth.

1235   Maddox, Brenda. *Who's Afraid of Elizabeth Taylor?* New York: M. Evans, 1977. 252 pp.
This is an objective account of both Taylor's private life and her acting career. Maddox is especially apt at describing the rising path the career followed.

1236   Sheppard, Dick. *Elizabeth: The Life and Career of Elizabeth Taylor*. New York: Doubleday Publishing, 1973. 507 pp.

Sheppard's biography provides a serious and detailed view of Taylor's life and career to 1973. He separates the facts from the legends about her, and he accurately assesses her acting talent.

1237   Waterbury, Ruth. *Elizabeth Taylor*. New York: Appleton-Century-Crofts, 1963. 310 pp.

This is a subjective book on Taylor's life and career. Although Waterbury had the cooperation of Taylor's mother in preparing this biography, no new facts or insights are included in the text.

Taylor, Laurette   1884–1946

1238   Courtney, Marguerite T. *Laurette*. New York: Rinehart, 1954. 433 pp.

Courtney provides a very complete biography of her mother. She describes both her private life and her acting career aptly and frankly.

Taylor, Maria Dyer   1837–1870

1239   Pollock, John C. *Hudson Taylor and Maria: Pioneers in China*. New York: McGraw-Hill, 1962. 212 pp.

Mrs. Taylor receives a good amount of space in this book, which describes her marriage in much detail. Pollock shows how her wisdom and sacrifices advanced her husband's work in China.

Teasdale, Sara   1884–1933

1240   Carpenter, Margaret H. *Sara Teasdale*. New York: Schulte, 1960. 377 pp.

Carpenter describes all of the stages of Teasdale's life, while only one chapter is devoted to reviewing her poetry. The biographer emphasizes the poet's relationship with Vachal Lindsay and quotes frequently from Teasdale's letters and diaries.

1241   Drake, William. *Sara Teasdale: Woman and Poet*. New York: Harper and Row, 1979. 304 pp.

Drake, a feminist critic, is deeply sympathetic to Teasdale. He describes her mental and physical illnesses by using newly discovered sources (ca. 1979). By analyzing the images in her poetry, he also evaluates her emotional life.

1242   Schoen, Carol B. *Sara Teasdale*. Boston: Twayne Publishers, 1986. 208 pp.

See entry 26.

Tekakwitha, Kateri   1656–1680

1243　Buehrle, Marie C. *Kateri of the Mohawks*. Milwaukee: Bruce Publishing, 1954. 192 pp.

This is a romanticized biography. The author is most straightforward when dealing with the facts of the subject's adult life, which were carefully researched.

1244　Sargent, Daniel. *Catherine Tekakwitha*. Boston: Longmans, Green, 1936. 246 pp.

Sargent, in his well-documented book, explains the culture and religion of Tekakwitha's tribe, as both are vital to understanding her life. He discusses her life in ample detail, considering the fact that little is known of her early years.

1245　Walworth, Ellen H. *The Life and Times of Kateri Tekakwitha, the Lily of the Mohawks, 1656–1680*. Buffalo: P. Paul and Brothers, 1891. 314 pp.

This is a complete and carefully documented account of Tekakwitha's life. The book also contains much information on her Mohawk tribe and New York state's colonial history.

Temple, Shirley   1928–

1246　Basinger, Jeanine. *Shirley Temple*. New York: Pyramid Publishers, 1975. 160 pp.

See entry 286.

1247　David, Lester, and Irene David. *The Shirley Temple Story*. New York: G. P. Putnam's Sons, 1983. 224 pp.

The Davids' book begins with Temple's birth and covers her entire life and career. Nothing negative is said about her in this text. Although the authors interviewed many people, including the actress's first husband, no insights into her character are given here.

1248　Eby, Lois. *Shirley Temple*. Derby, Conn.: Monarch Books, 1962. 143 pp.

This is a popular biography of Temple that focuses on her successful years as a child actress. It is a fairly well written book, but it is not useful to a serious student; it has no index.

1249　Edwards, Anne. *Shirley Temple: American Princess*. New York: William Morrow, 1988. 425 pp.

Edwards's book focuses on Temple's life after she left Hollywood and film-making. She presents many details about the actress's domestic life. Unfortunately, the book contains some inaccuracies.

Terry, Louisa Ward   See **Ward, Louisa**

Thanet, Octave   1850–1934

1250 McMichael, George. *Journey to Obscurity: The Life of Octave Thanet.* Lincoln: Univ. of Nebraska Press, 1965. 259 pp.
This is a scholarly and intelligent biography. Besides discussing all of Thanet's life, the biographer also details her writing career and the artistic changes that occurred in it.

Thaxter, Celia L.   1835–1894

1251 de Piza, Mary D. "Celia Thaxter, Poet of the Isles of Shoals." Dissertation. Univ. of Pennsylvania, 1955. 272 pp.
Using Thaxter's letters as her primary source, this biographer presents a highly detailed study of all the episodes of her subject's life, including her marriage and literary friendships. Her personality is described vividly in this study.

1252 Thaxter, Rosamond. *Sandpiper: The Life and Letters of Celia Thaxter.* Francestown, N.H.: M. Jones, 1963. 283 pp.
A relative of the poet chronicles all the eras of her life in this book. The biographer emphasizes Thaxter's intimate family relationships and her many literary friendships.

1253 Vallier, Jane E. *Poet on Demand: The Life, Letters and Works of Celia Thaxter.* Camden, Me.: Down East Books, 1982. 267 pp.
This is an accurate and sympathetic biography of the poet. The book's best feature is its useful secondary bibliography.

Thomas, Carey   1857–1935

1254 Finch, Edith. *Carey Thomas of Bryn Mawr.* New York: Harper and Brothers, 1947. 342 pp.
This is the standard biography of Thomas. It is penetrating and perceptive, especially on her early years. The book is also sympathetic to her work as a college administrator.

Thomas, Helen   1871–1956

1255 Flexner, James T. *An American Saga: The Story of Helen Thomas and Simon Flexner*. Boston: Little, Brown, 1984. 494 pp.

Flexner writes perceptively about his parents' marriage and their respective careers. His is a well-written, scholarly biography with an extensive bibliography included.

Thompson, Dorothy   1894–1961

1256 Sanders, Marion K. *Dorothy Thompson: A Legend in Her Time*. Boston: Houghton Mifflin, 1973. 428 pp.

Sanders admires her subject, yet remains objective in this biography; she describes Thompson's personality especially vividly. Thompson's personal life and career are covered fully by Sanders.

1257 Sheean, Vincent. *Dorothy and Red*. Boston: Houghton Mifflin, 1963. 363 pp.

Sheean relies heavily on Dorothy's letters and diaries to tell of her marriage to Sinclair Lewis; as a result, she receives more attention in this text than does her husband. Sheean is always sympathetic to Thompson and sensitive to her problems.

Thursby, Emma C.   1845–1931

1258 Gipson, Richard M. *The Life of Emma Thursby, 1845–1931*. New York: New York Historical Society, 1940. 470 pp.

This is a fairly objective and heavily detailed biography based on Thursby's private papers; Gipson quotes from her letters in this text. The book also includes a chronology of her career.

Tietjens, Eunice   1884–1944

1259 Love, Willie N. "Eunice Tietjens: A Biographical and Critical Study." Dissertation. Univ. of Maryland, 1960. 384 pp.

This thorough study discusses all of its subject's literary career and private life. It also includes an explanation of her genealogy and evaluates her contributions to American poetry.

Toklas, Alice B.   1877–1967

1260 Simon, Linda. *The Biography of Alice B. Toklas*. New York: Doubleday Publishing, 1977. 324 pp.

Although Simon covers all the stages of Toklas's life in this biography, she devotes more of the text to the years when her subject lived with Gertrude Stein. This book is based on newly discovered (ca. 1977), unpublished letters by Toklas; however, Simon quotes from them only briefly.

1261   Stein, Gertrude. *The Autobiography of Alice B. Toklas*. New York: Harcourt, Brace, 1933. 310 pp.

Stein, writing from the perspective of Toklas, describes their life together very vividly, particularly the years before World War I. Stein is very sympathetic to her subject. The reader must be warned that this book mixes fact with fiction.

Truman, Bess W.   1885–1982

1262   Truman, Margaret. *Bess W. Truman*. New York: Macmillan Publishing, 1986. 445 pp.

The author is perceptive and insightful on her parents' marriage and personalities. However, she does devote more space here to a discussion of her father; the book is based on 1,600 of his letters.

Truth, Sojourner   1797–1883

1263   Fauset, Arthur H. *Sojourner Truth: God's Faithful Pilgrim*. Chapel Hill: Univ. of North Carolina Press, 1938. 187 pp.

Although much good research was done for this book, the author's simplistic writing style and naive viewpoint render it less than adequate.

1264   Ortiz, Victoria. *Sojourner Truth, a Self-made Woman*. Philadelphia: J. B. Lippincott, 1974. 157 pp.

Ortiz describes all of Truth's life and career, from slavery to national prominence. She explains precisely the personal traits that made Truth's rise to leadership possible.

1265   Pauli, Hertha. *Her Name Was Sojourner Truth*. New York: Appleton-Century-Crofts, 1962. 250 pp.

Pauli reveals some new facts about Truth's life. She also employs fictionalized dialogues, which weaken the seriousness of this book.

Tubman, Harriet Ross   1826–1913

1266   Bradford, Sarah H. *Harriet Tubman, the Moses of Her People*. New York: Peter Smith, 1961. 149 pp.

Butler A. Jones writes a sympathetic portrait of Tubman in his introduction to this book. The text itself has a lengthy publishing history; it began as a sketch in 1869, with other material added later. It describes Tubman's nineteen trips into the South to help slaves escape.

1267   Conrad, Earl. *Harriet Tubman*. Washington, D.C.: Associated Publishers, 1943. 248 pp.

Conrad's study is based on much careful research; it is a well-documented, accurate book.

Tucker, Sophie   1884–1966

1268   Freedland, Michael. *Sophie: The Sophie Tucker Story*. Totowa, N.J.: Woburn Press, 1979. 221 pp.

Freedland had access to Tucker's letters in preparing this biography. By using them he sorts out the facts of her life from the legends about her. Unfortunately, this book lacks an index and a bibliography.

Turner, Lana   1920–

1269   Morella, Joe, and Edward Z. Epstein. *Lana: The Public and Private Lives of Miss Turner*. Secaucus, N.J.: Citadel Press, 1971. 297 pp.

This is an informal, unauthorized biography that relies too much on name-dropping and gossip to tell the story. Its sources are not documented.

Tyler, Julia G.   1820–1889

1270   Seager, Robert. *And Tyler Too: A Biography of John and Julia Gardiner Tyler*. New York: McGraw-Hill, 1963. 681 pp.

Seager describes all the stages of Mrs. Tyler's life in detail; he also clearly explains the politics of her era. He includes an insightful discussion of this first lady's influence on her husband.

Tyler, Priscilla C.   1816–1889

1271   Coleman, Elizabeth T. *Priscilla Cooper Tyler and the American Scene, 1816–1889*. University: Univ. of Alabama Press, 1955. 203 pp.

Since few facts are known about this woman, Coleman quotes frequently from Tyler's journals to round out her biography. Coleman draws a sympathetic and factual picture of his subject.

V

Van Alstyne, Frances   See **Crosby, Fanny**

Van Buren, Abigail   1918–

1272   Pottker, Jon, and Bob Speziale. *Dear Ann, Dear Abby: The Unauthorized Biography of Ann Landers and Abigail Van Buren.* New York: Dodd, Mead, 1987. 304 pp.
See under Landers, Ann.

Van Cott, Margaret N.   1830–1914

1273   Foster, John O. *The Life and Labours of Mrs. Maggie Newton Van Cott.* Cincinnati: Hitchcock and Walden, 1872. 339 pp.
Van Cott herself aided in the preparation of this book, which is mainly laudatory. Foster's details are not always specific enough, but he describes her early years well.

Vanderbilt, Consuelo   See **Balsan, Consuelo V.**

Vanderbilt, Gloria M.   1924–

1274   Goldsmith, Barbara. *Little Gloria . . . Happy at Last.* New York: Alfred A. Knopf, 1980. 650 pp.
Goldsmith provides all the basic data on Vanderbilt's life, but her focus is on the 1934 trial for the child's custody. The author quotes effectively from legal documents of that period, but weakens the book's seriousness by awkwardly employing psychoanalysis on its leading figures.

Vanderbilt, Grace Wilson   1870–1953

1275   Vanderbilt, Cornelius. *Queen of the Golden Age: The Fabulous Story of Grace Wilson Vanderbilt.* New York: McGraw-Hill, 1956. 311 pp.

This biography was written by the subject's son and contains many details of their family history and life-styles. Although he tries to write an honest and objective account of his mother, Cornelius shows his deep admiration for her.

Van Waters, Miriam   1887–1974

1276   Rowles, Burton J. *The Lady at Box 99: The Story of Miriam Van Waters*. New York: Seabury Press, 1962. 367 pp.

The author bases this book on records kept by Van Waters and on his interviews with her. He focuses mainly on her career in penology and social work. Throughout the text he is admiring of her high personal values and attractive character traits.

Vineyard, Mary Owens   1808–1877

1277   Carruthers, Olive. *Lincoln's Other Mary*. New York: Ziff-Davis, 1946. 229 pp.

Although the historical records about this woman are scant, Carruthers stays with only the certifiable facts in this book. (She does, however, use some imaginary settings to round out her account.) A useful appendix written by R. Gerald McMurtry describes the sources available on Mary Vineyard's life.

W

Wald, Lillian D. 1867–1940

1278 Daniels, Doris G. "Lillian D. Wald: The Progressive Woman and Feminism." Dissertation. City Univ. of New York, 1977. 345 pp.
Daniels describes Wald's early years briefly, before focusing on her progressive career of forty years. She shows in detail Wald's work for labor unions, settlement houses, female suffrage, and world peace.

1279 Duffus, Robert L. *Lillian Wald, Neighbor and Crusader*. New York: Macmillan Publishing, 1938. 371 pp.
Duffus has much admiration and praise for Wald, so his account of her work is somewhat biased. He sustains a clear, factual report of her career in settlement houses as he explains how they interacted with society.

1280 Reznick, Allan E. "Lillian Wald: The Years at Henry Street." Dissertation. Univ. of Wisconsin, 1973. 470 pp.
Reznick employs Wald's recently discovered (ca. 1973) personal papers to describe her early life. He then focuses in fine detail on the years 1893 to 1913 when she worked in New York City settlement houses.

Walker, Mary Edwards 1832–1919

1281 Snyder, Charles M. *Dr. Mary Walker: The Little Lady in Pants*. New York: Vantage Press, 1962. 166 pp.
Snyder draws his portrait of Walker and her career from unpublished materials he found in Oswego, New York, and its locale.

Walker, Mary Richardson 1811–1897

1282 Drury, Clifford M. *Elkanah and Mary Walker: Pioneers among the Spokanes*. Caldwell, Idaho: Caxton Printers, 1940. 283 pp.
Drury's emphasis is on the couple's work at their mission for the Spokane Indians. Most useful are his quotations from Mary's journals, as well as those from her diary.

Ward, Annie   1824–1895

1283   Tharp, Louise H. *Three Saints and a Sinner: Julia Ward Howe, Louisa, Annie and Sam Ward.* Boston: Little, Brown, 1956. 406 pp.
See under Howe, Julia Ward.

Ward, Louisa   1823–1897

1284   Tharp, Louise H. *Three Saints and a Sinner: Julia Ward Howe, Louisa, Annie and Sam Ward.* Boston: Little, Brown, 1956. 406 pp.
See under Howe, Julia Ward.

Warde, Frances   1810–1884

1285   Healy, Kathleen. *Frances Warde: American Founder of the Sisters of Mercy.* New York: Seabury Press, 1974. 480 pp.
This is the definitive biography written by a commission from her religious order, the Sisters of Mercy. Healy has done much research (including in the Vatican archives) in order to produce a complete account of her subject's life and works.

Warner, Anna B.   1827–1915

1286   Stokes, Olivia E. P. *Letters and Memories of Susan and Anna Bartlett Warner.* New York: G. P. Putnam's Sons, 1925. 229 pp.
Stokes, a longtime friend to her subjects, details their lives and characters in the first third of this book, then reprints their letters, and closes her account with a description of the pilgrimagelike trip she made to her subjects' homes after their deaths.

Warner, Edith   1891?–1951

1287   Church, Peggy P. *The House at Otowi Bridge: The Story of Edith Warner and Los Alamos.* Albuquerque: Univ. of New Mexico Press, 1960. 149 pp.
Church, a close friend to Warner, writes in tribute to her in this book. Its text is brief and focuses mainly on Warner's life in New Mexico and her many friendships.

Warner, Susan B.   1819–1885

1288   Stokes, Olivia E. P. *Letters and Memories of Susan and Anna Bartlett Warner.* New York: G. P. Putnam's Sons, 1925. 229 pp.
See under Warner, Anna B.

1289 Warner, Anna B. *Susan Warner*. New York: G. P. Putnam's Sons, 1909. 509 pp.

Anna Warner, a close companion to her older sister Susan for most of her life, provides in this text many intimate details of her sister's daily life and work habits.

Warren, Mercy Otis   1728–1814

1290 Anthony, Katharine S. *First Lady of the Revolution: The Life of Mercy Otis Warren*. New York: Doubleday Publishing, 1958. 258 pp.

Anthony does not narrow her focus enough on Warren to make this an adequate biography. Instead, she discusses Warren's husband and other family members at some length. The reader, therefore, cannot receive a clear understanding of Warren's personality.

1291 Brown, Alice. *Mercy Warren*. New York: Charles Scribner's Sons, 1896. 317 pp.

Brown depicts Warren fairly well in a flattering portrait. The book dwells heavily on the minute details of Warren's domestic life and the culture and mores of her era.

Washington, Dinah   1924–1963

1292 Haskins, Jim. *Queen of the Blues: The Story of Dinah Washington*. New York: William Morrow, 1987. 239 pp.

Haskins's lively narrative describes both Washington's career and her private life; emphasis is given to some important family relationships. The book may be too brief for use by a serious student.

Washington, Martha   1732–1802

1293 Beebe, Elswyth T. *Washington's Lady*. New York: Dodd, Mead, 1959. 368 pp.

Beebe (a pseudonym for Elswyth Thane) shows only his subject's good qualities, particularly her warm regard for her husband and family. The book contains some minor factual errors in its re-created scenes and dialogues. Some useful genealogy charts are included.

1294 Lossing, Benson J. *Mary and Martha: The Mother and the Wife of George Washington*. New York: Harper and Brothers, 1886. 348 pp.

Lossing's book is much more about Martha than about Mary. Since so little is known about either woman's personal life, he discusses them in relationship to George Washington and his public career.

1295   Wharton, Anne H. *Martha Washington.* New York: Charles Scribner's Sons, 1897. 306 pp.

Wharton praises Martha and her fine domestic qualities very highly. She also details the customs and manners of colonial Virginia, while avoiding much discussion of its politics.

Washington, Mary Ball   1708–1789

1296   Lossing, Benson J. *Mary and Martha: The Mother and the Wife of George Washington.* New York: Harper and Brothers, 1886. 348 pp.

See under Washington, Martha.

1297   Pryor, Sara A. R. *The Mother of Washington and Her Times.* New York: Macmillan Publishing, 1903. 367 pp.

Pryor idealizes her subject and praises all her virtues; the tone of the book is thoroughly romantic. Since few facts are known of Mrs. Washington's life, the lives of her ancestors are also described. The book lacks an index.

1298   Turner, Nancy B., and Sidney Gunn. *The Mother of Washington.* New York: Dodd, Mead, 1931. 284 pp.

Although the authors employ a somewhat informal writing style, their book is accurate on all the historical facts. They give an exceptionally good view of life in colonial Virginia.

Waters, Ethel   1900–1977

1299   Knaack, Twila. *Ethel Waters: I Touched a Sparrow.* Waco, Tex.: Word Books, 1978. 128 pp.

In this biography Knaack concentrates on the years 1957 to Waters's death in 1977 (the period in which Waters was a dedicated Christian). Knaack, who worked in the singer's household beginning in 1970, gives a sympathetic and not very objective view of the woman.

Welty, Eudora   1909–

1300   Evans, Elizabeth. *Eudora Welty.* New York: Frederick Ungar Publishing, 1981. 172 pp.

See entry 189.

1301 Vande Kieft, Ruth M. *Eudora Welty*. New York: Twayne Publishers, 1962. 203 pp.
See entry 26.

West, Jessamyn 1907–1984

1302 Shivers, Alfred S. *Jessamyn West*. New York: Twayne Publishers, 1972. 160 pp.
See entry 26.

West, Mae 1893–1980

1303 Bovar, Michael. *Mae West*. New York: Pyramid Publishers, 1975. 157 pp.
See entry 286.

1304 Eells, George, and Stanley Musgrove. *Mae West: A Biography*. New York: William Morrow, 1982. 351 pp.
The authors have based their biography on a large amount of research. One of their aims is to correct the facts that West misstated in her autobiography, which they do. They believe that her public image and her true personality were almost identical.

Wharton, Edith 1862–1937

1305 Auchincloss, Louis. *Edith Wharton: A Woman in Her Time*. New York: Viking Press, 1972. 191 pp.
Auchincloss is reticent on many of the intimate details of Wharton's life. He is best at describing her background and the influences on her, as well as the atmosphere of her society. This is really only a surface view of her life.

1306 Bell, Millicent. *Edith Wharton and Henry James: The Story of Their Friendship*. New York: George Braziller, 1965. 384 pp.
Bell's book relies on the letters of both writers to describe their friendship. She details well both their personal relationship and their literary relationship (especially how they influenced each other).

1307 Coolidge, Olivia E. *Edith Wharton, 1862–1937*. New York: Charles Scribner's Sons, 1964. 221 pp.

This is a concise biography that covers in an overview all the stages of Wharton's life. Coolidge makes a few small factual errors. The weakest feature of this biography is its unsophisticated language (at times close to a children's book level).

1308 Kellogg, Grace. *The Two Lives of Edith Wharton: The Woman and Her Work*. New York: Appleton-Century-Crofts, 1965. 332 pp.

This is chiefly a popular biography that describes clearly only Wharton's early years. Kellogg uses some fictionalized elements and makes errors of scholarship in this book.

1309 Lawson, Richard H. *Edith Wharton*. New York: Frederick Ungar Publishing, 1977. 118 pp.

See entry 189.

1310 Lewis, R. W. B. *Edith Wharton: A Biography*. New York: Harper and Row, 1975. 592 pp.

Lewis won a Pulitzer Prize for this outstanding, finely detailed biography of Wharton, which is based on her private papers. He brings her spirit alive in his text, yet remains an objective observer of her life and career.

1311 Lubbock, Percy. *A Portrait of Edith Wharton*. New York: Appleton-Century, 1947. 249 pp.

Lubbock focuses his attention on Wharton's personal character traits, revealing both the favorable and the unfavorable. He was her close friend, and highlights the period in England when they were together often. He does not recount anything controversial about her.

1312 McDowell, Margaret B. *Edith Wharton*. Boston: Twayne Publishers, 1976. 158 pp.

See entry 26.

1313 Wolff, Cynthia G. *A Feast of Words: The Triumph of Edith Wharton*. New York: Oxford Univ. Press, 1977. 453 pp.

This scholarly, meticulously researched book provides a good analysis of Wharton's inner life. Wolff provides meaningful insights into Wharton's character and her motivations for being a writer.

Wheatley, Phillis   1753–1784

1314 Renfro, G. Herbert. *The Life and Works of Phillis Wheatley*. Privately printed, 1916. n.p.

This early biography of Wheatley is best at describing her life in the Wheatley household and in detailing her states of mind in her last years. Some of Wheatley's letters are reprinted here, as well as a newspaper story covering her funeral.

1315 Richmond, M. A. *Bid the Vassal Soar*. Washington, D.C.: Howard Univ. Press, 1972. 216 pp.
Richmond relates all of the major events of Wheatley's life in one-half of this book; the rest of his text deals with George M. Horton, another slave poet. The book includes a bibliography.

1316 Robinson, William H. *Phillis Wheatley and Her Writings*. New York: Garland Publishing, 1984. 464 pp.
This is a basic sourcebook on the poet. It describes her life, reprints some criticism of her writings, and provides the texts of her poems. It also includes a bibliography.

1317 ———. *Phillis Wheatley and the Black American Beginnings*. Detroit: Broadside Press, 1975. 95 pp.
Robinson opens his book with a biographical sketch of Wheatley. He has two purposes in writing of her: he wishes to show her high quality as a poet and to analyze her awareness of blacks' suffering in early America. His text achieves these two goals.

Whistler, Anna M.   1804–1881

1318 Jones, Bessie J., and Elizabeth Herzog. *Whistler's Mother: The Life of Anna McNeill Whistler*. Boston: Little, Brown, 1939. 326 pp.
The two writers, using the pseudonym Elizabeth Mumford, employ their own diaries and letters to relate the facts of their subject's life. They are overly sentimental about and sympathetic to her; their quotations are not well documented.

White, Catherine Payne   d. 1903

1319 White, Owen P. *Frontier Mother*. New York: Minton, Balch, 1929. 101 pp.
Although White admires his mother, he is not overly sentimental in this book. He describes her personal traits well as he shows her struggles to raise a family on the Colorado frontier. The details he provides of her daily life are graphic.

White, Ellen Gould   1827–1915

1320 Canright, Dudley M. *The Life of Mrs. E. G. White, Seventh-Day Adventist Prophet: Her False Claims Refuted.* Cincinnati: Standard Publishing, 1919. 291 pp.

This is a hostile book written to refute White's teachings; Canright was once an Adventist but left the fold.

1321 Jemison, T. Housel. *A Prophet among You.* Mountain View, Calif.: Pacific Press Publishing Association, 1955. 505 pp.

Jemison provides in this book the official view of the Seventh-Day Adventist Church on their founder's life. He explains in much detail her gift of prophecy.

1322 Noorbergen, Rene. *Ellen G. White: Prophet of Destiny.* New Canaan, Conn.: Keats Publishing, 1972. 241 pp.

Noorbergen is completely biased in favor of White and her teachings. She covers all the stages of her subject's life, relying heavily on White's own books for the facts. The biographer also details White's ideas on diet and nutrition.

1323 Numbers, Ronald L. *Prophetess of Health: Ellen G. White.* New York: Harper and Row, 1976. 271 pp.

Numbers gives a frank account of White's writings on health topics and writes about the inner workings of the medical center that she and her husband founded.

1324 Spalding, Arthur W. *There Shines a Light: The Life and Work of Ellen G. White.* Nashville: Southern Publishing Association, 1953. 96 pp.

Spalding has nothing but praise for White and her career. Nevertheless, this book offers a brief, clear overview of her life.

White, Katharine S.   1892–1977

1325 Davis, Linda H. *Onward and Upward: A Biography of Katharine S. White.* New York: Harper and Row, 1987. 300 pp.

This is a well-written, comprehensive biography. Davis had the cooperation of the White family and the use of White's personal papers in the preparation of this book.

1326 Russell, Isabel. *Katharine and E. B. White: An Affectionate Memoir.* New York: W. W. Norton, 1988. 269 pp.

Russell worked as a secretary to this couple for eight years; she admires them but also writes rather candidly about them both. She is best at describing their marriage.

White, Pearl   1889–1938

1327 Weltman, Manuel, and Raymond Lee. *Pearl White: The Peerless Fearless Girl*. Cranbury, N.J.: A. S. Barnes, 1970. 266 pp.

This is a candid biography that is basically unsympathetic to White. It covers all of her career and adult romances, from her first acting job until her death. An appendix lists all the films in which she appeared.

Whitman, Narcissa P.   1808–1847

1328 Allen, Opal S. *Narcissa Whitman: An Historical Biography*. Portland, Ore.: Binfords and Mort, 1959. 325 pp.

This biography, which focuses on its subject's married years, details her life aptly. It is particularly good at presenting her in the settings of the pioneer Northwest. Although some fictionalized elements are used in the writing, none of the facts are changed.

1329 Drury, Clifford M. *Marcus and Narcissa Whitman and the Opening of Old Oregon*. Glendale, Calif.: Arthur H. Clark, 1973. 2 vols. 476 pp./435 pp.

This is a serious, complete biography on this couple and their pioneer life together. Although Drury is a thorough researcher, he does not place the Whitmans well in the context of their era. The book includes a bibliography that lists some new sources (ca. 1973).

Whitman, Sarah P.   1803–1878

1330 Ticknor, Caroline. *Poe's Helen*. New York: Charles Scribner's Sons, 1916. 292 pp.

Ticknor provides a detailed account of all of Whitman's life, but especially on her romance with and engagement to Edgar A. Poe. The book's basic source is the couple's love letters.

Whitney, Dorothy   1887–1968

1331 Swanberg, W. A. *Whitney Father, Whitney Heiress*. New York: Charles Scribner's Sons, 1980. 518 pp.

Swanberg covers both Whitneys' lives in this book; frequent quotations appear from the family's letters. The author also spends much space discussing Dorothy's husband and several of the more controversial members of their social circle, thus taking center stage away from Dorothy.

Whitney, Gertrude   1877–1942

1332 Friedman, Bernard H. *Gertrude Vanderbilt Whitney: A Biography.* New York: Doubleday Publishing, 1973. 684 pp.

This book is full of minute details on each year of Whitney's life. Friedman quotes at length from his subject's diary and discusses at length the custody trial of Gloria Vanderbilt.

Wiggin, Kate Douglas   1856–1923

1333 Smith, Nora A. *Kate Douglas Wiggin as Her Sister Knew Her.* Boston: Houghton Mifflin, 1925. 383 pp.

Smith has written a warm remembrance of her sister. She bases her book, in part, on unused notes Wiggin kept for an autobiography. Some of Wiggin's minor, personal poems are reprinted in this volume.

Wilcox, Ella Wheeler   1850–1919

1334 Ballou, Jenny. *Period Piece: The Life and Times of Ella Wheeler Wilcox.* Boston: Houghton Mifflin, 1940. 287 pp.

Ballou focuses on Wilcox's career rather than on her personal life. She analyzes the writer's place in the United States of her era while explaining why her light verse was so readily consumed and praised then.

Wilder, Laura Ingalls   1867–1957

1335 Spaeth, Janet. *Laura Ingalls Wilder.* Boston: Twayne Publishers, 1987. 120 pp.

See entry 26.

1336 Zochert, Donald. *Laura: The Life of Laura Ingalls Wilder.* Chicago: Henry Regnery, 1976. 260 pp.

Zochert has researched his subject well; although he covers all the years of her life, he is best at describing the early years. He also analyzes her use of autobiographical data in her writing.

Wilkinson, Jemima   1752–1819

1337 Hudson, David. *The History of Jemima Wilkinson.* Geneva, N.Y.: S. P. Hull, 1821. 208 pp.

Hudson's facts are often inaccurate. He wrote this book to lash out angrily at Wilkinson and her followers.

1338   Wisbey, Herbert. *A Pioneer Prophetess: Jemima Wilkinson, the Publick Universal Friend*. Ithaca: Cornell Univ. Press, 1964. 232 pp.

This is a brief, factual book on Wilkinson's career and on the religious community she founded. Wisbey is particularly apt at dismissing the many false legends about Wilkinson.

Willard, Emma Hart   1787–1870

1339   Lord, John. *The Life of Emma Willard*. New York: D. Appleton, 1873. 351 pp.

Dr. Lord, who knew his subject personally, greatly admires her; as a result, his book retains a sentimental tone throughout. While he emphasizes Willard's career, he also clearly describes her personal character.

1340   Lutz, Alma. *Emma Willard, Daughter of Democracy*. Boston: Houghton Mifflin, 1929. 291 pp.

This is a good biography that discusses Willard's personal life as well as her work for women's education. Her school at Troy, New York, is described in rich detail; since Lutz herself was a student there, she provides an especially vivid account of its functions and achievements.

Willard, Frances E.   1839–1898

1341   Bordin, Ruth. *Frances Willard: A Biography*. Chapel Hill: Univ. of North Carolina Press, 1986. 294 pp.

This is a well-documented book; for facts, Bordin researched Willard's private papers, including her recently released diaries (ca. 1986). The biographer uses psychology awkwardly to analyze Willard.

1342   Earhart, Mary, and Mary E. Dillon. *Frances Willard: From Prayer to Politics*. Chicago: Univ. of Chicago Press, 1944. 417 pp.

The biographers use a scholarly approach to their subject rather than a sentimental one (as did earlier biographers of Willard). They write objectively about their subject, separating the facts from the legends. A full bibliography of Willard's writings is included.

1343   Gordon, Anna A. *The Beautiful Life of Frances E. Willard, A Memorial Volume*. Chicago: Women's Temperance Publishing Association, 1898. 416 pp.

The first three hundred pages of this book are a complete but sentimental account of all of Willard's life, beginning with her ancestry. Gordon, who was Willard's private secretary for more than twenty years, shows deep admiration for the woman. The book closes with eulogies and tributes written for Willard.

1344   Strachey, Ray. *Frances Willard: Her Life and Work*. New York: Fleming H. Revell, 1912. 310 pp.

Ray Strachey is a pseudonym for Rachel Costello. She has written a basic biography on Willard's life and career, but no critical judgments are made.

1345   Trowbridge, Lydia J. *Frances Willard of Evanston*. Chicago: Willett, Clark, 1938. 209 pp.

Trowbridge, a close friend to Willard, writes this simple narrative as a tribute to her on the centennial of her birth.

Willebrandt, Mabel W.   1889–1963

1346   Brown, Dorothy M. *Mabel Walker Willebrandt: A Study of Power, Loyalty, and Law*. Knoxville: Univ. of Tennessee Press, 1984. 328 pp.

Brown begins at her subject's birth and relates all of her life with much personal detail included. Brown's research, in part based on Willebrandt family letters, is thorough. Her text also includes an enlightening discussion of this woman's career.

Wills, Helen   1905–

1347   Engelmann, Larry. *The Goddess and the American Girl: The Story of Suzanne Lenglen and Helen Wills*. New York: Oxford Univ. Press, 1988. 464 pp.

Engelmann highlights the lives of each of these athletes, but spends less time on their private lives than on their famous tennis matches (against each other especially). The author spoke to Wills personally; he describes her character very vividly.

Wilson, Augusta Evans   1835–1909

1348   Fidler, William P. *Augusta Evans Wilson, 1835–1909*. University: Univ. of Alabama Press, 1952. 251 pp.

Fidler describes all of Wilson's life accurately. He also analyzes the reasons for her success, particularly in light of the fact that she lacked sophisticated literary talent.

Wilson, Edith Bolling   1872–1961

1349   Hatch, Alden. *Edith Bolling Wilson: First Lady Extraordinary*. New York: Dodd, Mead, 1961. 285 pp.

This is a popular account of Mrs. Wilson, in which the author makes errors in using quotations. Hatch is totally biased in favor of his subject, about whom he provides no new information.

1350   Ross, Ishbel. *Power with Grace: The Life Story of Mrs. Woodrow Wilson*. New York: G. P. Putnam's Sons, 1975. 375 pp.

Ross's book is primarily concerned with the years 1915 to 1924. She describes the Wilsons' marriage well, but includes too many trivial details of domestics and fashions.

1351   Shachtman, Tom. *Edith and Woodrow: A Presidential Romance*. New York: G. P. Putnam's Sons. 1981. 299 pp.

Shachtman bases his book on the recently released (ca. 1981) diaries and letters of the couple; he quotes from them frequently. In this book, written for a general reader, the details of this marriage are rich and accurate.

Wilson, Ellen Axson   1860–1914

1352   Elliott, Margaret R. A. *My Aunt Louisa and Woodrow Wilson*. Chapel Hill: Univ. of North Carolina Press, 1944. 302 pp.

Elliott was the much younger sister of Wilson's first wife. In this book she recalls her early memories of the couple's life in the South and at Princeton.

1353   McAdoo, Eleanor R. W., and Margaret Y. Gaffey. *The Woodrow Wilsons*. New York: Macmillan Publishing, 1937. 301 pp.

This is an affectionate memoir written by the Wilsons' daughter, Mrs. McAdoo. She begins with her own childhood and covers all the years up to her mother's death in 1914. She highlights domestic details and her parents' relationship.

1354   Saunders, Frances W. *Ellen Axson Wilson: First Lady between Two Worlds*. Chapel Hill: Univ. of North Carolina Press, 1985. 359 pp.

This is a well-researched book that is based, in part, on Mrs. Wilson's letters. Saunders's approach is scholarly and her aim is to show this woman in her own light, not that of her husband.

Windsor, Wallis Simpson   1896–1986

1355   Birmingham, Stephen. *Duchess: The Story of Wallis Warfield Windsor*. Boston: Little, Brown, 1981. 344 pp.

Birmingham discusses in detail Wallis's life both before and after her celebrated marriage. When he discovers that an episode in her life is recalled differently by the many people he interviews, he records each version in his text.

1356   Bocca, Geoffrey. *The Woman Who Would Be Queen: A Biography of the Duchess of Windsor*. New York: Rinehart, 1954. 309 pp.

In this book, which employs fictionalization, Bocca concentrates on the events surrounding the king's abdication. He gives his reader a few intimate views of the Duchess's personality.

1357   Brookman, Laura L. *Her Name Was Wallis Warfield: The Life Story of Mrs. Ernest Simpson*. New York: E. P. Dutton, 1936. 117 pp.

Brookman offers many details of her subject's upbringing and early years in Baltimore. This information was obtained from a girlhood friend to Simpson.

1358   Bryan, J. and Charles J. V. Murphy. *The Windsor Story*. New York: William Morrow, 1979. 639 pp.

This well-documented book is more sympathetic to the duke than to the duchess, both of whom the authors knew. Their attempts to psychoanalyze the royal couple are weak.

1359   Garrett, Richard. *Mrs. Simpson*. New York: St. Martin's, 1980. 148 pp.

This book, based chiefly on its subject's autobiography, provides only a shallow view of her character. Only one interesting item is revealed about her; she was the dominant partner in her marriage to the duke.

1360   Higham, Charles. *The Duchess of Windsor: The Secret Life*. New York: McGraw-Hill, 1988. 520 pp.

Higham's version of his subject's life is based on gossip and rumor. He cannot verify his claims, some of which are quite fanciful: e.g., she once worked as a spy.

1361   Martin, Ralph G. *The Woman He Loved*. New York: Simon and Schuster, 1974. 543 pp.

Martin produces a clear and enlivened portrait of the duchess that is based on his firsthand knowledge of her. He is not laudatory, but instead shows both the weaknesses and strengths in her character.

1362   Mosley, Diana. *The Duchess of Windsor*. Briarcliff Manor, N.Y.: Stein and Day, 1980. 224 pp.

Mosley, who knew the royal couple socially, actually discusses them both in this book (despite its title). She is very sympathetic to the pair and defends them against their detractors.

1363   Thornton, Michael. *Royal Feud: The Dark Side of the Love Story of the Century*. New York: Simon and Schuster, 1985. 456 pp.
Thornton details all the circumstances leading up to Edward's abdication; he especially focuses on the royal family's adverse reaction to Wallis. He later describes the reconciliations of all the Windsors in the couple's last years.

1364   Warwick, Christopher. *Abdication*. London: Sidgwick and Jackson, 1986. 176 pp.
Warwick provides many details on the couple's love affair. He also describes, from a British point of view, the events leading up to Edward's abdication.

Winnemucca, Sarah   1844–1891

1365   Canfield, Gae W. *Sarah Winnemucca of the Northern Paiutes*. Norman: Univ. Of Oklahoma Press, 1983. 306 pp.
Canfield writes a sympathetic and detailed life of this woman. Since few factual records about her exist, the biographer rounds out the text with descriptions of tribal life and customs.

Winthrop, Margaret   ca. 1591–1647

1366   Earle, Alice M. *Margaret Winthrop*. New York: Charles Scribner's Sons, 1895. 341 pp.
Earle is totally sympathetic to Mrs. Winthrop and focuses only on her positive character traits. She makes use of the couple's letters to detail their private lives. The book is also filled with the customs and social life of early Boston.

Wood, Natalie   1939–1981

1367   Harris, Warren G. *Natalie and R. J.: A Hollywood Love Story*. New York: Doubleday Publishing, 1988. 264 pp.
Harris discusses Wood's childhood briefly, then focuses on the details of her courtship and marriage. However, the reader receives only a superficial view of this woman. Also, some of the author's claims cannot be substantiated.

1368   Wood, Lana. *Natalie: A Memoir by Her Sister*. New York: G. P. Putnam's Sons, 1984. 240 pp.

Lana Wood, Natalie's younger sister, writes a highly personal book that discusses both their lives. She honestly reveals both the good and the bad points in their relationship; she seems truly to understand her sister and the problems she faced.

Wood, Stella L.   1865–1949

1369   Bell, Marguerite N. *With Banners: A Biography of Stella L. Wood.* St. Paul, Minn.: Macalester College Press, 1954. 163 pp.

Bell, formerly a student of Wood's, writes affectionately and sentimentally of her. She covers all of Wood's life, but emphasizes her role as an educator and her influences on the American kindergarten.

Woodhull, Victoria C.   1838–1927

1370   Brough, James. *The Vixens: A Biography of Victoria and Tennessee Claflin.* New York: Simon and Schuster, 1981. 288 pp.

See under Claflin, Tennessee.

1371   Johnston, Johanna. *Mrs. Satan: The Incredible Saga of Victoria C. Woodhull.* New York: G. P. Putnam's Sons, 1967. 319 pp.

Johnston states that she bases her biography of Woodhull on that of Emanie Sachs in 1928 (see below). The best section of Johnston's book deals with her subject's work for women's rights. Unfortunately, the text lacks footnotes.

1372   Marberry, M. M. *Vicky: A Biography of Victoria C. Woodhull.* New York: Funk and Wagnalls, 1967. 344 pp.

This is a popular account of Woodhull's life that highlights the sensational events. Some of Marberry's facts differ from those in the Johnston book (see above). Although Marberry provides an extensive bibliography, her text lacks footnotes.

1373   Sachs, Emanie. *Terrible Siren: Victoria Woodhull (1838–1927).* New York: Harper and Brothers, 1928. 423 pp.

This is a well-researched book that presents the facts of Woodhull's life without analyzing her character or career. Sachs is especially apt at describing her subject's society.

Woodworth-Etter, Maria B.   1844–1924

1374   Warner, Wayne E. *The Woman Evangelist: The Life and Times of Charismatic Evangelist, Maria B. Woodworth-Etter.* Metuchen, N.J.: Scarecrow Press, 1986. 340 pp.

Using the newspapers of Woodworth-Etter's era, Warner supplies a well-documented study of her career, especially its controversies. He is apt at separating the facts of her life from the legends about her. However, he does not analyze her complex personality.

Woolley, Mary Emma   1863–1947

1375 Marks, Jeannette. *The Life and Letters of Mary Emma Woolley*. Washington, D.C.: Public Affairs Press, 1955. 300 pp.

Marks, her subject's intimate friend, writes an emotional and subjective account of Woolley's life. Marks had access to all of Woolley's private papers, and she reprints many selections from them here.

1376 Wells, Anna M. *Miss Marks and Miss Woolley*. Boston: Houghton Mifflin, 1978. 268 pp.

See under Marks, Jeannette.

Woolson, Constance F.   1840–1894

1377 Kern, John D. *Constance Fenimore Woolson: Literary Pioneer*. Philadelphia: Univ. of Pennsylvania Press, 1934. 198 pp.

This is a complete, scholarly biography that deals both with its subject's life and her career. The book also contains a full bibliography of Woolson's writings.

1378 Moore, Rayburn S. *Constance Fenimore Woolson*. New York: Twayne Publishers, 1963. 173 pp.

See entry 26.

Worrall, Olga R.   1906–

1379 Cerutti, Edwina. *Olga Worrall: The Mystic with a Healing Hand*. New York: Harper and Row, 1975. 169 pp.

Cerutti, who admires Worrall and her work, mostly describes her healing sessions in this book. She also provides extensive information about Worrall's seances with her deceased husband and former partner.

Wright, Patience   1725–1786

1380 Sellers, Charles C. *Patience Wright: American Artist and Spy in George III's London*. Middletown, Conn.: Wesleyan Univ. Press, 1976. 281 pp.

Sellers bases this book on much research and is able to detail how Wright sculpted in wax; the text also includes a catalog of her works. Sellers is effective at depicting Wright's life in London and its art world in the eighteenth century.

Wylie, Elinor Hoyt   1885–1928

1381   Farr, Judith. *The Life and Art of Elinor Wylie*. Baton Rouge: Louisiana State Univ. Press, 1983. 217 pp.

Farr praises Wylie as a first-rate American poet and writes in a flattering tone about her controversial character. The biographer also views Wylie as an early modern feminist who was misunderstood in her own era.

1382   Gray, Thomas A. *Elinor Wylie*. New York: Twayne Publishers, 1969. 171 pp.

See entry 26.

1383   Hoyt, Nancy. *Elinor Wylie: The Portrait of an Unknown Lady*. New York: Bobbs-Merrill, 1935. 203 pp.

Hoyt, Wylie's younger sister, has written a subjective recollection of her. She is especially precise on the poet's tastes, domestic life, and friendships.

1384   Olson, Stanley. *Elinor Wylie: A Life Apart*. New York: Dial Press, 1979. 376 pp.

All of this book is carefully and thoroughly researched. Olson is best at describing Wylie's character and the influences on her in her childhood (especially that of her mother). The biographer also provides new details on the poet's early years with Horace Wylie by consulting his personal papers.

Wyman, Jane   1914–

1385   Morella, Joe, and Edward Z. Epstein. *Jane Wyman: A Biography*. Boston: G. K. Hall, 1986. 350 pp.

Wyman's early life is reviewed hastily in this book. Instead, the authors dwell at length on her third husband, Ronald Reagan. This book, which tells its story by use of gossip and anecdotes, closes with a brief review of Wyman's recent television career (ca. 1986).

1386   Quirk, Lawrence J. *Jane Wyman: The Actress and the Woman*. New York: Dembner Books, 1986. 216 pp.

Quirk's book covers the various eras of Wyman's acting career, including her roles of the 1980s. All aspects of her personal life are also described in some detail: her marriages, her role as a mother, and her various friendships.

Y

Young, Ann Eliza   1844–1908+

1387   Wallace, Irving. *The Twenty-seventh Wife*. New York: Simon and Schuster, 1961. 443 pp.

This is an adequate, full-length biography of Young that is based on newly discovered sources (ca. 1961). The weaknesses of this book are its incomplete documentation and the lack of an index.

Young, Ella Flagg   1845–1918

1388   McManis, John T. *Ella Flagg Young and a Half-Century of the Chicago Public Schools*. Chicago: A. C. McClurg, 1916. 238 pp.

McManis has written a basic, all-inclusive book on Young's life and career, the latter receiving priority. He defends her controversial educational policies.

1389   Smith, Joan K. *Ella Flagg Young: Portrait of a Leader*. Ames: Iowa State Univ. Press, 1979. 272 pp.

Smith's book is based largely on the records of the Chicago Teachers' Federation, yet she adds little new information about Young's career. She also provides few details on the educator's private life.

Young, Loretta   1913–

1390   Morella, Joe, and Edward Z. Epstein. *Loretta Young: An Extraordinary Life*. New York: Delacorte Press, 1986. 288 pp.

The authors describe Young's personal life as well as all the stages of her career. They interviewed her former husband, Ted Lewis, for details about her domestic life. Unfortunately, the writing style in this book is full of clichés.

Z

Zaharias, Mildred "Babe"   1912–1956

1391 Johnson, William O., and Nancy P. Williamson. *"Whatta Gal!" The Babe Didrikson Story*. Boston: Little, Brown, 1977. 244 pp.

These two authors have written an honest account of the various hardships in Zaharias's life, beginning in her childhood. They reveal her true personality behind the public image and show her controversial relationships with other athletes.

Appendix
Women by Profession or Category

Abolitionists

Blackwell, Antoinette B.
Grimké, Angelina E.
Grimké, Sarah M.
Haviland, Laura S.
Holley, Sallie
Phillips, Ann Terry
Truth, Sojourner
Tubman, Harriet Ross

Actresses

Adams, Maude
Bacall, Lauren
Bancroft, Anne
Bankhead, Tallulah
Bow, Clara Gordon
Brooks, Louise
Clark, Marguerite
Colbert, Claudette
Cornell, Katharine
Crabtree, Lotta
Crawford, Joan
Cushman, Charlotte S.
Davies, Marion C.
Davis, Bette
de Havilland, Olivia
Draper, Ruth
Eagels, Jeanne
Elliott, Maxine
Farmer, Frances
Field, Kate
Fiske, Minnie M.
Fonda, Jane
Fontaine, Joan
Frederick, Pauline

Gardner, Ava
Gish, Dorothy
Gish, Lillian
Goddard, Paulette
Grable, Betty
Harlow, Jean
Hayes, Helen
Hayward, Susan
Hayworth, Rita
Hepburn, Katharine
Holliday, Judy
Hull, Josephine
Jones, Jennifer
Kelly, Grace
Lake, Veronica
Lombard, Carole
Mansfield, Jayne
Marlowe, Julia
Menken, Adah Isaacs
Miller, Marilyn
Monroe, Marilyn
Moorehead, Agnes
Morgan, Vicki
Mowatt, Anna Cora
Nesbit, Evelyn
Normand, Mabel
Pickford, Mary
Poe, Eliza(beth) A.
Seberg, Jean
Sedgwick, Edie
Skinner, Maud Durbin
Stanwyck, Barbara
Sullavan, Margaret
Swanson, Gloria
Talmadge, Constance
Talmadge, Natalie
Talmadge, Norma

Actresses (cont.)

Taylor, Elizabeth
Taylor, Laurette
Temple, Shirley
Turner, Lana
Tyler, Priscilla C.
West, Mae
White, Pearl
Wood, Natalie
Wyman, Jane
Young, Loretta

Adventurers and Explorers

Akeley, Delia
Boyd, Louise Arner
Earhart, Amelia M. (aviator)
Peck, Annie Smith
Pennell, Abby Reed (sailor)

Anthropologists

Benedict, Ruth F.
Fletcher, Alice C.
Mead, Margaret
Parsons, Elsie Clews

Architect

Morgan, Julia

Art Patrons

Cone, Claribel
Cone, Etta
Gardner, Isabella S.
Guggenheim, Marguerite "Peggy"
Harkness, Rebekah
Luhan, Mabel Dodge

Athletes

Wills, Helen
Zaharias, Mildred "Babe"

Authors

Alcott, Louisa May
Alexander, Francesca
Arnow, Harriette
Atherton, Gertrude
Austin, Mary Hunter
Bacon, Delia Salter
Barnes, Djuna
Barnes, Margaret Ayer
Barney, Natalie C.
Bates, Katharine Lee
Beattie, Ann
Bonner, Sherwood
Bowles, Jane A.
Boyle, Kay
Bradley, Marion Z.
Brown, Alice
Buck, Pearl S.
Burnett, Frances H.
Caldwell, (Janet) Taylor
Carver, Ada Jack
Cather, Willa S.
Chase, Mary Ellen
Chesnut, Mary B.
Chopin, Kate O.
Clemmer, Mary E.
Crothers, Rachel
Davis, Rebecca B.
Deland, Margaret
Didion, Joan
Dix, Beulah M.
Douglas, Harriet
Dunbar-Nelson, Alice
Elliott, Sarah B.
Ephron, Phoebe W.
Ferber, Edna
Fisher, Dorothy Canfield
Fitzgerald, Zelda Sayre
Foote, Mary Hallock
Freeman, Mary E. Wilkins
Fremont, Jessie Benton
Fuller, (Sarah) Margaret
Gág, Wanda

Gale, Zona
Gellhorn, Martha E.
Glasgow, Ellen
Glaspell, Susan
Gordon, Caroline
Grau, Shirley Ann
Guiney, Louise I.
Hafen, Ann W.
Hamilton, Edith
Hansberry, Lorraine
Harris, Corra May
Haven, Alice B.
Hellman, Lillian
Hemingway, Mary Welsh
Herbst, Josephine Frey
Hickok, Lorena A.
Hill, Grace L.
Holley, Marietta
Holley, Mary Austin
Hollingworth, Leta S.
Howe, Julia Ward
Hurston, Zora Neale
Jackson, Helen Hunt
Jackson, Shirley
Jewett, Sarah Orne
Johnson, Josephine W.
Johnston, Mary
Keller, Helen Adams
King, Grace E.
Larcom, Lucy
LeGuin, Ursula K.
Lennox, Charlotte R.
Lindbergh, Anne Morrow
Loos, Anita
McCarthy, Mary T.
McCullers, Carson S.
McGinley, Phyllis
Metalious, Grace
Miles, Emma Bell
Miller, Alice D.
Mitchell, Margaret
Moore, Anne Carroll
Murfree, Mary N.
Murray, Judith Sargent

Nin, Anais
Oates, Joyce Carol
O'Connor, Flannery
Ozick, Cynthia
Parker, Dorothy R.
Perkins, Lucy Fitch
Peterkin, Julia
Phelps, Elizabeth S.
Porter, Katherine Anne
Post, Emily
Prentiss, Elizabeth P.
Rand, Ayn
Rawlings, Marjorie Kinnan
Repplier, Agnes
Rinehart, Mary Roberts
Rives, Amélie
Roberts, Elizabeth Madox
Rourke, Constance M.
Rowson, Susanna H.
Sandoz, Mari
Sawyer, Ruth
Schlafly, Phyllis S.
Scott, Evelyn
Sedgwick, Catharine M.
Sinclair, Jo
Smedley, Agnes
Smith, Elizabeth Oakes
Smith, Lillian
Southworth, E. D. E. N.
Spencer, Elizabeth
Spofford, Harriet P.
Stafford, Jean
Stein, Gertrude
Stephens, Kate
Stowe, Harriet Beecher
Stratton-Porter, Gene
Stuart, Ruth McEnery
Suckow, Ruth
Susann, Jacqueline
Tarbell, Ida M.
Thanet, Octave
Toklas, Alice B.
Warner, Anna B.
Warner, Susan B.

Authors (cont.)

Welty, Eudora
West, Jessamyn
Wharton, Edith
Whitman, Sarah P.
Wiggin, Kate Douglas
Wilder, Laura Ingalls
Wilson, Augusta Evans
Woolson, Constance F.

Businesswomen

Arden, Elizabeth
Ayer, Harriet H.
Demorest, Ellen C.
Green, Hetty
Grossinger, Jennie
Lauder, Estée
Pinkham, Lydia E.
Rubinstein, Helena

Comediennes

Allen, Grace "Gracie"
Ball, Lucille
Brice, Fanny

Criminals

Borden, Lizzie A.
Chadwick, Elizabeth B.
Harris, Jean Witt
Parker, Bonnie
Starr, Shirley "Belle"
Surratt, Mary E.

Dancers

Baker, Josephine
Duncan, Isadora
Dunham, Katherine
Graham, Martha

Humphrey, Doris
Jamison, Judith
King, Eleanor
Lee, Gypsy Rose
Page, Ruth
Rogers, Ginger
St. Denis, Ruth
Tallchief, Maria

Designers

Bernstein, Aline F. (theatrical)
DeWolfe, Elsie (interior)
Draper, Dorothy (interior)
Hawes, Elizabeth (fashion)
Vanderbilt, Gloria M. (fashion)

Editors

Day, Dorothy
Hale, Sarah Josepha
Kirchwey, Freda
London, Charmian K.
Miller, Bertha Mahoney
White, Katharine S.

Educators

Agassiz, Elizabeth Cary
Banister, Zilphia P. G.
Beecher, Catharine E.
Berry, Martha M.
Bethune, Mary McLeod
Bevier, Isabel
Bridgman, Laura D.
Cooper, Anna J.
Crandall, Prudence
Dickey, Sarah Ann
Fahs, Sophia Lyon
Irwin, Agnes
Lyon, Mary
McAuliffe, (Sharon) Christa
Macy, Anne Sullivan
Macy, Henrietta Gardner

Mann, Mary Peabody
Marks, Jeannette A.
Maxwell, Martha
Mills, Susan Lincoln
Mitchell, Lucy Sprague
Mortimer, Mary
Norsworthy, Naomi
Palmer, Alice F.
Patrick, Mary Mills
Peabody, Elizabeth P.
Phelps, Almira Hart
Rorer, Sarah Tyson
Rutherford, Mildred L.
Sanford, Maria L.
Stone, Lucinda H.
Taft, Jessie
Thomas, Carey
Willard, Emma Hart
Wood, Stella L.
Woolley, Mary Emma
Young, Ella Flagg

Engineer

Gilbreth, Lillian M.

Feminists

Anthony, Susan B.
Blake, Lillie D.
Bloomer, Amelia Jenks
Catt, Carrie Chapman
Clay, Laura
Duniway, Abigail Scott
Gilman, Charlotte P.
Martin, Anne H.
Mott, Lucretia Coffin
Paul, Alice
Robinson, Harriet H.
Stanton, Elizabeth Cady
Stone, Lucy
Thomas, Helen

Fine Arts

Illustrators

McMein, Neysa
O'Neill, Rose Cecil
Smith, Jessie W.

Painters

Brooks, Romaine
Cassatt, Mary
Clark, Kate F.
Frankenthaler, Helen
Johnston, Henrietta
Moses, Grandma
Nieriker, May Alcott
O'Keeffe, Georgia
Peale, Sarah M.
Stettheimer, Florine

Potter

Martinez, Maria M.

Sculptors

Nevelson, Louise B.
Ream, Vinnie
Whitney, Gertrude
Wright, Patience

First Ladies

Adams, Abigail
Adams, Louisa J.
Carter, Rosalynn S.
Coolidge, Grace G.
Eisenhower, Mamie Doud
Ford, Elizabeth "Betty"
Grant, Julia Dent
Hayes, Lucy Webb
Jackson, Rachel D.
Johnson, Claudia "Lady Bird"
Kennedy, Jacqueline B.
Lincoln, Mary Todd

First Ladies (cont.)

McKinley, Ida Saxton
Madison, Dolly Payne
Nixon, Patricia Ryan
Polk, Sarah C.
Reagan, Nancy Davis
Roosevelt, Edith Kermit
Roosevelt, Eleanor R.
Truman, Bess W.
Tyler, Julia G.
Washington, Martha
Wilson, Edith Bolling
Wilson, Ellen Axson

Frontierwomen and Pioneers

Canary, Martha B. "Calamity Jane"
Hobson, Mary Quinn
Jemison, Mary (Indian captive)
Oakley, Annie
Slocum, Frances (Indian captive)
Tabor, Elizabeth "Baby Doe"
White, Catherine Payne

Government Officers

Dulles, Eleanor L.
Hanks, Nancy
Myerson, Bess
Perkins, Frances
Ragghianti, Marie
Willebrandt, Mabel W.

Heiresses

Curzon, Mary Leiter
Frazier, Brenda D.
Hearst, Patricia C.
Hill, Joan R.
Hutton, Barbara
Whitney, Dorothy

Historians

Beard, Mary Ritter
Brooks, Juanita
Hall, Sharlot M.
Salmon, Lucy Maynard
Tartt, Ruby Pickens (folklorist)
Warren, Mercy Otis

Hostesses

Fields, Annie A.
Murphy, Sara W.
Schuyler, Catherine V.
Warner, Edith

Journalists

Bly, Nellie
Claflin, Tennessee
Dix, Dorothy
Hopper, Hedda
Kilgallen, Dorothy
Landers, Ann
Parsons, Louella
Royall, Anne Newport
Savitch, Jessica (broadcaster)
Scripps, Ellen Browning
Strong, Anna L.
Thompson, Dorothy
Van Buren, Abigail
Woodhull, Victoria C.

Labor Leaders

Anderson, Mary
Jordan, Crystal Lee
Mason, Lucy Randolph

Lawyers

Allen, Florence E.
Holtzmann, Fanny E.

La Follette, Belle Case
Paige, Mabeth Hurd

Librarians

Coolbrith, Ina
Mudge, Isadore G.
Sharp, Katharine L.

Medicine

Abortionist

Lohman, Ann S.

Nurses

Barton, Clara H.
Bickerdyke, Mary
Goodrich, Annie W.
Nutting, Mary A.

Physicians

Blackwell, Elizabeth
Hamilton, Alice
Jacobi, Mary Putnam
Newcomb, Kate Pelham
Price, Nina Mae
Sabin, Florence Rena
Scudder, Ida Sophia
Swain, Clara A.
Walker, Mary Edwards

Musicians

Crosby, Fanny (hymnist)
Pittman, Portia M. (pianist)
Powell, Maud (violinist)

Native Americans

Hawaiians

Liliuokalani
Nāhienaena

Indians

Bright Eyes
Pocahontas
Sacajawea
Tekakwitha, Kateri
Winnemucca, Sarah

The Occult

Crandon, Mina S. (mystic)
Dixon, Jeane P. (astrologer)
Fox, Katherine "Kate" (spiritualist)
Fox, Margaret (spiritualist)
Garrett, Eileen J. (spiritualist)
Worrall, Olga R. (mystic)

Organization Founders

Low, Juliette Gordon
Phillips, Lena M.

Philanthropists

Blaine, Anita M.
Gould, Helen
Gratz, Rebecca
Guggenheimer, Minnie
Hearst, Phoebe A.
Lowell, Josephine S.
Post, Marjorie M.
Rockefeller, Abby A.
Smith, Sophia
Stanford, Jane Lathrop

Photographers

Abbott, Berenice
Arbus, Diane
Austen, Alice
Beals, Jessie Tarbox
Bourke-White, Margaret

Photographers (cont.)

Cunningham, Imogen
Gilpin, Laura
Lange, Dorothea N.

Poets

Bennett, Gwendolyn B.
Bishop, Elizabeth
Bogan, Louise
Bradstreet, Anne
Brooks, Gwendolyn
Cary, Alice
Cary, Phoebe
Crapsey, Adelaide
Davidson, Margaret M.
Dickinson, Emily
Doolittle, Hilda (H.D.)
Lazarus, Emma
Levertov, Denise
Lowell, Amy
Loy, Mina
Millay, Edna St. Vincent
Monroe, Harriet
Moore, Marianne C.
Morton, Sarah W.
Moulton, Louise C.
Plath, Sylvia
Preston, Margaret J.
Sarton, May
Sigourney, Lydia H.
Spencer, Anne
Teasdale, Sara
Thaxter, Celia L.
Tietjens, Eunice
Wheatley, Phillis
Wilcox, Ella Wheeler
Wylie, Elinor Hoyt

Political Activists

Boudin, Katherine "Kathy"
Bryant, Louise Stevens

Carroll, Anna E.
Davis, Angela Y.
Goldman, Emma
Oughton, Diana
Parsons, Lucy E.
Szold, Henrietta (Zionist)

Politicians

Astor, Nancy L.
Bolton, Frances P.
Bosone, Reva Beck
Byrne, Jane Burke
Felton, Rebecca L.
Ferguson, Miriam A.
Ferraro, Geraldine
Flynn, Elizabeth G. (organizer)
Luce, Clare Boothe
Mankin, Helen Douglas
Moskowitz, Belle (organizer)
Rankin, Jeannette
Robertson, Alice Mary
Smith, Margaret Chase

Publishers

Beach, Sylvia W.
Graham, Katharine M.
Leslie, Miriam F.
Patterson, Eleanor "Cissy"
Rivers, Pearl
Schiff, Dorothy
Sheed, Maisie Ward

Relatives of Famous People

Daughters

Johnson, Luci
Johnson, Lynda
Longworth, Alice Roosevelt
Roosevelt, Anna Eleanor
Smith, Abigail Adams
Starr, Pearl

Mothers

Alcott, Abigail
Churchill, Jennie Jerome
Clemens, Jane L.
Hemingway, Grace Hall
Henry, Sarah Winston
Kennedy, Rose F.
Lincoln, Nancy Hanks
Pinckney, Eliza(beth) L.
Roosevelt, Sara Delano
Washington, Mary Ball
Whistler, Anna M.

Sisters

Cowles, Anne Roosevelt
Howells, Annie
James, Alice
Kennedy, Kathleen
Mecom, Jane Franklin

Wives

Adams, Marion "Clover"
Arnold, Margaret S.
Audubon, Lucy G.
Bell, Mabel
Crane, Cora H.
Davis, Varina Howell
Edwards, Sarah P.
Emerson, Ellen T.
Emerson, Lidian J.
Hawthorne, Sophia P.
Hemingway, Hadley
Hemingway, Pauline Pfeiffer
Houston, Margaret L.
Kennedy, Ethel S.
Kennedy, Joan B.
Lesley, Susan
Mitchell, Martha Beall
Moody, Harriet C. T.
O'Neill, Carlotta Monterey
Seward, Frances M.
Sherman, Ellen Ewing

Steichen, Lillian
Winthrop, Margaret

Friend to Famous Man

Vineyard, Mary Owens

Religion

Missionaries

Denton, Mary F.
Fiske, Fidelia
Forsberg, Vivian
Judson, Ann H.
Judson, Emily C.
Judson, Sarah B.
Moon, Lottie D.
Nelson, Rebecca J.
Smith, Amanda Berry
Taylor, Maria Dyer
Walker, Mary Richardson
Whitman, Narcissa P.

Religious Leaders

Butler, Mother Marie Joseph
Cannon, Harriet Starr
Collson, Mary
Connelly, Cornelia
Eddy, Mary Baker
Hardey, Mary A.
Hutchinson, Anne
Jackson, Rebecca Cox
Kuhlman, Kathryn
Lathrop, Rose Hawthorne
Livermore, Harriet
Meyer, Lucy Rider
Rogers, Mary J.
Seton, Elizabeth A. Bayley (saint)
Smith, Emma Hall
Van Cott, Margaret N.
Warde, Frances
White, Ellen Gould
Wilkinson, Jemima
Woodworth-Etter, Maria B.

Scientists

Brown, Rachel Fuller (biochemist)
Carson, Rachel Louise (biologist)
Hazen, Elizabeth Lee
    (bacteriologist)
Lawrence, Margaret (psychoanalyst)
McClintock, Barbara (geneticist)
Martin, Lillien J. (psychoanalyst)
Mitchell, Maria (astronomer)
Slye, Maud (zoologist)
Swallow, Ellen H. (chemist)

Singers

Abbott, Emma
Anderson, Marian
Callas, Maria
Fitzgerald, Ella
Garland, Judy
Hackley, E(mma) Azalia
Holiday, Billie
Holman, Libby
Homer, Louise
Horne,Lena
Hunter, Alberta
Jackson, Mahalia
Joplin, Janis
MacDonald, Jeanette
Mercer, Mabel
Minnelli, Liza
Moore, Grace
Nordica, Lillian
Phillipps, Adelaide
Rainey, Gertrude "Ma"
Russell, Lillian
Shore, Dinah
Smith, Bessie
Streisand, Barbra
Thursby, Emma C.
Tucker, Sophie
Washington, Dinah
Waters, Ethel

Social Reformers

Balch, Emily G.
Booth, Maud B.
Breckinridge, Madeline M.
Child, Lydia Maria
Dix, Dorothea Lynde
Emery, Sarah E. V.
Hooks, Julia Ann
Kelley, Florence
King, Coretta Scott
Munford, Mary Cooke
Nation, Carry
Robins, Margaret D.
Sanger, Margaret H.
Willard, Frances E.
Young, Ann Eliza

Social Workers

Addams, Jane
Bethune, Joanna G.
Cameron, Donaldina M.
Cratty, Mabel
Dodge, Grace H.
Felton, Katharine C.
Lathrop, Julia
McDowell, Mary E.
McMain, Eleanor L.
Peter, Sarah W.
Richmond, Mary
Van Waters, Miriam
Wald, Lillian D.

Society Leaders

Balsan, Consuelo V.
Bell, Helen Choate
Bonaparte, Elisabeth P.
Burr, Theodosia
Chase, Kate
Eaton, Margaret "Peggy"
Jumel, Eliza Bowen

MacKay, Marie L.
Palmer, Bertha
Pennybacker, Anna J.
Vanderbilt, Grace Wilson
Ward, Annie
Ward, Louisa
Windsor, Wallis Simpson

Rosenberg, Ethel
Seelye, Sarah Emma

Theatrical Directors

Flanagan, Hallie
Morgan, Anna

Spies

Boyd, Belle
Cushman, Pauline
Greenhow, Rose O.
Harrison, Marguerite

War Heroines and Patriots

Corbin, Margaret C. (soldier)
Lewis, Ida (lighthousekeeper)
Ross, Betsy G. (flagmaker)
Sampson, Deborah (soldier)

Index

All references are to entry numbers, not page numbers.